THE OVERLANDING VEHICLE

BUILDER'S GUIDE

Don Alexander

S-A DESIGN

CarTech®

CarTech®

CarTech®, Inc.
6118 Main Street
North Branch, MN 55056
Phone: 651-277-1200 or 800-551-4754
Fax: 651-277-1203
www.cartechbooks.com

Edit by Bob Wilson
Layout by Connie DeFlorin

ISBN 978-1-61325-748-7
Item No. SA529

Library of Congress Cataloging-in-Publication Data Available

Written, edited, and designed in the U.S.A.
Printed in China
10 9 8 7 6 5 4 3 2 1

All photos are courtesy Don Alexander unless otherwise noted.

DISTRIBUTION BY:

Europe
PGUK
63 Hatton Garden
London EC1N 8LE, England
Phone: 020 7061 1980 • Fax: 020 7242 3725
www.pguk.co.uk

Australia
Renniks Publications Ltd.
3/37-39 Green Street
Banksmeadow, NSW 2109, Australia
Phone: 2 9695 7055 • Fax: 2 9695 7355
www.renniks.com

Canada
Login Canada
300 Saulteaux Crescent
Winnipeg, MB, R3J 3T2 Canada
Phone: 800 665 1148 • Fax: 800 665 0103
www.lb.ca

CONTENTS

Acknowledgments

Thank you to my wife, Christie Helm, for your support.

Thank you to Bob Wilson, editor at CarTech; the Bear Valley Overland crew, Corey and Casey; Bill Stephens for help with testing and installation; Wendy Stephens for testing and spotting help; Toby Jho for great photography; Desi Hauer at Big Bear Jeep Experience; and Paul Crawford at J.P. Molnar for photography help.

Thank you to my friends and associates in the awesome Jeep aftermarket: Ray Currie and Casey Currie of Currie Enterprises; John Currie, Brandon Currie, Brian Shepard, and Tiny Stark of RockJock 4x4; Paul Jho, Jay Lee, and John Hagen of Nexen Tires; Henk Van Dongen and Ryan Michael of Rugged Ridge; Tom Allen of PSC Motorsports; Neal Hollingsworth of Yukon Gear & Axle; Terry Jurgens of Ultra Vision Lighting; Greg Mulkey of Raceline Wheels; Steve Sasaki and Tyler Sasaki of Power Tank; Dave Luman, Kevin Smith, and Tom Trotter of Rock Slide Engineering; Jason Stanton, Tim Cowher, and Jon Mason of NovaWinch; James Barth of Rockhard 4x4; Justin Andrews of Factor 55; Shari McCullough Arfons of McCullough Public Relations and Tuffy Security; Jim Reel of JE Reel Drivelines; Steve von Seggern of Bilstein Shocks; Scott Brown of Stellantis Jeep Public Relations; Henry Valesquez of BRP Wheels; Steve Dowden of Hi-Lift Jacks; Don Sneddon and Willie Woo of Mickey Thompson Tires; Elizabeth Granada of Midland Radio Corp.; Brittany and Kevin Willaims of LiteBrite Nation; Jeff Greene of Rough Country; Gale Banks of Banks Power; Jason Buckles of Bolt Lock; Matson Breakey of Metal Cloak; Dave Schlossberg of Synergy Manufacturing; Brad McCarthy of MaxTrax; Don McMillan of Daystar; and Max Gremillion of Pull Pal.

INTRODUCTION

Before overlanding, there was expedition travel, and before expeditions, there were safaris. When I was much younger, we camped out of our vehicles. We called the activity "camping." The principles have not changed. However, the equipment and vehicles have—a lot!

Back in the day, I took sleeping bags, a tent, cooler, and possibly a small stove and lantern. At that time, most "overlanding" was conducted in campgrounds, hopefully with bathrooms and a shower. As campgrounds became overcrowded, dispersed camping and camping in the backcountry with no amenities became more popular. More gear was desirable due to the lack of facilities. Demand creates supply, and overlanding is no different.

The modern version of overlanding took off in 2007 with the creation of *The Overland Journal* magazine and the Overland Expo event that was founded by a couple named Roseann and Jonathan Hanson. The first Overland Expo in Prescott, Arizona, had 900 attendees and a few vendors. Fast-forward to 2022, and the Overland Expo West hosted over 30,000 attendees and nearly 500 vendors. In addition, the Overland Expo has grown to four events across the US.

Fifteen years ago, overlanding participants were rarely seen in the backcountry. Growth was slow. When the pandemic struck, people looked for ways to get out of their houses while avoiding the serious risk of becoming a Covid-19 statistic. Overlanding captured the imagination of many individuals who were looking for a safe, beautiful, and peaceful getaway. Participation has grown at a large rate the last few years. Now, overlanders populate the forests, deserts, and other scenic backcountry locales on weekends and over longer periods of time. Many dispersed camping spots make it easy to find a great, isolated, and scenic location for an overlanding adventure.

While participation has grown steadily, the vehicles and gear available to the overlanding community are simply overwhelming. Almost weekly, vehicle manufacturers are introducing new off-road-capable vehicles that are targeted to the overlanding market. Tire manufacturers are launching off-road tires that are aimed at overlanding. Many TV commercials, especially from vehicle makers, showcase overlanding activities.

However, the largest growth segment is gear for overlanding. Every imaginable product is available to enhance the overlanding experience. More than 1,000 companies offer gear for overlanding. More than 100 companies sell rooftop tents. Dozens of product categories populate the overlanding market. The number of new products at the Overland Expo West in May 2022 compared to the September 2021 expo was staggering. Overland Expo offers the Overland source book with nearly 250 pages full of overlanding product information: overlandexpo.com/overland-sourcebook/.

The overlanding purists scoff at the idea of weekend or short adventures. Real overlanders travel for weeks, months, or even years according to the die-hard old-school crowd. Many would love to travel for extended periods, but few can afford that luxury. The important goal is to seek adventure. Whether it's a day-trip picnic, a weekend in your favorite area, or a long vacation for months of adventures, go explore. Your adventure does not need to meet anyone else's rules or expectations. Have fun!

What Is Overlanding?

Since the dawn of the human race, exploration has lurked within the human spirit. Finding food sources, water, and shelter demanded searching for new resources. Stretching boundaries always involved adventure. Exploration and adventure are ingrained in the human DNA.

Today, finding food and shelter hardly requires exploration. While searching for a parking spot and fighting rush-hour traffic may have elements of adventure, those activities hardly elevate the human spirit. Humans need adventure with challenges that enliven the mind, body, and soul. We need something beyond exploring the web or playing computer games and something outside to take on and explore the natural world.

For a rapidly growing segment of the US population, overlanding fills the need for adventure. For several decades, many sociologists reported concerns about the disconnect from nature for many Americans. To oversimplify their conclusions, many were afraid of the outdoors and nature. This disconnect caused measurable emotional, physical, and psychological issues. This trend is changing, and overlanding is an outlet for a newfound desire for outdoor adventure.

While overlanding has been around since mechanized travel began, the activity grew in popularity as the 21st century began. Twenty years into the new millennium, the growth of overlanding is nothing short of explosive. The isolation brought about by the Covid-19 pandemic pushed people to seek safe outlets for adventure. Overlanding fits the bill nicely.

What elements define overlanding? Overlanding requires the use of a mechanized vehicle as opposed to human or animal-powered travel.

Overlanding opportunities abound across North America and around the globe. A capable stock 4WD vehicle, such as the Jeep Wrangler Rubicon (JL), coupled with an Opus trailer is a great setup for exploring the backcountry. The ease of setup and the ability to establish a base camp but explore unencumbered makes this combination ideal for short- and long-term adventures. This Jeep is also a daily driver. (Photo Courtesy J.P. Molnar)

This includes mountain bikes, motorcycles, and four-wheeled (or more) vehicles. In this book, we focus on four-wheeled vehicles. Overlanding also requires complete self-sufficiency. This is similar to backpacking, where the participant must carry food, water, shelter, clothing, and hygiene supplies for the duration of an adventure.

Unlike backpacking, overlanding requires participants to also carry fuel, tools for repairs and for getting unstuck, navigation gear, and

The combination of a rooftop tent with a Toyota vehicle is popular for overlanding. The Toyota 4Runner allows comfortable exploration on all but the most difficult trails.

Overlanding History

Overlanding attracts scores of newcomers every year. To many, overlanding is a new phenomenon, but this is not true. The chuck wagon dates back to 1875 in the Big Bear Valley in California. Sleeping accommodations were generally simple canvas A-frame tents. Settlers and miners traveled many miles to look for homesteads and gold.

Even earlier, the Serrano tribe traveled over land from the desert to the mountains to look for water, food, supplies, and more ideal temperatures. On foot, by horse, and later with carts and wagons, travel on local Big Bear trails dates back more than 300 years. ■

A chuck wagon is on display at the Eleanor Abbott Museum in Big Bear, California.

A-frame tents similar to these were used by overlanders in the 1800s. These are on display at the Eleanor Abbott Museum in Big Bear, California.

The Toyota Tundra is a capable overlanding vehicle. It shines in desert environments and is best suited for easy to moderate terrain.

The Subaru Outback offers good overland performance on easy-to-moderate trails.

a method for communication. For the most part, overlanding uses unpaved roads for travel and avoids developed campgrounds or RV parks. Off-highway travel is paramount to overlanding, and off-highway travel makes overlanding a subset of off-roading in general.

By definition, off-roading is the use of a motorized vehicle on unpaved routes usually on public lands. Public land may be managed by the United States Department of Agriculture (USDA) Forest Service, Bureau of Land

Rooftop tents are a great option for overlanding accommodations, especially on vehicles like the Jeep Gladiator.

Management (BLM), or state, county, or municipal agencies. Off-roading often occurs on private land, usually in off-road parks, especially east of the Mississippi.

Many longtime overlanders do not consider themselves to be part of the off-roading community. This belief can lead to ignoring some of the basic ethics and courtesies that have been long established for using motorized vehicles on public lands. Non-adherence to the rules, laws, and courtesies that guide the off-road community can lead to route closures and disasters.

Some definitions of overlanding suggest that an overlanding trip must be a long-term adventure that lasts more than a few days. Weekend or even one-night adventures in the backcountry certainly qualify as overlanding. Some overlanding die-hards believe that fully decked-out rigs are a necessity. This is also untrue. Any vehicle with good ground clearance that can drive on easy routes in dry weather can be used for overlanding. While four-wheel-drive (4WD) is desirable, it is not needed on easy terrain when the roads are dry. Two-wheel-drive (2WD) trucks, vans, and SUVs will work. All-wheel-drive

Large off-road-capable trailers make overlanding more comfortable. While pulling them through challenging terrain is not ideal, big trailers are the perfect option for base camp when extended stays at one location are planned.

Expedition-style rigs provide the ultimate long-range overlanding experience. However, their massive size and weight limit the type of terrain that these behemoths can tackle, and the cost for one of these rigs is astronomical.

Ready-made off-road-capable camper vans feature ease of setup and good capability on all but the most difficult terrain

Traditional truck-based campers provide comfortable accommodations with the durability of a truck platform. Their size and weight are drawbacks.

(AWD) is helpful, and 4WD is desirable. Good ground clearance is mandatory. Low-ground-clearance vehicles are susceptible to underside damage and can easily become stuck on rough terrain. Here are some items needed to participate in overlanding adventures:

- A vehicle with good ground clearance (preferably 4WD or at minimum AWD)
- Food
- Water
- Sleeping gear
- Clothing appropriate for the weather
- Maps or global positioning system (GPS)-based smartphone applications for a phone or tablet

Of course, this is a minimal list of items, but it is all that is really necessary for mild weather and easy dry roads and trails. Most people have a vehicle and minimal gear on hand to set off on an overlanding trip. This approach is a great way to determine if overlanding is an activity to pursue. However, be aware that overlanding can be expensive. Modifying a 4x4 vehicle can cost thousands of dollars even before you invest more thousands in cool overlanding gear.

If you are new to overlanding, here are several questions to ask yourself:

- How much off-roading experience do I have?
- What level and type of terrain would I like to tackle?
- How comfortable do I wish to be while exploring?
- What is the duration of adventure that I would like to tackle?
- What is my budget?

If you have never been on an overlanding adventure, take a short overnight or weekend trip to help you decide if overlanding is something that you want to pursue. Hopefully, it will answer some of the key questions. If you do not have vehicle capable of easy overlanding, rent an SUV, van, or truck for a weekend. Look online for overlanding or off-roading spots close to home. Chances are good that you will have a great time on your first short adventure.

If you are an experienced off-roader with a fairly capable 4x4 rig but have no overlanding experience, pack some food, a sleeping bag, and a tent and give it a try. You probably know some great dispersed

An all-wheel-drive SUV, such as a Subaru Outback, with good tires and adequate ground clearance makes a good overlanding vehicle.

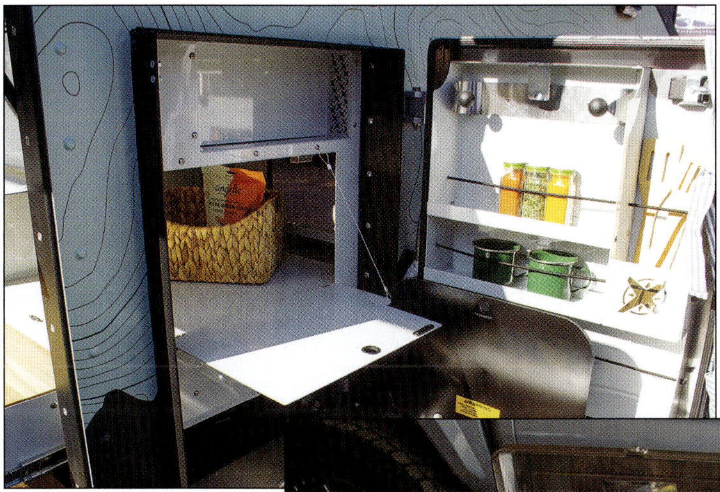

Storage space for food is a must. This elaborate kitchen setup in a trailer is nice, but it's not a necessity for basic overlanding adventures.

Water supplies may be the most important items to carry for an overlander. Potable water can be carried in containers, such as these RotopaX.

Food preparation and cooking are key elements of overlanding. This simple kitchen setup is portable, easy to store, lightweight, inexpensive, and capable of producing delicious meals.

Most stock 4WD trucks, SUVs, and AWD crossover vehicles can handle easy but beautiful terrain. (Photo Courtesy Stellantis)

When the terrain becomes challenging, a more-capable stock vehicle or one with modifications is necessary.

camping spots along some of your favorite trails. Otherwise, you can tackle those trails that are too long to complete in a day trip.

If you decide to go all in for the ultimate overlanding rig for a prime overlanding adventure, you are in the right place. This book will help guide you through the fun, exciting, and challenging process. Each chapter covers important information to help you make decisions about shopping for a new or used rig, modifying your vehicle, and selecting equipment.

Extreme terrain requires a more-capable rig. Some stock vehicles can tackle this type of terrain, but most vehicles need upgrades. Better tires, more ground clearance, and better protection make tackling this type of terrain more manageable. (Photo Courtesy Stellantis)

Here is a quick preview of many issues that you need to address and choices that require careful deliberation:

- Do I own a vehicle that is capable of overlanding?
- If I purchase a rig for overlanding, will it serve as a daily driver as well?
- Do I currently own any camping gear?
- Am I more likely to stay in one location for several days?
- Will I be moving to new spots daily?
- Do I have any physical limitations?
- What is a reasonable budget for my overland build?
- What is my experience level for camping and off-roading?
- Do I have access to training or groups where I can gain experience more easily?
- What overlanding opportunities are present in my geographical location?

Tent camping is a great way to try overlanding for little or no investment. Use your existing vehicle and try an easy trail for an overnight trip.

The Freedom to Explore, Responsibilities, and Consequences

Overlanding offers the freedom to explore some of the most beautiful places on the planet. Scenery, serenity, and some driving challenges make overlanding a wonderful form of adventure travel. Not surprisingly, the explosive growth of overlanding creates problems. The most significant issues cause damage to the land. Driving and parking off of designated routes causes serious damage to the terrain. Tire tracks on undisturbed ground can cause damage to plant and animal life. It accelerates erosion due to the loosening of soil and damage to ground cover, and adversely affects animal habitat.

Damage takes years, even decades, to repair. Driving off of designated routes is also illegal on public lands with potential hefty fines. Illegal campfires can lead to devastating destruction. Leaving behind trash, including human waste, is a growing problem that should never be an issue. Poor driving practices, such as excessive wheelspin, accelerate erosion, which creates damage to the road surfaces and surrounding terrain.

Fences are installed along designated routes for a reason, usually to protect a sensitive area of land. Damaging a fence to bypass a difficult section of road is illegal. It is also the quickest way to get that trail closed to motorized-vehicle travel.

Locations such as this are good for camping. It is near a designated route, so parking a vehicle here is legal.

Responsibility on Public Lands

Using public lands requires users to be responsible for preserving that land and to leave it in the same or better condition than it was previously. A pervasive attitude among a segment of our population causes serious problems. "It's my land, and I'll do whatever I want," is the sentiment. Well, it's not your land. It belongs to everyone. I know that you, the reader, are responsible. You are not part of the problem, but you can be part of the solution by setting a positive example, educating others in a positive and kind manner, and collecting others' discarded trash. No one wants trash dumped on their property or poop left in their yard.

Land managers, such as the BLM and USDA Forest Service, have limited resources due in part to extreme budget cuts. Most road maintenance on public lands is conducted by volunteers from clubs and Adopt-A-Trail programs. Do your part by not adding to the workload or you can become a volunteer.

Consequences

No one wants to drive into a beautiful overlanding camping spot only to discover a pile of trash left behind by irresponsible users. Don't be that person.

No one wants to see thousands of acres of pristine forest destroyed by a devastating fire. While some wildfires are caused by lightning strikes, most are caused by humans. Know the local fire regulations and restrictions and learn how to properly extinguish a campfire. Everyone loves a campfire, but the risks are high, especially in the western US. Some of our favorite trails have been obliterated by human-caused wildfires.

Stay on designated routes. Not

An illegal campfire caused a blaze that obliterated this great trail and overlanding area. While some fires are caused by lightning, most are caused by humans.

The Barker Ranch in Death Valley, the site where Charles Manson was captured, burned from a fire that was set by careless campers.

doing so is the best way to get roads and trails closed to motorized vehicle recreation. Most managing agencies for public lands provide maps (printed and/or digital) that show designated legal routes. The BLM offers maps of regions and subregions on its website. The USDA Forest Service provides the Motorized Vehicle Use Map (MVUM) for every national forest in the US.

The consequences of irresponsible motorized vehicle use on public lands include:

- Loss of access
- Destruction of pristine forest land from wildfires and subsequent erosion from flooding
- Damage in environmentally sensitive areas
- Unsightly trash left behind that can harm wildlife

Dispersed Camping

Dispersed camping is simply camping in undeveloped locations. Dispersed camping implies that one can camp anywhere. While it's mostly accurate, camping anywhere is not allowed. Here are some rules for dispersed camping:

- Camp 100 feet away from any water source
- Camp within 150 feet of a roadway (do not drive on undisturbed ground)
- Camp outside of a 1-mile radius of any designated campsite
- Don't camp at a site for more than 14 days
- Camp where others have camped before. Look for worn down dirt and rock clusters that have been formed to keep fires in check where fires are allowed.
- Don't leave behind trash or anything else you carry in with you. Pack it in and pack it out.
- Check beforehand for any restrictions, especially open-fire

restrictions. Depending on the administering agency, what the weather has been like, and other various factors, specific rules may be in place.

Leave No Trace

These rules are in place for a reason. Bulldozing your way through the woods, setting up camp wherever you please, destroying plants, and scaring wildlife as you go has a significant impact on the environment. By being respectful and following the rules, you are protecting these public lands for future campers.

Pay attention to the signs. If a 4x4, high-ground-clearance rig is recommended, there is a reason. Camping and campfires are not allowed in this area.

This group of Adopt-A-Trail volunteers is repairing fencing that was knocked down by illegal vehicle travel. The San Bernardino National Forest Adopt-A-Trail program is the largest in the US with more than 50 clubs and a volunteer corps that puts in up to 25,000 man-hours annually to maintain the road and trail system. If you want to be part of the solution, the battle is to maintain motorized vehicle access on public lands. Join a club and volunteer in an Adopt-A-Trail program.

Tread Lightly!

Tread Lightly! is a nonprofit organization that promotes the responsible use of public lands. The Tread Lightly! principles offer excellent guidelines for responsible off-roading and overlanding:

Travel Responsibly

- Travel responsibly on designated roads, trails, or areas.
- Travel only in areas open to 4WD vehicles.
- For your safety, travel straight up or down hills.
- Drive over (not around) obstacles to avoid widening the trail.
- Straddle ruts, gullies, and washouts even if they are wider than your vehicle.
- Cross streams only at designated fording points where the road crosses the stream.
- When possible, avoid mud.
- In soft terrain, go easy on the gas to avoid wheelspin, which can cause ruts.
- Don't turn around on narrow roads, steep terrain, or unstable ground. Back up until you find a safe place to turn around.
- Stop frequently and scout ahead on foot.
- To help with traction, balance your load and lower tire pressure to where you see a bulge.
- Know where the differential or the lowest point on your vehicle is located. This will help negotiate terrain and prevent vehicle damage that may result in oil and fluid spills on the trail.
- Maintain a reasonable distance between vehicles.
- Comply with all signs and respect barriers.
- Travel with a group of two or more vehicles. Driving solo can leave you vulnerable if you have an accident or breakdown.
- Designate meeting areas in case of separation.
- Choose the appropriate winch for your vehicle size.
- Attach the towing cable, tree strap, or chain as low as possible to the object that is being winched.
- Let the winch do the work; never drive the winch.
- When winching, always inspect your equipment, use the right winch for the situation, find a good secure anchor, and never winch with less than five wraps of wire rope around the drum.
- When using a tree as an anchor, use a wide tree strap to avoid damaging the trunk of the tree.
- Don't mix driving with alcohol or drugs.

Tread Lightly! *continued*

Respect the Rights of Others

- Respect the rights of others, including private property owners, all recreational trail users, campers, and others so they can enjoy their recreational activities undisturbed.
- Be considerate of others on the road or trail. Learn the basics of trail etiquette.
- Leave gates as you find them.
- If crossing private property, be sure to ask permission from the landowner(s).
- Yield the right of way to those who pass you while traveling uphill.
- Yield to mountain bikers, hikers, horses, and pack animals. Proceed with caution.
- When encountering horses on the trail, move to the side of the trail, stop, turn off your engine, remove your helmet, and speak. You want the horse to know you are human.
- Ask the rider the best way to proceed.
- Sudden, unfamiliar activity may spook animals and possibly cause injury to animals, handlers, and others on the trail.
- Do not idly ride around in camping, picnicking, trailhead, or residential areas.
- Keep speeds low around crowds and in camping areas.
- Keep the noise and dust down.

Educate Yourself

- Educate yourself prior to the trip. Obtain travel maps and regulations from public agencies, take recreation skills classes, and know how to operate your equipment safely.
- Obtain a map of your destination and determine which areas are open to off-highway vehicles.
- Make a realistic plan and stick to it.
- Always tell someone of your travel plans.
- Contact the land manager for area restrictions, closures, and permit requirements.
- Check the weather forecast before you go.
- Prepare for the unexpected by packing necessary emergency items.
- Buckle up! Seat belts are mandatory.
- Know your limitations.
- Watch your time, fuel, and energy.
- Take an off-highway driver's course to learn more about negotiating terrain in a 4WD vehicle.
- Make sure your vehicle is mechanically up to task.
- Be prepared with tools, supplies, spares, and a spill kit for trailside repairs.

Avoid Sensitive Areas

- Avoid sensitive areas, such as meadows, lake shores, wetlands, and streams.
- Stay on designated routes.
- Other sensitive habitats to avoid include living desert soils, tundra, and seasonal nesting or breeding areas.
- Do not disturb historical, archeological, or paleontological sites.
- Avoid startling livestock and wildlife that you encounter and keep your distance.
- Motorized and mechanized vehicles are not allowed in designated wilderness areas.
- Pack out what you pack in and carry a trash bag to pick up litter left by others.
- Respected access is open access.

Do Your Part

- Do your part by modeling appropriate behavior, leaving the area the same or better than you found it, properly disposing of waste, minimizing the use of fire, avoiding the spread of invasive species, and restoring degraded areas.
- Practice minimum impact camping by using established sites and camping 200 feet from water sources and trails.
- Observe proper sanitary waste disposal or pack your waste out.
- Protect the soundscape by preventing unnecessary noise created by a poorly tuned vehicle or revving your engine.
- Before and after a ride, wash your vehicle to reduce the spread of invasive species.
- Build a trail community.
- Get to know other types of recreationists that share your favorite trail. ■

Overlanding Vehicles

The good news is that dozens of vehicles can be turned into great overlanding rigs. You may already own one. The bad news is that before you buy, several decisions must be made to make sure that you have a vehicle that meets your needs.

Important Questions

Your answers to the following six questions will help you prepare for an overlanding adventure.

Any vehicle with 4WD or AWD and decent ground clearance, such as the Jeep Gladiator, can explore easy roads.

What Type of Terrain Will You Travel?

Many off-road trails are rated for difficulty. Some use symbols, and others use a numbering system. Symbols include a green circle for easy, a blue square for difficult, and a black diamond for very difficult. In some areas, a double black diamond means extreme. Some areas, such as Moab, Utah, use a numbering system to rate trails on a 1 to 10 scale with 1 being very easy and 10 being a difficult trail for purpose-built off-road buggies. Some areas, especially BLM areas, do not rate trails at all.

Let's give this some perspective. Hundreds of thousands of miles of dirt roads and trails exist in the United States. California alone has about 100,000 miles of trails and dirt roads. Overall, over 90 percent of the roads and trails fall into the easy green circle category or 1 through 3 on the number scales. Almost any SUV or truck with 4WD or AWD can navigate the easy trails in all but the most severe weather conditions.

However, there is a catch. Most of these roads and trails receive little or no maintenance. What this means is that the trails, while still easy, can be very rough with exposed rocks, bumps, ruts, side slopes, and washboard and whoop-de-doo surfaces. What causes these uncomfortable and possibly damaging road surfaces? Erosion is at the top of the list. Wind, rain, and melting snow wash away dirt, expose rocks, and create ruts and bumps. Vehicle traffic contributes to the erosion by loosening the dirt and moving rocks and debris. Driver-induced wheelspin makes the situation worse by increasing the dirt movement and digging holes. The frequency of vehicles traveling at various speeds on dirt roads helps create washboard and whoop-de-doo surfaces. Road maintenance can alleviate most of these issues, but maintenance is sparse, especially on federal lands managed by the USDA Forest Service, BLM, and the National Park Service.

The lack of maintenance is a direct result of severe budgets cuts for federal land management agencies. At the last report, my local forest (the San Bernardino National Forest) had a budget of only $50,000 to maintain over 600 miles of roads and trails. A $1 million budget would barely cover the needs. The local Adopt-A-Trail program picks up some of the slack, but even with upward of 25,000 volunteer hours of maintenance work each year, the work accomplished only covers what can be done with hand tools. The volunteers cannot operate heavy equipment, such as road graders and bulldozers. The deterioration of the road surfaces is exacerbated by the stunning increase in traffic that is attributed to the rapidly growing popularity of overlanding and utility terrain vehicle (UTV) use.

What does this mean in relation to the selection process of purchasing an overlanding vehicle? Most of the vehicles that are suitable for off-road travel (even on the easy trails and roads) do not have good off-road tires, and their suspension systems are not up to handling the rigors of rough, rutted, and rocky terrain. A lack of ground clearance is also a concern. Does this mean they cannot be used off-road? Of course not. It does mean that going will be slow and a little uncomfortable at times and that maintenance and upgrades are required.

Many vehicles can handle difficult terrain. Most require modifications to tackle extreme hillclimbs, descents, and rocks.

How Much Gear Will You Carry?

How much gear will be carried is a tough question for two reasons. First, we always end up with more gear than we think. Second, estimating the weight and space for that gear is difficult until the gear is in hand. More gear means a bigger rig. Be sure that your vehicle has the load capacity to handle your planned gear, and add a healthy safety margin.

Will Your Overlanding Rig Also Be a Daily Driver?

If your overlanding rig will also be a primary daily driver, consider a vehicle that allows easy removal of overlanding gear, especially gear carried on roof racks. Lugging extra gear around for daily activities increases wear and tear and hurts fuel economy.

How Many People Will be Traveling Together?

This one is simple. You need seating for all occupants and space for their gear. You also need food and water for everyone. The more people, the bigger the vehicle that is required.

What is Your Budget for a Vehicle and Overlanding Gear?

New overlanding rigs are expensive. Add the cost of all the necessary gear, and it is quite high. If your budget is tight, consider purchasing a used 4x4 vehicle that has already been built for overlanding.

How Long Do You Intend to Spend on Your Overlanding Adventures?

This is another simple question. Long trips require more food, water, and supplies, which means they require more storage, especially if you plan to be off-grid for long periods of time.

4WD versus AWD

Most 4WD trucks and SUVs have transfer cases with low-range gearing, but many do not. A 4WD system offers the advantages of being able to select when to use 4WD. Many have automatic selection when traction is limited. Some use dials and/or switches to select modes specifically for various terrain, such as mud, snow and ice, rocks, or sand. The 4WD vehicles that offer a transfer case with low-range gearing can provide more torque (power) for climbing hill and rocks as well as more engine braking for steep descents and abrupt drop-offs. Vehicles with a 2-speed transfer case have a greater capability to tackle difficult terrain.

AWD vehicles receive constant power to the tires. AWD vehicles work great in low-traction situations with rain, snow, and ice. They work well off-road on most surfaces as long as road grades are not too steep. Most crossover vehicles use AWD, which is one factor that limits these vehicles to easier roads and trails.

Solid Axle versus Independent Front Suspension

Most current 4x4 vehicles feature independent front suspension. Some also have independent rear suspension. The entire line of Jeep Wranglers and Gladiators are the only 4x4s that come with solid axles. While many argue that independent front suspension is fine for off-roading, reality says no.

Axle articulation improves off-road performance in rough terrain. Independent suspension limits axle articulation considerably. Solid axles can flex significantly more and allow the tires to better follow rugged terrain and keep all four tires on the ground. See Chapter 6 to learn about sway bars and why sway-bar disconnects or off-road sway bars are recommended for many vehicles.

Independent front suspension can traverse most rutted terrain and fairly large rocks, but tires will often be lifted off the ground, sometimes by as much as 2 feet. On level ground or a slight incline, this is not dangerous. However, on steeper sections, especially if the driver has chosen the wrong line, a rollover is a remote possibility. Independent suspension is significantly better for ride comfort and handling on paved roads. While any vehicle used off-road can have steering issues, vehicles equipped with independent suspension use rack-and-pinion steering boxes and relatively small-diameter tie-rod ends. Both are weak links in the system. New Bronco owners are experiencing broken tie-rod ends and failed rack-and-pinion steering boxes.

Roof Weight-Bearing Capacity

Roofs on vehicles have weight limits. There are two types of limits. Static load capacity refers to the weight that a vehicle roof can handle while it is stationary. The dynamic load capacity refers to the weight the vehicle can hold while in motion.

Every state has laws pertaining to

All vehicles have weight-carrying limits. Two limits indicate loads for static (vehicle stationary) and dynamic (vehicle moving) loads. The average dynamic roof load limit is about 160 pounds. A truck with racks mounted to the bed rails has much greater load capacity. Keep in mind that high loads on any vehicle raise the center of gravity and diminish resistance to rollovers.

Overlanding-Capable Vehicle Categories

Each category of overlanding vehicle has positive and negative attributes.

4WD Compact SUVs	
Pros	**Cons**
• Low cost • Easier maneuverability, especially on narrow trails • Reasonable ground clearance • Many wheel and tire combination options • Good selection of suspension and shock-absorber upgrades	• Limited space • Low ground clearance • Larger tires may be limited due to clearance issues • Limited to easy roads and trails • Many small SUVs do not have a transfer case with four-low gearing

4WD Full-Size SUVs	
Pros	**Cons**
• Good storage capacity • Reasonable ground clearance • Many wheel and tire options • Good selection of suspension and shock-absorber upgrades • Better capabilities for somewhat more difficult adventures	• More expensive than compact SUVs • May not be able to navigate tight spots on narrow trails

4WD Midsize Trucks	
Pros	**Cons**
• Easier maneuverability, especially on narrow trails • Reasonable ground clearance • Many wheel and tire options • Good selection of suspension and shock-absorber upgrades	• Limited space • Low ground clearance • Larger tires may be limited due to clearance issues • Limited to easy and moderate roads and trails • Some small trucks do not have a transfer case with four-low gearing

Midsize pickups are a great platform for overlanding. The crew-cab design offers good passenger accommodations. The truck bed provides great storage, and the bed rails are a stable and strong platform for rooftop tents and other gear. The Chevy Colorado has growing aftermarket support for an already-capable truck.

4WD Full-Size Trucks	
Pros	**Cons**
• Excellent storage capacity • Generally good ground clearance • Many wheel and tire options • Ability to fit much larger tires • Good selection of suspension and shock-absorber upgrades • Better capabilities for more difficult adventures • Most have transfer cases with four-low gearing	• More costly • May not be able to negotiate tight spots on narrow trails

Crossovers	
Pros	**Cons**
• Cost • Good maneuverability • Some wheel and tire options • Reasonable selection of suspension and shock-absorber upgrades	• Limited space • Very low ground clearance • Larger tires may be limited due to clearance issues • Limited to easy roads and trails • Most crossovers do not have a transfer case with four-low gearing

4WD Vans	
Pros	**Cons**
• Excellent storage capacity • Everything is self-contained • Fast setup • Comfortable • Excellent in bad weather	• Cost • Tall tops make trails with low-hanging branches challenging • Low ground clearance • Larger tires may be limited due to clearance issues • Limited to easy roads and trails • Some vans do not have a transfer case with four-low gearing

Van Conversions and Campers	
Pros	**Cons**
• Excellent storage capacity • Everything is self-contained • Fast setup • Comfortable • Excellent in bad weather	• Expensive • Tall tops make trails with low-hanging branches challenging • Low ground clearance • Heavy • Larger tires may be limited due to clearance issues • Limited to easy roads and trails • Some vans do not have a transfer case with four-low gearing

Purpose-Built Expedition Vehicles (Van Conversions and Campers)	
Pros	**Cons**
• Excellent storage capacity • Everything is self-contained • Fast setup • Comfortable • Excellent in bad weather • Very capable on open terrain	• Extremely expensive • Large • Heavy • Limited to wide open spaces with lots of clearance • Not suited for daily driving

Truck campers offer great room. Pop-up campers collapse for a lower profile. The camper can be removed and stored to allow the truck to be a comfortable daily driver and hauler.

Designed for open spaces and desert terrain, these expedition trail rigs are not ideal for narrow mountain trails and roads. The Hunter Acela Predator EXP costs over $300,000. The Earth Cruiser V-8 4x4 starts at $350,000. The Mercedes-built Unimog has a long history as a military vehicle that is good for overland trips in open spaces—or as the ultimate mall crawler.

Overlanding-Capable Vehicle Categories *continued*

Used Vehicles	
Pros	**Cons**
• Cost: many good deals, especially on built vehicles • Many have good equipment for off-road adventures and may already be overland-equipped	• Many need maintenance soon after purchase • May have been abused • Beware of scams • Should be inspected by a professional

Hummers are roomy and capable except for their size, which limits trail access.

The out-of-production Nissan Xterra (especially the earlier Off-Road model and the newer Pro4X model) is a great overlanding vehicle.

If you want something different and cool, look for Jeep Forward Control (FC). The FC is a great overlanding rig for pretty extreme terrain. The FC is rare and expensive.

The Land Rover Discovery I and Discovery II models from the late 1990s and early 2000s helped start the overlanding movement. They are inexpensive, which makes them great as low-cost overlanding rigs. Carry spares, especially electrical-system parts, if you have these vehicles.

The Toyota FJ Cruiser is another out-of-production 4WD vehicle with good overlanding potential.

roof weight limits. You can find roof-load weight limit information in the owner's manual. In general, the dynamic load capacity, which is lower than the static capacity, on average is 110 pounds. The static roof load capacity average is about 165 pounds. If you have a rooftop tent, don't exceed the dynamic load when the tent is stored. When occupied, stay within the static weight limit. The reason for the lower static weight capacity includes aerodynamic forces, especially lifts. Shockingly, according to AAA, there are about 200,000 motor vehicle accidents each year that are caused by road debris that result in about 500 deaths. Exceeding weight limits is dangerous and can damage your vehicle and gear.

Brands and Models

Here is an incomplete list of vehicles that are suitable for overlanding when equipped with 4WD or AWD. This can be used as a starting point for your search.

Make	Model
Chevrolet	Colorado ZR2, Silverado
Ford	F-150, Ranger, Bronco, Explorer, Expedition, Transit (van)
Dodge	Durango, Ram, Ram 1500, Sprinter (van)
Jeep	Wrangler, Cherokee (TrailHawk model), Grand Cherokee (TrailHawk model), Renegade (TrailHawk model). Non-TrailHawk models with 4WD can be used for very easy off-road trails and roads but lack ground clearance and tire size increase options.
Toyota	Tacoma, 4-Runner, FJ Cruiser, Land Cruiser
Lexus	GX 470, GX 460
Nissan	Frontier PRO 4X, Pathfinder, Xterra PRO
Land Rover/ Range Rover	Defenders and older Discovery 1 and 2 models
Hummer	H1, H2, and H3

The Ford Bronco checks every box for overlanding adventures. With six versions, even the entry-level base model can tackle moderate trails with good tires. The Badlands trim is designed for extreme off-roading, and the Wildtrak is more desert oriented. The optional Sasquatch package kicks the off-road performance up a few notches.

Chevrolet offers several variations of the Colorado model. The ZR2 package comes with many off-road-specific features, such as skidplates and rock sliders, upgraded suspension, and many options from the factory. Aftermarket support is strong.

The Ram 1500 TRX is an off-road beast with great on-road performance as well. While its size may keep it off some trails, its off-road performance starts with more than 11 inches of ground clearance with the air suspension and ride controlled by Bilstein Active Terrain Dynamic shocks. It also has a locking rear differential and skidplates.

No factory 4x4 matches the Jeep Wrangler Rubicon with the Xtreme Recon package for off-road performance. In stock trim, the Rubicon Xtreme Recon can tackle all but the most extreme trails. If taking on challenging terrain is part of the overlanding plan, the Rubicon is a great platform for rooftop tents or off-road trailer towing. Non-Rubicon models provide good off-road capability on easier trails.

Any trim level of the Jeep Cherokee with 4WD can take on easy off-road trails. The Cherokee TrailHawk model can take on difficult terrain with increased ground clearance and several important off-road features. (Photo Courtesy Stellantis)

The 2022 Jeep Grand Cherokee TrailHawk offers luxury and off-road capability. It features air suspension with a maximum ground clearance of 11.4 inches, several off-road modes, skidplates, and a front sway-bar disconnect. It also offers good storage capacity, excellent in-class tow ratings (especially with the Hemi V-8 option), and a luxurious interior. (Photo Courtesy Stellantis)

Small SUVs lack storage capacity, but with careful gear selection and packing, little SUVs (such as the Jeep Renegade TrailHawk) can cover 90 percent of the dirt roads and trails to allow a wide range of overlanding adventures. (Photo Courtesy Stellantis)

The Toyota Land Cruiser is a good platform to make modifications so that you can take on difficult terrain. It is also a solid platform for overlanding gear.

The discontinuation of this Toyota surprised many people, especially overlanders. The FJ Cruiser makes an excellent overlanding rig for easy-to-difficult trails. They are still popular as used vehicles.

Before the term "overlanding" was coined, Land Rovers dominated expedition travel. The Land Rover Defender was the ultimate expedition rig.

Today, the Land Rover Defender is a luxurious version of the earlier Defender, but it maintains its off-road heritage as a good-but-expensive overlanding platform.

Overlanding Newcomer Tips

Off-roading can be daunting to a newcomer. It is a very different environment compared to driving on the highway. The fear of getting lost or stuck keeps many newcomers from experiencing the adventures that four-wheeling offers. There is much to learn, and some elements of driving off-road are counterintuitive. While nothing is better than hands-on experience, these tips point you in the right direction and open a whole new world of adventure, challenge, and beauty. These tips were developed for students at the Trails 411 Off-Road Training programs in Big Bear Lake, California.

Driving Tips

The following section features tips that will help you drive on your overlanding adventure.

Learn the Controls

Knowing what your controls are used for and how to operate them is critical. Before heading out to a trail, familiarize yourself with the operation of the transfer case for 2WD and 4WD high range and low range. Know how to shift an automatic transmission in manual mode if so equipped. Does your 4x4 have manual controls or electronic? Learn how to engage and disengage axle lockers.

Off-road driving presents many challenges. For a newcomer, the challenges can be overwhelming. Adding the additional weight of overlanding gear makes the challenge greater. The basics of driving, vehicle gear, and the environment are all key to enjoying the experience in places, such as the legendary Rubicon trail.

The Wrangler JL Rubicon has many electronic controls. It is important to fully understand all the off-road controls to get the most from your 4WD vehicle. (Photo Courtesy Stellantis)

Know how the hill assist is engaged. Hill assist uses the onboard computer and antilock-braking system to control downhill speed without applying the brakes. Each system is a little different, but it all depends on the transmission gear and the transfer-case ratio. If your 4x4 is new, there is a good chance that the salesperson did not go over the 4x4 controls when you purchased the vehicle. Read the owner's manual. The same applies to used vehicles.

Visual Fields

Where you look is often where you go. Most newcomers have a tendency to look right in front of the hood. Expand your visual field to scan the terrain in front of you as far as possible. Also, take in the terrain to the sides and the rear. An additional trick is to rotate your side mirrors down so that you can see the rear tire contact patches in rocky terrain. Keep your eyes moving and attempt to anticipate the terrain and line you need to drive to avoid obstacles and stay safe.

A slight distraction on a narrow trail can lead to disaster. Paying attention makes off-road driving much safer. (Photo Courtesy Stellantis)

Pay Attention

Many trails are narrow. Inattention, even for a split second, creates a situation where a tire can breach the edge of the road. This can lead to getting stuck or going over the side. Lack of attention can also allow a bad line into ruts, bumps, whoop-de-doos, rocks, tree stumps, and other unfriendly objects that can lead to damage and an unpleasant ride.

The driver's hands should be positioned on top of the steering wheel. Thumbs should be on top of the wheel, not wrapped around the wheel. Steering wheel kick-back over rough terrain can cause injuries to thumbs and wrists.

Keep your eyes moving to take in as much of the terrain as possible. Most of the time, your eyes will be in the green zone monitoring obstacles. The yellow zone allows you to determine the optimal line before you need to maneuver. The red zones include the sides and rearview mirrors. Watch these areas occasionally.

Place Tires for Ground Clearance

Straddling obstacles is intuitive for most new off-road drivers. Increased ground clearance reduces the chance of getting hung up on obstacles and damaging critical underside components. Place the vehicle's tires on the obstacles to gain ground clearance. By practicing tire placement on small rocks, you learn where your tire contact patches are located. Knowing how much ground clearance you have is also helpful. If in doubt, reduce speed and place the tires on the rock or obstacle.

Place the tires on obstacles to gain ground clearance. The natural tendency is to straddle the obstacles, which often leads to getting the vehicle high-centered and stuck.

Look for Traction

Different surfaces have varying degrees of traction. Dry surfaces offer good traction, and wet and muddy surfaces provide less traction. It's even worse in snow, and traction can be non-existent on ice. Sandy sections have less traction than dry dirt, which has less traction than rocky terrain. Brush and debris along the edge of a trail may protrude through ice, snow, or mud and can improve traction. Look for traction when the vehicle slips and slides and excessive wheelspin occurs.

Steering

While how much and when to turn the steering wheel seems basic, some elements of steering are not intuitive. Off-roading often requires full-lock steering maneuvers in tight quarters. If the steering wheel is turned too much too soon, body damage can occur when the vehicle hits trees, rocks, brush, and other obstacles.

When steering, the rear tires do not follow in the tracks of the front tires. The rear tires track inside the path of the front tires. The sharper the turn, the more pronounced this becomes. The rule of thumb for short-wheelbase rigs, such as two-door Jeep Wranglers, Suzuki Samurais, and Toyota FJ40s, is to begin rotating the vehicle when the obstacle is at the A-pillar of the windshield. For longer-wheelbase

Loose rocks provide less traction than those that are planted solidly in the ground. (Photo Courtesy Stellantis)

Snow may require some momentum to move forward. Too much wheelspin will dig the tires deeper into the ground. (Photo Courtesy Currie Enterprises)

vehicles, such as four-door Jeep Wranglers, SUVs, and trucks, rotation should wait until the obstacle is at the B-pillar (or the driver's shoulder).

Gear/Transfer-Case Ratio

Newcomers always ask what gear to use in the transfer case. Never use 4WD on dry pavement. I always recommend 4WD on the dirt for improved control. High range is fine for most situations. Use low range when climbing or descending hills, especially steep hills. Use four-low range in rocks where speeds are low. If engine RPM exceeds about 3,000 in top gear in low range, stop and shift back into high-range 4WD. Use a transmission gear that keeps your engine RPM near optimal torque, which is usually between 1,500 and 2,500.

Braking Downhill

Driving down a steep hill causes weight to transfer from the rear tires to the front tires. Braking causes more weight to transfer forward. The reduced weight on the rear tires makes them prone to lock. If the rear tires lock up while steering, the rear of the vehicle can begin to slide sideways. If uncorrected, the tires can catch in the dirt, rocks, or ruts and cause a rollover. This can even happen with antilock brakes. Counter-steering the wheel and easing off the brakes can allow a sideways slide to be corrected. Gentle acceleration can also help. Carrying extra speed may be uncomfortable, but that is preferred over tipping over.

Angle through Ruts

Getting high-centered on bumps and ruts is annoying and embarrassing. Minimize the risk by crossing bumps and ruts at an angle. The goal is to place one tire at a time over the bump or through the rut to maximize ground clearance. In a series of undulating ruts and bumps, take the line that will keep the vehicle as level as possible.

Plan the line through ruts and over bumps so that the vehicle stays as level as possible.

Drive at an angle through the ruts so that only one tire at a time crosses the deepest section. (Photo Courtesy Currie Enterprises)

Watch the Tilt

When driving over obstacles with only one side of your 4x4, be aware of the tilt angle of the vehicle. This can happen over rocks, bumps, tree roots, and side slopes. In tight quarters, the low side of the vehicle can tilt enough to cause damage to the roof, mirror, or other body panels. Slow speeds will reduce bouncing, which in turn reduces the tilt or lean of the vehicle. If you hit the bump or obstruction too quickly, the amount of tilt and bounce increases along with the risk of damage. So, go slow in tight quarters and on uneven terrain.

Speed for Hillclimbs

Most hillclimbs are best undertaken at low speeds: 3 to 6 mph. Very

Minor wheelspin on hillclimbs is okay as long as momentum is maintained.

Dropping down steep ledges requires hard braking to keep the front springs from compressing too much while unloading the rear springs. Try to steer straight or downhill if possible (to the left in the photo) to stabilize the vehicle.

steep hills require more momentum. Keep wheelspin to a minimum with a light foot on the throttle. Know what is at the top of the climb, even if it means hiking to the top. Many climbs require a sharp turn as the climb is crested. Missing the turn or carrying too much speed can lead to an uncomfortable and dangerous ride.

Wheel lock-up on a descent is dangerous. The deep ruts here keep the Jeep from sliding sideways.

Dropping Down Ledges

Hard braking is required when dropping down ledges or off rocks. The tires should roll down slowly and not bounce. Weight transfer off the rear tires occurs when descending. Even more weight transfers forward if the front tires bounce down hard. Rollovers occur on steep drop-offs when too much speed is carried. An additional factor occurs when one tire drops down before the other. The natural tendency is to steer toward the uphill (or higher) tire. If the right front tire drops down before the left, the instinct is to steer left, but this causes the right front downhill tire to become a fulcrum. This will make a rollover more likely. Keeping the steering wheel straight reduces the risk. If possible, steering downhill helps stabilize the vehicle and reduces the risk of a rollover even more.

Use a Spotter

Use a spotter when the terrain is complicated, the line is difficult, or the driver can't see. A spotter becomes the driver's eyes outside the vehicle. A spotter can see obstacles and determine the best path when the driver is unable to see the terrain. Spotters must use clear, concise hand signals when the vehicle is moving and only use verbal communication when the vehicle is stationary.

The driver must be able to clearly see hand signals. Bystanders must move out of harm's way, and the spotter needs to be ready to move quickly if the driver makes a mistake with the steering, throttle, or brakes.

Pay attention to the path of the rear tires as well as front. For longer vehicles, such as the Jeep Wrangler Unlimited, the rear tires will track inside the front tires by a full half-width of the vehicle in a full-lock turn.

The spotter is signaling the driver to stop. Verbal communication should only occur when the vehicle is not moving.

The spotter signals to the driver that a large obstacle is about to be climbed. A hands-up motion does this effectively. A hands-down motion means that the vehicle is dropping down an obstacle and the driver should apply the brakes hard to roll down the drop-off.

Hand signals from the spotter provide the best and most precise communication with the driver. We use signals that allow the driver to mirror the hand signals of the spotter. The spotter's hands are held as if he or she is holding a steering wheel. Steering motions are mirrored by the driver. This type of hand signal indicates both direction and how far to turn the steering wheel.

Vehicle Tips

The following section features tips for off-road driving.

Inflating and Deflating Tires

Tires are aired down (tire pressure reduced) for four reasons: 1) improved traction by allowing the tire contact patch to spread over a greater area, 2) an improved ride since the tires are softer, 3) reduced risk of a puncture because the tire tread and sidewall have more compliance, and 4) reduced damage to the road surface because the weight on each tire is spread out over a greater area of the tire contact patch.

The optimal tire pressure for an off-road situation varies by the stiffness and height of the tire sidewall, the weight of the vehicle, the type of wheels being used, and the road surface and conditions. For example, a 33-inch-diameter tire on a 17-inch wheel has a sidewall about 7 inches tall at optimal highway tire pressure. That tire can be aired down so the sidewall height is reduced by 10 to 12 percent or 3/4 inch. This is a safe tire pressure for most conditions. Never go below 12 psi without beadlock wheels.

Airing up requires an air source. Inexpensive 12-volt car air compressors can be purchased in hardware stores or online. If all else fails, driving a short distance (no more than 5 miles) at a low speed (40 mph maximum) to an air source is safe with tires in good condition. The big issue is overheating the tires. On hot days in the desert, shorter distances and lower speeds are required.

Disconnect the Front Sway Bar

Two sway bars control body roll when cornering. Limiting body roll on the highway is important on the highway, but when off-roading, sway bars limit axle articulation. If the axles cannot move freely up and down, it is likely to lift one or two tires off the ground in big ruts, bumps, and rocks. This happens in some truck and SUV TV commercials.

For safety and your blood pressure, keeping all four tires planted on terra firma is a sound idea. Disconnecting sway bars reduces the likelihood of lifting tires off the ground and teeter-tottering. In rare cases, a rollover is possible. Disconnecting the front sway bar is the most important. If you have a Jeep Wrangler Rubicon, there is an electric sway-bar disconnect. If not, sway-bar-disconnect kits provide an inexpensive solution to the issue.

Learn Basic Navigation

GPS provides valuable information for off-road navigation, but electronics can fail. Always carry a paper map for the area where you travel off-road. Learn how to read a map and understand the basics of navigation. Free paper maps are available from most government land managers, including the US Forest Service Motor Vehicle Use Maps (https://www.fs.fed.us/recreation/programs/ohv/ohv_maps.shtml) and BLM (blm.gov/maps). Paper maps are available at visitor centers, ranger stations, and field offices.

Gear Tips

Eventually, everyone gets stuck. This section is an overview of basic recovery gear that can help you get unstuck.

A Hi-Lift jack is often the first recovery tool that is purchased by newcomers. The Hi-Lift jack offers valuable versatility.

Tire deflators, such as the Currie EZ Deflator, make airing down quick and easy. Using a deflator is one of the most inexpensive ways to improve the off-road experience.

The Handle-All kit from Hi-Lift provides several helpful tool heads that interchange on a single handle.

Tow straps are used to pull stuck vehicles or tow broken-down rigs. They should not be used for yanking a stuck vehicle. Use a kinetic strap for yanking.

Recovery Gear

The previously mentioned tow strap and shackle top the list. A shovel can allow you to dig your vehicle out of a tough situation. A portable jack with a wheel lift attachment, such as the Hi-Lift jack, allows you to lift a wheel and tire off the ground. You can then stack rocks or debris under the tire to gain ground clearance when you are high-centered.

Winches have a major cool factor and are a great tool. Extraction boards can quickly get you unstuck from soft surfaces, including sand, mud, and snow. A ground anchor, such as the Pull Pal, allows you to use a winch when no other vehicles, trees, or other objects are available to winch against.

Tow Strap and Shackles

It is naive to count on a passerby to help if you get stuck or suffer a breakdown, so be prepared. A good Samaritan may be willing to help but may not have the tow strap and shackles that are needed to get your vehicle pulled out of trouble. Carry these items with you. A good tow strap is cheap insurance. Only use tow straps with stitched loops at the ends. Never use straps with metal hooks. They can fail and are dangerous.

Other Tips

It is important to travel in a group so that members of the group can provide assistance when other members get stuck, break down, or have a medical emergency. Club 4x4 runs and professional events, such as Jeep Jamborees, are a great way to learn the ropes.

If you are hell-bent on going solo, satellite locators can help in the case of an emergency. At the very least, notify someone who you can count on about your planned route and estimated time of return. If you fail to report by a designated time, that person can look for you or contact the local authorities.

Even if you plan on a short hour-or-two excursion into the backcountry, carry plenty of water. While we can survive for several days, even weeks, without food, survival without water is limited to two to three days. The rule of thumb is to carry 1 gallon of water per person per day. Carry at least a two-day supply of water for a one-day trip off-road, and more if you are wheeling in hot conditions. Carry snacks for comfort.

Most areas of prime off-road terrain are in mountain or desert regions. Significant temperature swings are common. A 90°F desert day can become a chilly 40°F overnight. Dress in layers. Carry blankets just in case. Even lightweight emergency foil mylar blankets can help. Cheap rain ponchos can help keep you dry in unexpected summer thunderstorms.

Folding camp chairs are more comfortable than rocks and logs and take up little space. Hand wipes, paper towels, toilet paper, and hand sanitizer come in handy when exploring the backcountry. Carry trash bags to leave no trace.

The most dangerous element of off-roading is scampering around on rocks, hills, and ruts. Scrapes and cuts are common. A basic first-aid kit is a necessity for backcountry travel. Learning how to use first aid is a good

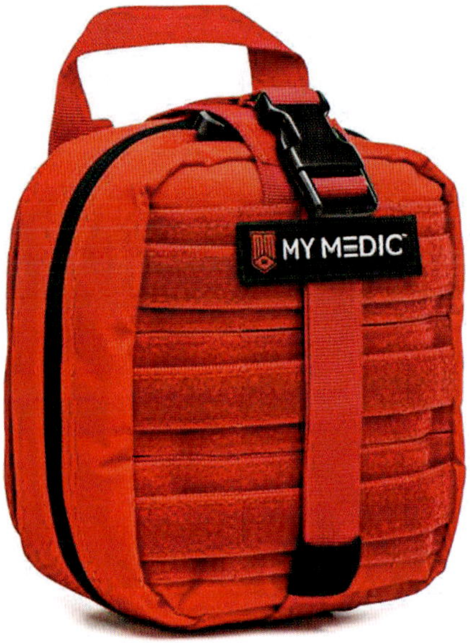

A simple first-aid kit makes attending minor wounds easy. Most trail injuries are cuts, scrapes, and bruises when outside the vehicle.

Leaving trash in the backcountry harms the environment, degrades the experience for others, and leads to closed access. Pack out your trash.

idea. At least read the instructions in your first-aid kit, preferably prior to using it in the field. A first-aid smartphone application, such as the SAS Survival Guide, can offer guidance.

Leaving trash in the backcountry can result in closed access for off-road vehicles. Carry out any trash that you create, and help out the environment by picking up trash left by thoughtless individuals. You would be shocked by the gross items that people leave behind.

If a route is not marked or on an official map, it is probably not a legal route. Stay on legal routes. One of the biggest threats to motorized vehicle access on public land is travel on illegal routes. If you're not sure, don't go there.

Land management agencies, such as the US Forest Service and the Bureau of Land Management, provide signage on most legal routes.

CHAPTER 4

Overlanding Trailers, Adventure Vans, Truck-Bed Campers, and Expedition Rigs

Purpose-built vehicles for camping, such as trailers, vans, and expedition rigs, offer significant advantages and several drawbacks. Self-contained living quarters provide a high level of convenience.

Vans require camp breakdown and gear stowage before heading out on an adventure or into the nearest town for supplies. Trailers can be left in camp while the tow rig ventures out for a day trip from base camp.

Overlanding trailers, such as the Opus Lite Off-Road, can be used as a base camp when camping for multiple days. This allows the 4x4 rig to explore without breaking camp. (Photo Courtesy J.P. Molnar)

Camper vans are a solid platform for camping in comfort and exploring easy terrain. The luxury comes with a big price tag.

Even small utility-style trailers that have been converted for overlanding can provide advantages, especially when equipped with a rooftop tent on a rack. The biggest disadvantage in most cases is the cost. Overlanding van conversions and off-road-capable trailers can be quite expensive.

Trailers

Overlanding trailers have a huge advantage because they can be disconnected and left at base camp. The biggest disadvantage is needing a vehicle that is capable of towing the trailer and being able to negotiate terrain that is as challenging as the trailer can handle.

Overlanding trailers are available in a wide range of designs and sizes and with a variety of different accommodations and equipment. The smallest trailers are based on old military utility-trailer designs. The small trailers can be fitted with large off-road tires for exceptional off-road performance, but they lack the amenities of larger units, such as sleeping quarters, an indoor kitchen facility, and a bathroom. They use rooftop tents for the sleeping quarters, a privacy shelter or annex room for the bathroom, and a slide-out kitchen for cooking. The lack of amenities is made up for with less weight (meaning that tow rigs with less towing capacity can be used) and greater off-road capability.

Low-profile designs, usually lower than the top of a tow vehicle even with a rooftop tent, allows the smaller

Large off-road-capable camping trailers have considerable space and comfortable accommodations for sleeping and cooking as well as bathroom facilities. They require a larger tow rig, but once the trailer has been set up and detached, the tow rig is free to explore.

Mission Overland offers the Summit off-road trailer, which features a pop-up clam-shell-style top with up to 76 inches of headroom, 22 inches of ground clearance, a slide-out kitchen, and a queen-sized bed with an additional bunk bed.

The Kimberly Kamper RLT Edition off-road camper trailer features a unique floor plan. The forward section unfolds for the galley, and the rear section opens up to provide sleeping quarters for two people. A toilet and hot water shower round out the amenities of this capable off-road trailer.

trailers to navigate tight quarters and low-hanging tree branches without the same risk of damage or getting stuck. If rock crawling is on your agenda for overlanding adventures, the small trailers can be set up to tackle any terrain that your 4x4 rig can handle.

Large trailers offer distinct comfort advantages, including indoor sleeping, cooking, and bathroom/shower facilities. Large off-road trailers, such as the Black Series trailers, offer sizes up to 21 feet in length, which is about the longest and largest trailer capable of negotiating the tight quarters and rough, rutted trails that exist in the backcountry. Even a 21-foot-long trailer has limitations. Big trailers require more towing capacity, are more difficult to maneuver, cost more to buy and maintain, and have limited off-road capability. The larger the trailer, the more these issues apply. The trade-off is that they have greatly improved comfort when compared to a small trailer. Several important considerations should be taken into account when shopping for an overlanding trailer.

Sleeping Accommodations

Arguably the most important consideration is sleeping capacity. Sleeping accommodations for each individual is important. Small, nimble trailers have no accommodations, so a rooftop tent or swag tent will be necessary. For larger groups, more than one tent can be used. Larger trailers, either pop-up or full size, have sleeping quarters for two to eight people inside. All of the trailers can utilize annex rooms to accommodate more individuals for sleeping.

Floor Plan

A wide range of floor plans exists for off-road trailers. Study the plans and spend some time inside a trailer to get an idea of how well the setup works for your situation. Consider the sleeping layouts and privacy, bathroom layouts, the galley setup and dining accommodations, storage, and the ease of entry and exit.

Tow-Rig Towing Capacity

The total weight of a trailer plus gear, supplies, and cargo for overlanding must be considered. The total weight towed should never exceed the towing capacity recommended by the vehicle manufacturer. Additionally, the gross vehicle weight rating (GVWR), which is the total weight carried within the tow vehicle including passengers, fuel, gear, and trailer tongue weight, should never be exceeded. Ideal trailer tongue weight is 10 percent of the total trailer weight. More or less tongue weight can cause handling to deteriorate to the point of being dangerous. Consult with the manufacturer of the tow rig and the trailer for more specific information.

Amenities

Amenities require careful consideration. Does a bathroom have a stand-up shower? Is the toilet a flush style? What is the black-water and gray-water capacity? How much fresh water can be carried onboard? What is the electrical capacity? What are the battery-charging options? Can the refrigerator run on solar power, 12-volt power, and propane power?

Traveling light has advantages. The Patrol XC from Rustic Mountain Overland offers a compact, highly capable off-road trailer with a size that is similar to early military trailers. This design is ideal for tackling rough terrain.

The 1950s retro teardrop-style trailer offers protected sleeping accommodations but minimal storage. Ground clearance is also minimal, so this type of trailer is limited to easy roads and trails.

The Expedition 2.0 off-road camper by Off Grid Trailers provides the amenities of much larger trailers by utilizing inside sleeping quarters with outdoor annex rooms and awnings. The all-steel construction of the trailer provides great durability for rough off-road adventures. Ground clearance is 21 inches to help navigate ruts and obstacles.

What is the capacity of the refrigerator? Is there a freezer? Is there a heater, and can it handle the lowest temperatures you will encounter? Is there air conditioning? How large is the stove? Is there an oven? How about a closet? How effective is interior and exterior lighting?

Off-road trailers, such as the Kimberly Kampers RLT Edition, provide great room with the attached annex tents. Although it's perfect for multi-night stays at base camp, the RLT takes some time for setup and teardown.

Patriot Campers enjoys a stellar reputation in the overlanding trailer market. Offering several compact designs with a long list of features, the Patriot line is great off-road on tough terrain due to clever design features, such as the slanted tail on some models, which allows a great departure angle.

Black Series HQ off-road capable trailers range in length from about 19 feet to nearly 29 feet in overall length. The extensive list of features and options comes with a downside: cost and the need for a large tow vehicle.

Storage

Regardless of the size of the trailer, storage is a key consideration. In addition to refrigerator capacity, water, and waste-tank capacity, what can be stored? Consider these items:

- Bedding and sleeping bags
- Towels
- Nonperishable food items
- Clothes

Lance has been in the RV trailer business for decades. It is one of the few RV companies to move into the overlanding market. Its trailer offers some great features but lacks good ground clearance for many of the roads and trails on public lands.

Opus Campers USA makes a range of compact off-road trailers that feature air tent technology. Instead of using struts and bars to support the pop-up tent structure, Opus uses tubes inflated with compressed air. Setup is easy, and weight is kept to a minimum.

Even the Opus Lite, the smallest trailer in the Opus line, offers a dining area with a removable table and a pull-out queen-sized bed. (Photo Courtesy J.P. Molnar)

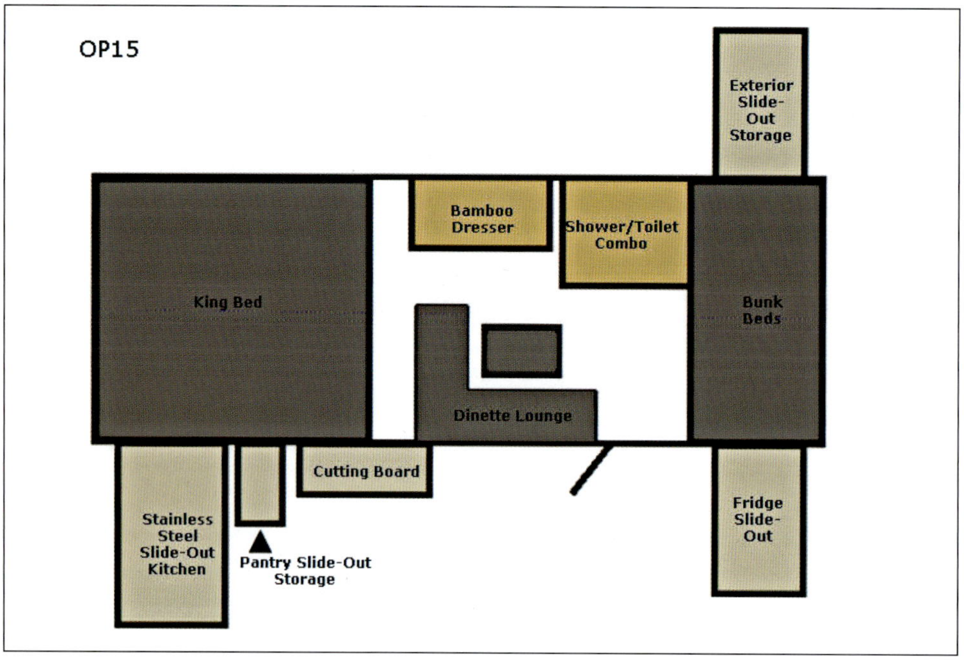

The Opus 15 off-road trailer offers great comfort and amenities while maintaining good off-road capabilities for a large trailer. This floor plan shows how much space the Opus 15 has. When shopping for a trailer or van, look at floor plans early in the selection process.

- Outdoor-activity gear
- Dishes, pots, pans, and cooking gear
- Cleaning and bathroom supplies and paper products

Off-Road Capability

In general, the larger the trailer, the less capable it is off-road. Ground clearance, approach and departure angles, turning angles, and weight should be considered relative to the types of trails that you plan to tackle. Small, nimble trailers can take on relatively extreme terrain with a good setup and easily match the performance of a well-equipped, rock-crawling-capable 4x4 rig.

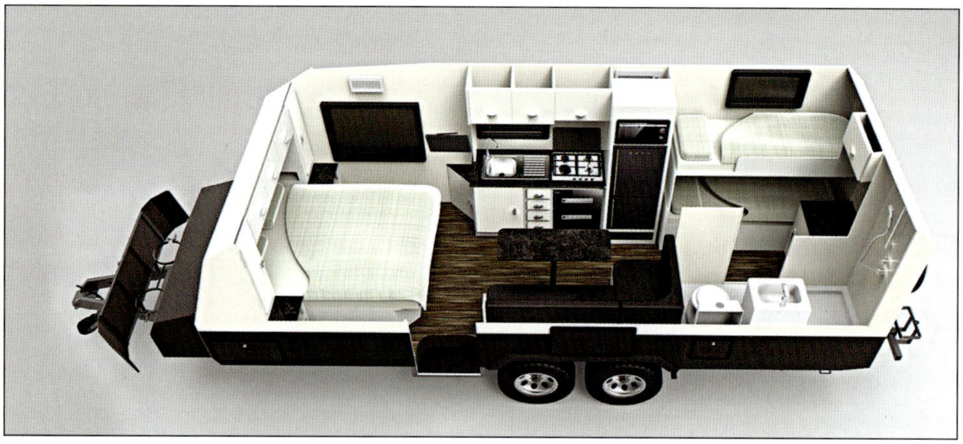

Cutaway illustrations, such as this one from Econocampor, provide insight into a trailer's layout.

Axle and Trailer Articulation

Even easy trails can become rutted, and rocks can become exposed. Erosion and the lack of maintenance budgets available to public land managers are factors that cause deterioration of backcountry roads and trails. Well-maintained roads are a real treat, but count on the need to negotiate ruts and rough patches. Tow-rig axle articulation is important, as is trailer axle articulation. Most off-road trailers utilize some form of suspension with good articulation. Many use an independent swing-arm suspension that offers

Off-road toy haulers with tilt-down rear doors can haul bikes, ATVs, and supplies for base camp.

Full-size trailers offer one big advantage: space for a full-size indoor shower.

Large trailers, such as the Black Series HQ17, are great base-camp setups but take considerable setup and tear-down time. They also require larger, more powerful tow vehicles.

Large indoor kitchens in some full-height trailers provide protection from the elements while cooking.

After a day of exploring, arriving back at base camp to a cozy setup, such as this one created around the Opus Lite trailer, is what overlanding is all about. (Photo Courtesy J.P. Molnar)

Indoor dining is a nice feature of large trailers. When the weather turns cold or wet, inside meals are a welcome feature.

An interior toilet is an amenity that is available in large trailers. A built-in washing machine is a little over the top.

good articulation. Large trailers suffer from reduced articulation.

Trailer tongue articulation is often overlooked. A standard 2- or $2\frac{5}{8}$-inch ball hitch has limited rotation that can be exceeded. When the limits of travel at the ball are reached, the trailer-hitch arms cannot rotate and often flex, which puts great loads on the tubes and can lead to failure over time. Even worse is that a trailer tire (or tires on multi-axle trailers) can lift off the road surface in heavily rutted terrain which can lead to a rollover. Modern off-road trailers use a hitch system that works like a universal joint to allow greater and smoother trailer articulation. If a trailer is not equipped with this hitch, the aftermarket offers rotating hitches that replace the ball-style hitch in the hitch receiver on the tow vehicle. For heavier trailers, look into load-bearing and weight-distribution hitch systems.

Small trailers with outdoor galleys are the essence of camping. Note the capable off-road tires and the slanted tail, which offers a great departure angle for taking on big ruts, rocks, and rough terrain.

Australia is the birthplace of the overlanding movement. The Pursuit off-road trailer from BRS Off-Road offers innovative design features.

If exploring the backcountry is the primary goal, trailers such as the Opus Lite can tackle any terrain that the tow rig can take on while providing a high level of comfort at camp. (Photo Courtesy J.P. Molnar)

Opus trailers excel off-road. They are equipped with aggressive off-road tires, a spare tire, independent-trailing-arm coil suspension with dual shock absorbers, a front rock guard to protect from damage and debris, underbody armor with diamond plating to navigate over rocky terrain, a significant rear departure angle for added clearance, and electric brakes. (Photo Courtesy J.P. Molnar)

Articulation is critical for off-road vehicles in rough, rutted, and rocky terrain. The same applies to the trailer, especially the hitch. Lack of articulation can damage the trailer and trailer hitch. It can even unload and lift tires on the tow vehicle. Lock N' Roll trailer hitches allow full articulation by using a three-axis rotation on the hitch and a unique locking device that eliminates slop in the hitch connection. The design also makes backing and maneuvering into tight spaces much easier.

Adventure Vans

Fully self-contained camper vans provide a high degree of comfort and utility for long-term overlanding adventures. Many manufacturers, models, and styles offer overlanders a great selection of floor plans, sleeping accommodations, and amenities. The great features and comfort come at a cost. Adventure vans are expensive but provide enough space and amenities for extended travel or living on the backcountry roads.

While they are great for extended travel and comfort, adventure vans have significant drawbacks. Vans are large with a high center of gravity, tall profile, and high total weight. Adventure vans are limited to less-challenging roads and trails. Most vans are limited to smaller tire sizes. Axle articulation is limited. The tall structure, high center of gravity, and limited articulation limit travel to easier roads with good overhead clearance.

When shopping for an adventure van, consider all of the criteria that was outlined earlier in this chapter for selecting overlanding trailers.

Truck-Bed Campers

Campers for pickup trucks come in a wide range of sizes and accommodations. Ranging from a simple camper shell to a large, comfortable, self-contained unit that is similar to an adventure van, truck-bed campers are a great option for any adventure plan and budget.

Camper shells are great for low-cost, short-term adventures where sleeping in the truck bed is an option. For more extensive travel, large campers offer similar benefits

Vans are a great for overlanding adventures on easy-to-moderately-difficult trails and roads. Many variations and floor plans are available from several manufacturers.

Swiveling seats behind the front-row seats allow passengers to face forward while on the move but face backward or inward for dining, relaxing, and conversations.

Underbed storage drawers that are accessible from the rear doors provide storage space for important gear and supplies.

Solid-shell, high-top vans feature improved headroom with structural integrity. However, the increased frontal area affects performance and hurts fuel economy.

Small truck-bed camper shells protect gear and can act as a cover for sleeping bags in the bed.

to overlanding trailers with a wide variety of sleeping, galley, and bathroom facilities. As with adventure vans, campers are self-contained with the same need to stow gear and pack before breaking camp to undertake even a short adventure from base camp.

Truck-bed campers offer some significant advantages over adventure vans. The camper can be removed so that the truck can be used as a daily driver without the large, heavy load on board. Trucks offer more robust platforms than vans and often have better suspension, increased articulation capability, and a stout 4WD system. Large off-road tires can also be fitted to allow the camper and truck combination to take on more challenging terrain. The same limitations that apply to truck campers also apply to trailers. Larger-sized rigs face more difficulty on narrow, rutted trails with minimal overhead clearance.

Huge truck-bed campers offer great comfort for adventures. Their sheer size makes travel on many roads impossible due to the height and width of the rig. A heavy-duty truck is required, and fuel economy is poor.

Pop-up campers allow a low profile when driving and good space when they are opened at camp. With awnings and considerable storage space, pop-up campers are a great alternative and can be easily removed for more utility and daily driving with the base truck.

When shopping for a truck camper, consider all of the criteria outlined in the "Trailers" section earlier in this chapter.

Expedition Rigs

Nothing tops an expedition rig on the cool-factor scale. With costs ranging into the mid-six figure category, nothing tops the cost, either. Besides cost, size is the overwhelming downside for an expedition rig. Intended for open country and desert environments, expedition rigs are too large to fit on many of the roads and trails that are popular for overlanding or your favorite fast-food drive-thru.

The Hawk edition camper from Four Wheel Campers mounts to a flatbed truck, offers improved ground clearance, and pops up enough to increase headroom.

Behemoths, such as this expedition rig from Adrenalin Industries, can be luxurious and capable. However, their sheer size makes them impractical for many trails and roads in forested areas. They are designed mostly for open desert terrain. Prices are astronomical.

CHAPTER 5

BUILDING AN OVERLANDING RIG

A key question for anyone contemplating going overlanding is if your current vehicle will work well for overlanding.

In Chapter 2, overlanding vehicles were covered in some detail. If you currently own one of those 4x4s, trucks, SUVs, or vans, you are set to go overlanding. Depending on the vehicle, easy short-term adventures are easily undertaken in a stock vehicle with overlanding gear, including:

- Sleeping Bag
- Tent
- Water
- Food
- Cooler

A vehicle such as the new Ford Bronco is an excellent platform for an overlanding rig. Most truck and SUV manufacturers offer vehicles that are good for off-road adventures.

Toyota makes a range of SUVs and trucks that are ideal for overlanding. Aftermarket support is excellent for these vehicles.

One of the best new rigs for overlanding is the Chevy Colorado ZR2. This pickup can carry loads on the bed rack and in the bed. It can also easily tow an off-road trailer.

- Cooking Gear
- Basic Recovery Gear (a tow strap, soft or D-ring shackles, and recovery points on the vehicle)

Basic gear for overlanding allows adventures for short periods, such as weekends, on easy terrain in good weather. More extensive and difficult long-term overlanding trips require more gear and a vehicle with greater off-road capability.

A Jeep Wrangler is hard to beat as the basis for an overlanding rig, especially if extreme terrain is on the to-do list. No vehicle in history has better support from the aftermarket to allow for the creation of an extreme rock crawler with excellent overlanding capabilities.

In spite of the immense popularity of rooftop tents, ground tents offer a viable, lightweight, and inexpensive alternative for sleeping accommodations. Modern ground tents are easy to set up and store, and they can be left behind at base camp without having to break them down for travel.

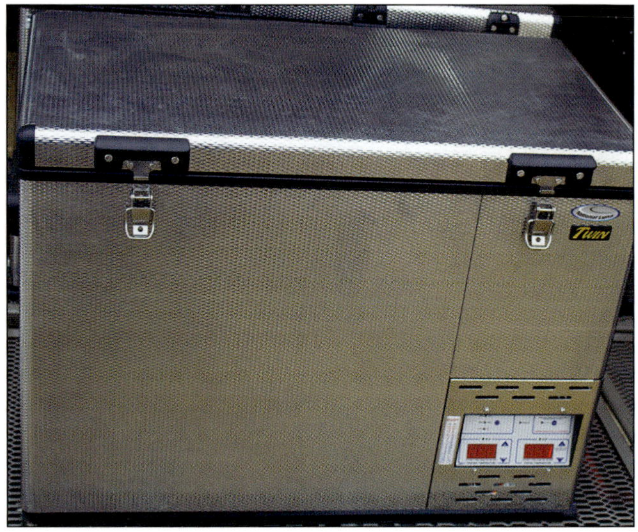

Electric refrigerators are available in several sizes to fit almost any overlanding vehicle. When planning an overlanding adventure, cold-food replenishment stops should be determined.

Water storage is easy, and many options are available for potable and non-potable water. As a rule of survival in the backcountry, carry 1 gallon of water per person per day for the duration of your trip or until water can be replenished.

Food storage requires some security. A 12-volt refrigerator is nice, but hard- and soft-sided coolers using ice or freezer blocks work well for short overlanding adventures.

Soft shackles allow for the attachment of winches to hard mounts on bumpers, tow points, and a variety of other recovery gear.

D-ring shackles are important to have, as soft shackles do not always work.

Strong tow hooks that are rigidly mounted to the vehicle's frame structure are mandatory for towing and other forms of vehicle recovery.

Portable stoves are a better solution than packing sandwiches and cold cereal for cooking in the backcountry. Propane stoves are available in many sizes and a variety of price points.

A good, sturdy tow strap is mandatory recovery gear for any off-road vehicle. Use only tow straps with stitched loop ends—not ones with metal hooks.

Determine the Type of Overlanding You Prefer

Ask yourself whether you plan to use your existing vehicle or purchase a vehicle for overlanding. Will the vehicle used for overlanding also be a daily driver? Next, decide on the type of terrain that you plan to encounter on your adventures. Capable off-road vehicles can easily be built for highway use as well. Keep in mind that even roads rated as "easy" can be rutted and rocky. Ground clearance is important and so is traction. Vehicle load needs to be considered as well. Carrying several hundred pounds of overlanding gear and passengers can overload a stock vehicle and will reduce ground clearance. Carrying more gear requires suspension modifications. At the minimum, a lift kit to allow the loaded rig to maintain the stock ride height is important. More lift over the stock height allows the use of larger tires and increases ground clearance.

The types of roads and trails that will be used will determine the extent of the modifications that are needed. For example, more extreme trails will possibly require additional armor for underside protection, a winch and winch bumper, and additional recovery gear. Traveling in small groups means that some recovery gear can be shared. Solo travel requires carrying everything onboard. One of the points of overlanding is to travel self-sufficiently. Learning to use the gear that is carried is also a must.

If rock crawling fits into your plans, a more-capable rig is in order. Items such as axle upgrades, steering upgrades, and larger tires and wheels need to be added to the list. At our off-road school, many students who say that they are not really interested in rock crawling change their minds after being exposed to some basic rock crawling challenges. Rock crawling requires a very-capable rig. Even if rock crawling is not a high priority, a rig capable of tackling the rocks with reliability means that the rig will stand up to the rigors of overlanding with ease.

A late 1990s Land Rover Discovery I on 33-inch tires and a 2-inch suspension lift can easily tackle a difficult trail. Most 4x4 vehicles with good ground clearance and off-road tires can master trails like this.

Any Jeep Wrangler can tackle most difficult trails with sensible modifications.

Taking on difficult trails in a luxury vehicle looks (and is) easy in a vehicle such as the 2022 Jeep Grand Cherokee TrailHawk.

Cause and Effect

As loads increase and trails become more challenging, the need to upgrade also increases. Here are some examples:

- Larger tires may require a suspension lift.
- A suspension lift may require steering-geometry correction. This is especially true with independent front suspension with lifts of more than 2 to 2.5 inches.
- Larger tires likely require stronger axles. Heavier loads also require stronger axles.
- Axle housings need to be upgraded or reinforced as the load, tire size, and trail difficulty increase.
- More load and bigger tires make brake upgrades a good idea.
- More load may require a winch with greater pulling power.
- Shock-absorber upgrades are necessary to control the suspension lift and heavier loads.
- Gear-ratio changes are necessary with bigger tires and greater loads, especially if hilly terrain, rocks, and trailer towing are on the agenda.

Build Options

Options for building overlanding vehicles are nearly endless. Many trucks, SUVs, and crossovers provide a suitable platform for overlanding. Vehicle choices range from very-capable used vehicles, such as early Toyota pickups, many models of Jeeps, and early Land Rover Discovery 1s to $300,000-plus Earth Roamers. The choice of the vehicle is based mostly on the intended use, budget, and type of trails.

Almost any 4WD or AWD vehicle with adequate ground clearance is suitable for overlanding on easy trails. Ground clearance is crucial given the deterioration of the trails caused by erosion and high levels of use. As trails become more difficult (the ruts get deeper, the bumps get taller, the hills get steeper, and the rocks get bigger), more capable vehicles are a necessity. Crossover vehicles and many stock SUVs and pickups do not have the ground clearance or protective armor to be ideal for difficult roads and trails. Modifications can allow these vehicles to tackle difficult terrain.

Progressing to the most difficult trails where rock crawling is common, hills are steeper, and the ruts can swallow a small car, few stock vehicles are up to the task. Modified Jeep Wranglers are the most common selection for extreme off-roading. The Ford Bronco is a good choice, and a wide range of Toyotas can handle modifications to take on the rough terrain. As overlanding becomes more popular, more aftermarket parts will become available to allow smaller vehicles to tackle difficult terrain.

Axle articulation, or flex capability, is one of the important elements needed to make a sound choice if extreme off-roading is one of the overlanding goals for a build. Articulation is covered in detail in Chapter 6.

The reality is that solid-axle vehicles articulate better than vehicles with an independent suspension. Many earlier 4x4 trucks and some SUVs came equipped with solid front and rear axles. Jeep Wranglers and some pickup trucks are currently the only new vehicles with solid axle configurations. The Jeep Wrangler and Gladiator in stock form, especially the Rubicon model, offer far superior flex or articulation. While vehicles with independent front suspension can be used on the tough stuff, the solid front axle will outperform the independent-front-suspension-equipped vehicles handily in difficult terrain. Independent-front-suspension vehicles require modifications to take on more challenging terrain. Independent-front-suspension systems usually have rack-and-pinion steering which is not ideal for the rigors of off-road adventures. The gears are not as strong, and the tie-rod ends are generally too small. Upgrades, when available, offer better performance and are less likely to wear prematurely or fail. Steering failures on the trail are difficult to overcome.

Aftermarket parts availability is also a factor when planning an overlanding build. Some vehicles have a huge aftermarket, while others have limited parts available for upgrading. The Jeep Wrangler models have more aftermarket parts options than any other vehicle in history. Toyota, Nissan, and Land Rover have good options. Other brands have availability, but not all products are ideal for overlanding. The Ford Bronco and Chevy Colorado are newer models with a rapidly growing aftermarket.

Overlanding gear, including rooftop tents, storage, tools, and recovery gear, is not usually brand specific. The dimensions of some items, such as storage solutions, will be a factor for fitment, but most items for overlanding will work on most overlanding-suitable vehicles.

New Vehicle

Many new vehicles are great for overlanding right off the showroom floor, including the Ford Bronco, Jeep Wrangler and Gladiator (espe-

The full-size Ford Bronco is available in a variety of trim levels. There are seven in all, with the Sasquatch package available on most. The aftermarket products that are available for the Bronco increases daily, but the Badlands version with the Sasquatch package has capabilities to tackle some challenging terrain in stock form.

The Jeep Gladiator offers plenty of options for overlanding and has extensive aftermarket support. The Gladiator, like any pickup truck, offers great storage space and can carry heavier loads on a bed rail–mounted rack.

cially the Rubicon models), Toyota Tacoma, Chevrolet Colorado, Nissan Frontier, and Subaru Outback and Forester. The one important factor is the gear load. Too much weight in a stock vehicle can reduce ground clearance; stress the driveline, engine, and transmission; and overload the brakes. Each of these issues need to be addressed. In most cases, upgrades to suspension, drivelines, and brakes can overcome the stock vehicle's deficiencies.

The biggest downside to starting with a new vehicle is the cost. The addition of overlanding gear is about the same regardless of the vehicle, but modifications and upgrades can be costly. Starting with a vehicle that is already capable will cost more upfront but will require fewer modifications to prepare for the desired level of off-road adventures.

If difficult black-diamond trails are part of your overland adventure plan and making minimal modifications appeals to you, no vehicle is better than the Jeep Rubicon with the Extreme Recon package. In addition to all of the Rubicon features, the Extreme Recon package includes 35-inch tires and 4.56:1 ring-and-pinion gear ratios.

Luxury SUVs are considered candidates for overlanding. The Land Rover Defender falls into the "good" category, but the new 2022 Jeep Grand Cherokee TrailHawk is possibly even better. With the air-ride suspension fully lifted, the TrailHawk has 11.4 inches of ground clearance and a towing capacity of 6,200 pounds with the Pentastar V-6 (7,200 pounds with the Hemi V-8). The Grand Cherokee is a good candidate for hauling an overland trailer and exploring difficult terrain.

Used Vehicle

Great deals can often be found on used vehicles suitable for overlanding or vehicles that have already been modified for difficult off-road trails and overlanding. To take advantage of these deals, know in advance the exact make and model of the vehicle that you prefer as well as the range of model years.

More homework is required when looking for a used modified vehicle. Research the best aftermarket products available for the desired vehicle. Finding a vehicle that offers the desired equipment will be challenging. Being

Land Rover Discovery I and II models from the late 1990s into the early 2000s are capable off-road vehicles with reasonable aftermarket support. They're also inexpensive.

International Harvester Scouts are hard to find, but they are capable for overlanding.

Another low-cost entry-level overland-capable vehicle is the Jeep Cherokee XJ. Costs are low and many parts are available for upgrades.

flexible may help, but don't accept substandard parts or a poorly maintained vehicle just because you're eager to get out on the trail.

Modifying a Current Vehicle

If you have a vehicle that is suitable for overlanding, what modifications are needed to ensure improved performance and reliability? If you start with a used vehicle, make sure that the running gear, engine, transmission, transfer case, axles, suspension, and brakes are in good working order. These items should not be an issue with a new vehicle.

Tires

A few new 4x4 vehicles come with good off-road tires from the factory. The Jeep Gladiator Rubicon comes with the Falken WildPeak AT3W, the Jeep Rubicon JL comes with the BFGoodrich All-Terrain T/A, the Chevy Colorado ZR2 is equipped with the Goodyear Wrangler DuraTrac, and the Ford Bronco uses the Goodyear Territory (Wrangler) M/T tires.

Most other 4WD and AWD overlanding-suitable vehicles come with less-than-ideal tires for overlanding. For most overlanding applications, a good all-terrain tire will perform off-road to a much higher level while maintaining good on-road characteristics. In nearly all cases, a large-diameter tire can be fitted. For example, the Chevy Colorado ZR2 comes with a 30.4-inch tire, but a 33-inch-diameter tire can be fitted with no modifications. A Jeep Wrangler Rubicon can easily run a 35-inch-tall tire compared to the stock size just below 33 inches.

Larger-diameter tires can be used with most suitable overlanding vehicles. Large tires offer several benefits, including more ground clearance and the ability to run lower tire pressure. See Chapter 7 for more details.

Most vehicles capable of overlanding do not come equipped with good off-road tires. All-terrain tires are a good compromise between highway driving and good off-road performance. Mud-terrain tires offer improved performance for challenging terrain. The hybrid Rugged Terrain (RT) tire is becoming more common for overlanding rigs and is a great compromise.

Wheels

Stock wheels are generally adequate for small increases in tire size. Many newer vehicles come with 18-inch-or-larger-diameter wheels. Larger diameter wheels mean smaller tire sidewalls and less ability to lower tire pressures for optimal traction off-road. Ideally, the wheel diameter should be 50 percent or less than the tire diameter. See Chapter 7 for more details.

Suspension

Most overlanding vehicles can have a suspension lift installed. Aftermarket suspension companies offer a wide range of lifts for many overlanding-capable vehicles. Suspension lifts are beneficial for several reasons:

- Increased ground clearance
- Fitment of taller, wider tires
- Increased gear-carrying capacity without lowering the ride height of the vehicle

Many companies offer suspension lifts for most overland vehicles. Lifts increase ground clearance and allow the installation of taller tires. Lifts on independent suspension must be limited to about 2 inches to keep the axle driveshafts from running at too much of an angle.

On the negative side, the center of gravity height increases, which increases the potential for a rollover. Suspension lifts on vehicles with independent suspension have important limitations to how high the lift can be. Driveshafts on vehicles with an independent suspension are sensitive to angles. Suspension lifts create greater angularity, which puts increased loads on CV joints and steering components. This effect is minimal on lifts of 2 inches or less. See Chapter 6 for more information.

Shock Absorbers

Stock shock absorbers always leave something to be desired from a durability standpoint. Most overlanding vehicles benefit from the

More and more 4x4 vehicles are being equipped with premium, high-tech shock absorbers from the factory. For those with less capable or worn-out shocks, most shock-absorber companies offer a wide range of shocks for a variety of travel ranges as well as different valving based on the type of terrain traveled.

use of more-capable off-road shocks. Better shocks improve ride quality and help improve traction during transitions when overlanding. If suspension lifts are employed, longer shocks may be necessary to ensure full suspension travel. Many lift kits include shock absorbers. See Chapter 6 for more details.

Brakes

Modern vehicles have vastly improved brakes for the gross vehicle weight of the given product. Vehicles that drive on steep terrain, carry heavy loads of overlanding gear, or tow overlanding trailers benefit from brake upgrades. High-performance brake pads and rotors are available for nearly any vehicle. Complete brake upgrade kits improve overall braking performance for heavily loaded overlanding rigs. For more information, see Chapter 6.

Gearing

Lower (numerically higher) ring-and-pinion ratios help to compensate for taller tires and heavier loads. Changing the ring-and-pinion gear ratios is a daunting task that requires special tools and a high degree of knowledge and skill. Increasing the tire diameter by 5 to 10 percent does not require a ring-and-pinion gear-ratio change in most cases. A large increase in load for overlanding gear combined with taller tires makes a ring-and-pinion ratio change more necessary.

Driveline

Driveshafts and axles take a beating off-road, especially when the terrain becomes rugged and overlanding gear loads add additional strain to the drivetrain. With an increased tire size and additional weight added for overlanding gear, axle and driveshaft upgrades are worthwhile. More information regarding the driveline is in Chapter 11.

Steering

Steering upgrades for stock vehicles are usually not necessary. Some exceptions include the aluminum steering found on 2018–2020 Jeep Wranglers and the rack-and-pinion steering on the new full-size Ford Bronco. Tie-rod ends can be a weak link on most vehicles. Vehicles equipped with independent front suspension are the most vulnerable. Heavy loads and larger tires increase the strain on the steering system. Look for upgrades for your vehicle to improve off-road reliability. More information regarding steering is in Chapter 6.

Armor and Protection

Many overlanding-capable vehicles come from the factory with some

Extensive off-road builds that are designed for extreme terrain benefit from an upgraded steering system, power steering pump, hydraulic assist, and steering box.

underside protection. Skid plates protect vital components, such as fuel tanks, the transmission pan, and the oil pan. However, not all of the important underside components are protected even when some skid plates are provided. Check your vehicle for underside protection and add skid plates if they are available for your rig.

Another vulnerable area is the rocker panels. These panels below the side doors are easily damaged on rocky trails and heavily rutted sections where ground clearance is inadequate. Repairs to rocker panels are quite expensive. Adding rock sliders (rocker slides) provides protection for the rocker panels.

Armor (skidplates, bumpers, rock sliders, and fenders) reduces the risk of damage to expensive and important components. While not really necessary for easy roads, difficult trails generally require protection upgrades.

CHAPTER 6

Suspension, Steering, and Brakes

Adding overlanding gear to a stock 4x4 increases the stress and workload on critical components, such as the suspension, steering, and brakes. Weight additions to a stock vehicle lowers the ground clearance, places additional stress on the steering system, and increases the stopping distance. The more weight that is added to an overlanding rig, the more important it becomes to upgrade the suspension, steering, and braking systems for improved off-road performance and for safety both on- and off-road.

So many 4x4 and AWD vehicles are suitable for overlanding that it is impossible to go into detail for each. This chapter covers general concepts, and guidance is offered regarding modifications that improve off-road performance.

Aftermarket suspension companies, such as Ironman 4x4, offer kits to increase clearance for larger tires, improve ride and traction, and allow better articulation even with independent front suspension. (Photo Courtesy Ironman 4x4)

Suspension Components

The suspension system on a vehicle is designed to allow the controlled vertical movement of the tires while providing a degree of stability by controlling body roll and a balance between front and rear tire traction.

The need for on-road driving and off-road travel are similar but not completely compatible. On-road travel makes use of a stiffer suspension because paved roads are smoother. Off-road driving requires more ground clearance and suspension travel as well as a much softer suspension to allow the tires to stay on the road surface over a wide variety of ruts, bumps, rocks, and soft surfaces. Highway vehicles with off-road capability present a serious challenge to suspension engineers.

Various vehicles from different manufacturers make a wide range of compromises that range from being good on the highway and okay off-road, to really good off-road with not so great on the highway.

Let's look at the major suspension components and what they do.

Ironman 4x4 offers its Stage 1 foam-cell pro suspension kit for the Toyota 4Runner from 2003–2009 and the Lexus GX 470 non-kinetic dynamic suspension system (KDSS), which features front coilover springs and shocks. (Photo Courtesy Ironman 4x4)

Ironman 4x4 offers its Stage 2 foam-cell pro suspension kit for the Toyota 4Runner from 2003–2009 and the Lexus GX 470 non-KDSS version. The Stage 2 kit includes forged front upper control arms. (Photo Courtesy Ironman 4x4)

Springs

Springs support the weight of the vehicle. If the weight of a rig with overlanding gear is increased, stiffer, taller springs are needed to handle the additional weight. Springs also absorb bumps and ruts. They absorb shock loads from road-surface irregularities. So, if springs absorb shock loads, what do shock absorbers do?

Fabtech offers a wide range of suspension packages for trucks, SUVs, and Jeeps. Some kits come with Dirt Logic reservoir shock absorbers that help keep the shock oil cool over rough terrain.

Most small SUVs and crossover vehicles use strut suspension. Several companies offer small lift kits for strut-equipped vehicles, such as this ATS Subaru suspension kit from Ironman 4x4. (Photo Courtesy Ironman 4x4)

Icon Vehicle Dynamics makes coilover and other suspension packages for a variety of overlanding capable trucks and SUVs. Some of its kits include remote-reservoir shocks and hydraulic bump stops to soften the ride on the harsh, rutted roads and trails that are often encountered when overlanding.

They dampen vibrations (oscillations), which is why the technical term for shock absorbers is "vibration dampers."

The most important job of the springs is to keep the tire contact patches on the road surface as much as possible and provide ride comfort. If the springs are too stiff, the ride is harsh, and the tires often lose contact with the road surface. If the springs are too soft, the vehicle will bottom out on the suspension or ground, wallow, and feel unstable. Springs are used to lift a 4x4 for improved tire and ground clearance and more axle articulation. Spring rates should be near stock or slightly stiffer.

Offset bushings, such as these from Ironman 4x4, have mounting holes offset so that the bushing can be rotated in the bracket to adjust caster. (Photo Courtesy Ironman 4x4)

Suspension Control Arms

Suspension control arms and linkages can be trailing arms on a solid axle or A-arms on independent suspension. Suspension arms control the movement of the wheels and tires in vertical travel. They affect the amount of wheel travel and articulation. Trailing arms are used on solid axles to control the vertical travel of the wheels and tires. The longer the arms, the larger the arc of travel becomes. Longer arms mean that longitudinal movement is minimized during suspension travel. Longer arms also allow better axle articulation within the range of suspension travel up (compression or bump travel) and down (extension or rebound travel).

Aftermarket upper control arms in kits with coilover springs and shocks, such as this setup from Fabtech, improve suspension geometry, clearances, and add strength and reliability. (Photo Courtesy Fabtech)

Independent suspension uses A-arm-style control arms. The geometry of the upper and lower control arms determines the lateral arc in which the wheel and tire travel. The relative length of the control arms affects the amount of up and down travel available, which in turn affects articulation.

Travel

While not a component, suspension travel dictates off-road suspension performance. Travel is limited by spring height, stiffness, and design; shock absorber travel; tire clearance in the fender wells; A-arm and control-arm travel limitations, and angularity on independent-suspension axle shaft joints.

Longer springs increase suspension travel if the other limitations are properly addressed to allow increased travel. Coilover springs and shocks

Suspension travel plays a key role in ride quality, articulation, and tire traction. The Ironman 4x4 kit for the Jeep Gladiator demonstrates good travel and articulation. (Photo Courtesy Ironman 4x4)

While this Jeep Wrangler is not exactly an overlanding rig, axle articulation and suspension travel are far better with solid-axle assemblies.

Remote-reservoir, bypass, adjustable shock absorbers allow fine tuning for a variety of on- and off-road situations. High-end shocks are ideal for overlanding when vehicle weight changes and road surface conditions vary. Fox Factory manufactures various shocks for multiple applications.

may allow ride-height adjustments (raise or lower the body/chassis) with adjustable spring perches. They do not increase suspension travel unless the coilover spring and shock are longer and allow more travel. Raising the spring perch on a coilover raises the vehicle (increases ground clearance) but does not increase vertical suspension travel. Raising the spring perch changes the ride height but increases "up" travel and decreases "down" travel.

Shock Absorbers

Shock absorbers control the oscillation, or bouncing of the spring. In other words, the shock dampens vibrations of the spring. The vehicle will wallow and bounce if the shocks are too soft, and it will be an uncomfortable ride if they are too stiff. The shock absorber on an overlanding rig is subject to extreme loads. Quality dampers always serve you better than the low-cost and often low-quality shocks.

If a shock is too stiff, tire contact with the ground is reduced, as is articulation. If a shock is too short on a lifted 4x4, vertical travel and articulation are reduced.

Shock-absorber damping rates control how quickly weight is transferred from one tire to another when cornering, braking, and accelerating as well as when the axles are articulating. This affects the transitional handling balance and how quickly weight moves from a tire when it encounters a rock to a tire that is still

Jeep Wranglers have extensive options for the suspension system and shock absorbers. My Wrangler JLU rides on RockJock by John Currie springs, control arms with Johnny joints, track bars, and Antirock sway bars that do not require disconnection to achieve full axle articulation. The Bilstein B8 8100 bypass shocks utilize a remote reservoir and are fully adjustable in both compression and rebound.

The Bilstein B8 8100 bypass shocks feature knurled knobs to adjust compression and rebound to make damping-rate adjustments quick and easy. Each adjustment has about 45 clicks for fine tuning.

loaded. Shock rates are controlled by valves that allow fluid to bleed. Various valve sets come into play at different shaft speeds. Some shocks use additional bypass bleed ports within the bore of the shock.

Various valves and bypasses control the damping rates for different shaft and piston speeds. This allows fine-tuning of the valves to accommodate different situations that range from twisty mountain roads to rock crawling and rolling bumps in the desert. Valving in a shock should be compatible with the loads to which the shock is subjected. What works on a stock 4x4 vehicle is not adequate for a heavily-laden overlanding rig.

Lifted rigs need longer shocks to take advantage of the increased

The Bilstein 5160 remote-reservoir shocks are ideal for overlanding. These premium shocks offer great performance at a reasonable price.

The Ford Bronco is a great overlanding vehicle on easy-to-moderate roads and trails or in the desert. Some suspension modifications make it better on difficult and rocky terrain (Photo Courtesy Fabtech)

Icon Vehicle Dynamics makes an extensive line of coilover shock suspension systems, including upper control arms for independent-front-suspension vehicles.

Fabtech offers a complete kit for the Bronco, including coilover springs, Dirt Logic remote-reservoir shocks, front upper control arms, and adjustable rear lower links. (Photo Courtesy Fabtech)

The front suspension package with the Fabtech kit provides improved durability, better suspension geometry, and superior ride comfort in rough terrain. (Photo Courtesy Fabtech)

The system from Fabtech is much stronger than stock. The control arms allow adjustment for better axle alignment. The coilover springs and shocks allow ride-height adjustments to be made, which makes lifting and leveling easy. (Photo Courtesy Fabtech)

spring travel and articulation. When choosing a lift kit for your rig, purchase one that has both springs and shocks as a coordinated package along with any necessary control arms, bushings, and other hardware. Shock travel should be limited in extension so that the shock cannot fully extend and damage the piston and internal valving. In compression, bump stops are used to limit travel so that damage to the shock internals is avoided.

The RockJock by John Currie and Antirock sway bars for Jeep Wranglers and Gladiators (and soon for the Bronco) do not require disconnects to achieve full articulation. The sway bars are balanced from front to rear to optimize weight transfer and tire loads, which maximizes traction while allowing full articulation.

Sway Bars

Sway bars (also called anti-roll bars) control body roll when cornering. The sway bars affect handling balance by affecting where the weight transfers to the front or rear while cornering. However, for off-road travel, sway bars greatly reduce the ability of the axles to articulate by reducing travel. Essentially, sway bars limit suspension travel. Sway bars also increase ride harshness in the bumpy conditions that are encountered off-road.

The massive front sway bar controls body roll on the highway. The stiffness severely limits articulation. A front sway-bar disconnect solves the issue.

Several companies make sway-bar disconnect end links that allow highway roll control when connected and good articulation when disconnected. Quick-release pins make disconnecting the bar quick and easy.

Disconnecting the sway bars helps articulation when off-road but negatively affects handling and stability on-road. The front sway bar is much stiffer than the rear. For this reason, disconnecting only the front bar is necessary. Most vehicles have attaching bolts on the sway-bar end links that can be easily removed when going off-road. One of the first modifications recommended for off-road is a front sway bar disconnect. Several companies offer front sway-bar-disconnect kits for many overlanding vehicles.

How Suspension Works

The job of the suspension system requires many compromises among several components. Balancing ride comfort, the ability to keep the tires in contact with the road surface, and maximizing tire traction is a tricky task for suspension engineers. Getting springs, shocks absorbers, sway bars, and suspension geometry to work together can be an elusive goal.

Suspension Travel

Lift kits that use taller springs (as opposed to spacers) and longer shocks with more travel increase the suspension travel. More travel improves traction by allowing the tire contact patches to remain on the ground over rough terrain.

Axle articulation is the ability of the axle to rotate vertically on solid-axle vehicles and for independent suspension to travel as much as possible to help keep tires on the ground over rocks, bumps, and ruts. Suspension lifts allow more axle articulation as long as the sway bars are disconnected or aftermarket sway bars are used. Bump stops should always be used to keep compression travel limited so that the springs and shocks do not bottom out. Rebound travel should be limited to keep the springs seated and the shocks from being fully extended during full extension or rebound travel. Shock absorbers can be damaged if they are fully compressed or extended.

Articulation

Axle articulation affects tire traction and vehicle stability. Articulation allows the axles of a 4x4 to move in the largest possible arc. This allows the body to stay more level over large obstacles, such as rocks, ruts, and bumps. Good articulation improves vehicle stability and tire traction by keeping all four tires in contact with the ground.

Factors that affect axle articulation include sway bars, spring rates, suspension travel, and the pivot arc of the suspension. Sway bars, or anti-roll bars, minimize body roll when cornering. They also minimize axle articulation. Axle articulation is the measure of the full vertical travel of the tire in both compression and extension travel. Taller springs allow more travel. Shock absorbers that are

The stock Jeep Gladiator Rubicon comes with an electric front sway-bar disconnect that allows good articulation off-road. Ford Broncos use a similar sway-bar-disconnect system. (Photo Courtesy Stellantis)

too short for the springs limit travel, as does the sway bar. The sway bar can be disconnected to improve travel.

Articulation is important for allowing the axles and axle housings to rotate more freely on uneven terrain when driving through ruts and over bumps and rocks. More axle articulation means keeping both left- and right-side tires in contact with the ground over larger obstacles. If the axle can rotate more freely, the vehicle will stay more level. More articulation improves stability and traction. The sway bars should be reconnected before driving any distance or at speed on the highway.

Solid axles articulate more freely than independent-suspension axles. Solid axles handle more extreme surfaces like large ruts, bumps, and rocks. Free rotational movement of the front and rear axles allow the tire contact patches to stay on the road or trail surface over uneven terrain. This improves traction, helps stabilize the vehicle, and reduces the likelihood of suspension damage if the airborne tires/wheel/suspension slams back to the ground. It is important to keep the tire contact patches on the ground as long as possible, even if the load is minimal on one tire. When the tire lifts off the ground, it must return at some point. Often the tire and wheel will return to earth harshly, which can cause damage to the suspension and create a situation with reduced stability.

Independent-suspension systems have much shorter pivot arcs due to the axle length and control-arm pivot point. The control arms determine the arc of vertical suspension travel, which is much shorter (over 50 percent compared to a solid axle) and can cause the tires to lift off the ground much sooner and higher than with solid axle setups. Even with longer springs and shocks on an independent suspension, articulation is seriously limited.

Full suspension travel with the front sway bar disconnected allows full articulation when negotiating big ruts, bumps, and rocks. Tire traction improves and so does the heart rates of the driver and passenger.

My Jeep Wrangler Rubicon is outfitted for rock crawling and serves double duty for overlanding adventures on extreme trails, such as the John Bull Jeep Badge of Honor trail or the Rubicon.

Solid Axle versus Independent Suspension

The Jeep Wrangler is the only current SUV-class vehicle that utilizes a solid front axle. Some heavy-duty trucks still use solid front axles. Most late model trucks and SUVs use independent front suspension. Even the new Bronco has independent front suspension. Each has advantages and disadvantages. Here is what to look for.

Highway Handling

Independent suspension, at least on the front, offers superior handing and ride comfort on the highway. The geometry of an independent suspension allows better camber angle control. The tire will better conform to the road surface with independent suspension. This improves the cornering traction and overall handling characteristics. Solid axles experience more camber change when cornering, which results in slightly reduced cornering capability.

Ride on Rough Surfaces

Independent suspension systems reduce unsprung weight significantly. Unsprung weight is the

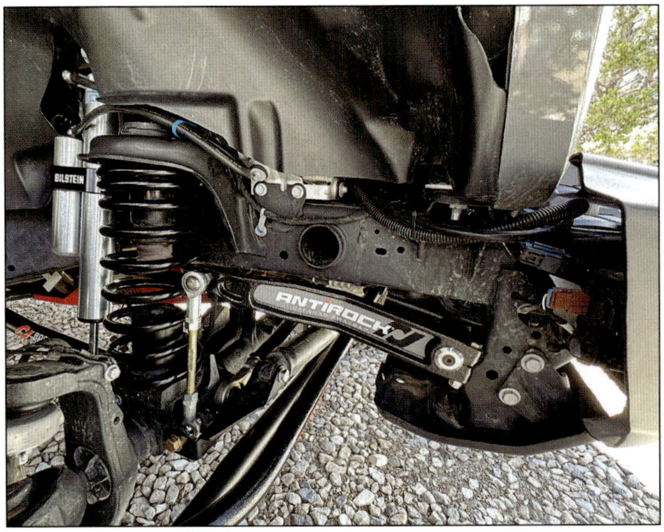

RockJock 4x4 suspension systems and Bilstein shock absorbers work well together for overlanding Jeep Wranglers and Gladiators and Ford Broncos. The RockJock kit includes 3.5-inch lift springs, upper and lower front and rear control arms with Johnny joints, CurrectLync steering, and Antirock sway bars.

The Bilstein 5160 remote-reservoir shock absorbers have damping characteristics for low to medium speeds on rough terrain. The high-speed valving works well on the highway for a comfortable ride while maintaining good handling characteristics.

weight that is not supported by the springs. Unsprung weight includes wheels, tires, brakes, hubs, and axles. Only half the weight of components like axle shafts and suspension control arms are unsprung on independent-suspension setups.

The reduced unsprung weight on independent-suspension systems improves ride quality over bumps, through ruts, and over small rocks. Ride improves on washboard roads and whoop-de-dos as well. Independent suspensions perform better than solid-axle systems on easy-but-rough terrain with superior ride comfort and slightly better traction on rough terrain.

Ground Clearance

Suspension lifts are installed for more ground clearance, which mostly means fitting taller tires. A lift with stock-size tires offers only marginal increases in ground clearance, mostly under the third member of independent-suspension systems. While this certainly helps, taller tires provide the most increase in ground clearance.

Most overland-capable rigs are severely limited in tire size increases due to fender and chassis clearance limitations. This is especially true for vans, such as the Transit and Sprinter. At the other extreme, some vehicles, such as the Jeep Wrangler and the full-size Ford Bronco, allow more room for larger tires but are still limited, even with a lift.

For overlanding, the ideal lift is the smallest lift that allows the fitment of taller tires that fit within the stock fenders and do not interfere with the frame, suspension, or inner body panels. More lift will only raise the center of gravity to make the rig more tippy. One important lift consideration requires determining the load added to the vehicle with overlanding and recovery gear. Some lift is needed to return the vehicle back to the original ride height and ground clearance.

Lift Limitations

Rigs with front and rear solid-axle assemblies are more easily lifted higher than rigs with independent front suspension. Solid-axle vehicles, such as Jeep Wranglers and early Broncos and Blazers, can generally be lifted up to 5 inches to allow larger tires and create significant increases in ground clearance. A practical limit is 4 inches to keep the center of gravity at a more sane level and reduce rollover risks. For example, the new Jeep Wrangler JL can run up to a 42-inch-tall tire with a spring and shock lift of about 4 inches. A stock JL Wrangler Rubicon can run up a 37-inch-taller tire with no lift or fender modifications.

Independent suspension systems cause another set of issues. The biggest concern for lifts on an independent suspension is the angle of the driveshafts. The driveshafts running from the ring-and-pinion center section to the wheel hubs are fairly level at rest on a stock rig. Lifting the ride

The Nissan Xterra performs quite well for overlanding. Ironman 4x4 offers its foam cell pro Stage 2 suspension kit for the 2005–2015 Nissan Xterra. (Photo Courtesy Ironman 4x4)

Icon Vehicle Dynamics makes 2.5 Aluminum Series shocks for a wide range of vehicles from Toyota, Ford, GM, Jeep, and Ram. These are the rear 2.5 shocks for the Toyota FJ Cruiser and 4Runner from 2003–2022.

The E-Clik 2.5-inch Piggyback shock features automatic rate adjustment with controlled settings that are available to the driver on the fly. The E-Clik shocks are available for Toyota, Jeep, and Raptor vehicles.

height changes the angle of the axle shafts so that they run downhill from the ring-and-pinion housing.

Two problems can occur. First, the increased angle induces more stress on the joints that allow the axle shafts to swing up and down. The higher the lift, the more stress is put on the shafts, and the more likely a joint can experience accelerated wear or fail. Lifts of more than 2.5 inches put excessive loads on the rotating joints. Pickups with tall lifts (up to 8 to 10 inches) use kits using a drop bracket to lower the ring-and-pinion center-section housing to bring the axle shaft angles closer to stock, but then the additional ground clearance is lost.

A second negative factor affects suspension travel. The angles of the axle shafts and suspension control arms change. The downward angle of the components reduces the "down" travel (extension or rebound) while increasing "up" travel. The amount of total travel remains the same, assuming that there is adequate tire clearance in the fenders. The percentage of up-versus-down travel changes, which hurts axle articulation even more. This applies to coilover springs as well as conventional springs.

Coilover spring/shock systems with a threaded collar allow easy ride-height adjustments. A corner of the rig can be raised or lowered to gain ground clearance, fit larger tires, and level the vehicle. However, when the ride height is raised, which is often called preloading the spring, bump (or compression) "up" travel is reduced while "down" travel (rebound or extension) is increased.

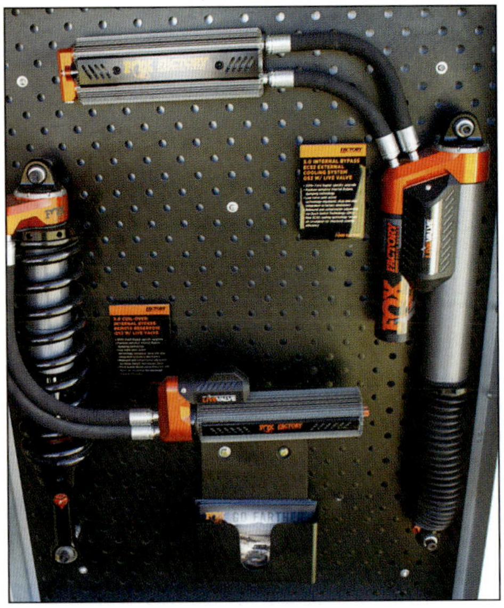

Fox Factory offers several styles of shocks from smooth body shocks to external bypass, electronically controlled coilover shocks. The range of products cover Chevy, Ford, GMC, Jeep, Nissan, Ram, and Toyota.

Suspension control arms need strength to survive the rigors of overlanding. Many SUVs use lightweight control arms. Fabtech and other companies offer beefier control arms, including these rear lower-link arms for the 2021–2022 Ford Bronco 4WD. (Photo Courtesy Fabtech)

The Ford Bronco's off-road performance improves with a lift. Fabtech offers a kit that works well on the backcountry trails and looks good on the road. (Photo Courtesy Fabtech)

Overlanding vans benefit from a lift to improve the ride, traction, and tire clearance. Fabtech offers a kit for the 2015–2021 Mercedes Sprinter 3500 4WD. The 1.5-inch coil assist kit uses Bilstein B6 front struts with lift springs and Dirt Logic 2.25-inch Resi assists. At the rear, Dirt Logic 2.25-inch shocks control the rear leaf springs with spring spacers, longer U-bolts, and wheel spacers. (Photo Courtesy Fabtech)

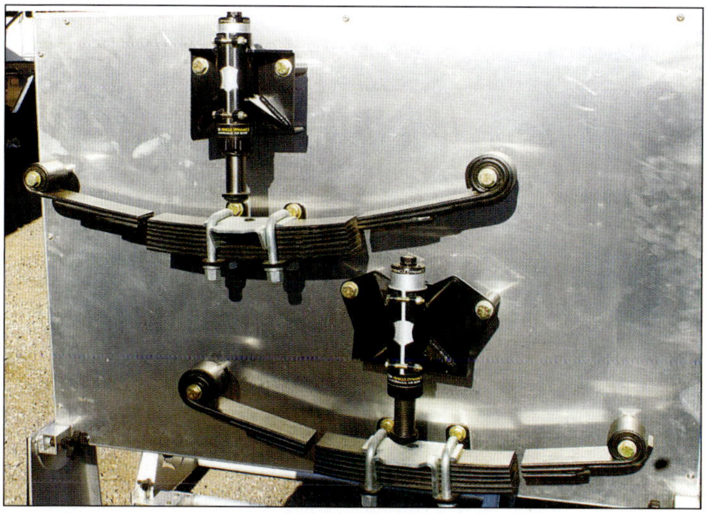

Leaf springs are old school but are still found on many truck and SUV rear suspensions. The additional weight of overlanding gear many require stiffer springs to handle the additional load. Icon Vehicle Dynamics, among others, offers stiffer leaf springs for many applications. Icon also offers the unique hydraulic bump stop to help cushion the compression of the spring while driving over harsh bumps.

Pickups make great overlanding rigs on all but the narrowest trails. An aftermarket suspension system adds traction and allows for more tire clearance. Fabtech makes a 3-inch upper-control-arm lift kit with Dirt Logic 2.5-inch coilover shocks on the front and 2.25-inch Dirt Logic shocks on the rear for the 2019–2021 Ram 1500 Rebel 2WD and 4WD trucks and other applications. (Photo Courtesy Fabtech)

Steering

Independent-suspension steering systems vary somewhat from solid-axle front ends. While the components are similar and perform the same functions, the mechanical aspects are considerably different. While the solid-axle setup uses a single tie-rod with a drag link to transfer steering motions from the steering box to the wheel hubs, an independent suspension system uses two tie-rods that link each end of the rack-and-pinion steering box to the front wheels.

Each system offers advantages and disadvantages. Rack-and-pinion steering on independent front suspension provides superior handling and feel on the highway. Off-road, the independent suspension system is more fragile. Both systems leave something to be desired when used off-road. More weight, larger tires, and difficult terrain makes the rack-and-pinion steering systems prone to damage and failure. The more robust recirculating ball steering boxes on solid-axle steering aren't free from failure, either.

Short of a major crash, such as a rollover, steering failures quickly ruin a trip. Repairs can be difficult (assuming spare parts are readily available) and recoveries, like towing, are extremely challenging. The most vulnerable components on all steering systems are stock tie-rods, the tie-rod and drag link on solid axle setups, and tie-rod ends. The tie-rods on rack-and-pinion steering systems invite failure due to the lightweight designs of the rods and tie-rod ends. Solid-axle steering is more robust but only a little. For serious overlanding adventures, especially on rough terrain, it is prudent to take advantage of the offerings by many aftermarket companies that offer tie-rod and drag-link upgrades. An alternative is to carry spare tie-rods and tie-rod ends.

When a tie rod is bent, toe settings usually change by a great amount to the point that steering is nearly impossible. The tie-rod is weakened, so even if the rod can be straightened, it becomes more prone to further damage or failure. Damage and failures occur in bumpy, rutted terrain and in the rocks. Damage often occurs because a rut, rock, steep shelf obstacle, or bump has been hit at too fast of a speed.

The components are more vulnerable when the vehicle is turning. Tie-rod shafts can bend, and rod ends can bend or break. Even minor damage where the toe alignment is thrown off can cause major issues with steering movement and render the vehicle undrivable. Being towed by another rig does not work unless it's a tow truck that can lift the front end off the ground. While bent or broken tie-rods and tie-rod ends can occur on any vehicle, the lighterweight components on independent-front-axle steering are more vulnerable.

For example, take the new Ford Bronco. Tie-rod failures have become somewhat common on the new Bronco. When tie-rods fail, damage often occurs to the constant velocity (CV) joints as well. Fortunately, several aftermarket companies offer strong components to reduce the risk of failure. The aftermarket offers stronger steering components for most overlanding-capable vehicles.

Steering boxes take rotational movement from the steering wheel and turn it into lateral movement of the tie-rods on independent front suspension (or the tie-rod and drag link on solid axles). Most vehicles equipped with independent front suspension use rack-and-pinion steering boxes. The pinion gear is rotated when the steering wheel is turned. The pinion gear moves the rack (a toothed, flat bar), which, in turn, moves the tie roads laterally. The tie-rods move the wheels and tires to steer the vehicle. On most solid-axle 4x4s, the steering box uses a recirculating-ball system to initiate steering. The recirculating-ball steering box is much more robust than a rack-and-pinion steering box.

Any steering system can fail. Failure is more likely when the terrain becomes more severe and larger tires are utilized.

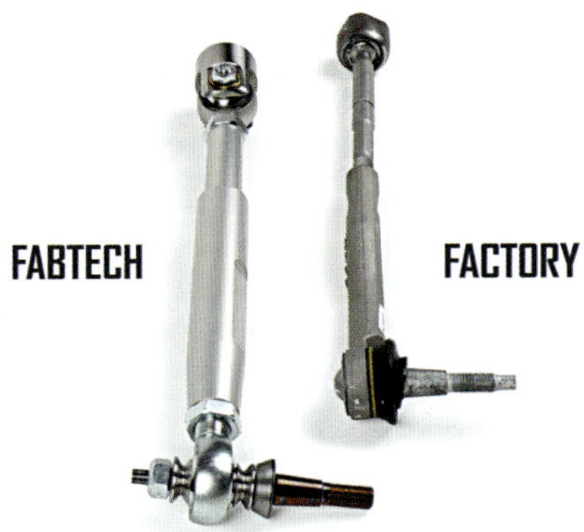

The Ford Bronco, as with many independent-front-suspension-equipped 4WD vehicles, suffers from weak steering tie-rods. They are prone to breaking even under moderate loads. When a tie-rod end fails, it most often damages or destroys the CV joint and adds more trauma to an already-bad situation. Trying to recover a vehicle with broken steering is not pleasant. Fabtech has made great strides in solving this issue. Compare the Fabtech tie-rod end to the factory version. Fabtech offers a complete kit including the billet aluminum tie-rods, clevises, rod ends, boots, and hardware. (Photo Courtesy Fabtech)

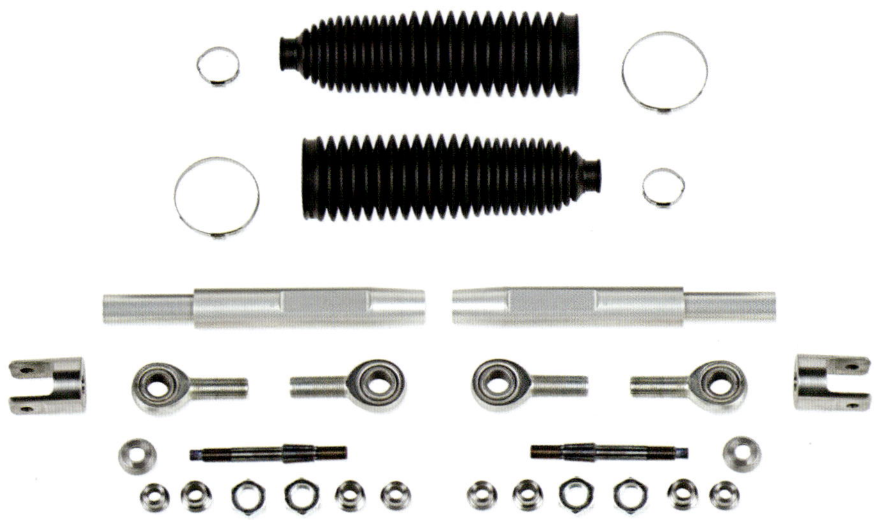

When the Jeep Wrangler JL was introduced in 2018, it was equipped with an aluminum steering box. The aluminum expanded with heat to allow the steel sector shaft that attaches to the steering arm to wobble enough to cause shimmy. Newer JLs use cast-iron steering boxes. The best solution is the PSC heavy-duty steering box.

PSC makes a complete power steering kit for many Jeeps, including the 2018–current JL series. The kit includes a new power-steering pump, hoses, power ram, heavy-duty steering box, main reservoir, and fill tank.

Potential Problems and Common Failure Points

- Steering gear wear
- Tie-rods
- Tie-rod ends
- Ball joints
- Steering arms
- Knuckles/spindles
- Steering box mounting bolts

Issues Unique to Rack-and-Pinion Steering

- Rack housing flex
- Rack bushing displacement that renders the steering useless
- Rack failure from major loads on rough terrain

Issues Unique to Recirculating-Ball Steering

- Sector-shaft breakage
- Steering-arm breakage

At the Moab Easter Jeep Safari, Loren Healy (the 2022 winner of the Everyman Challenge at King of Hammers in a Bronco) carried three sets of spare tie-rods in a nearly stock Bronco because they break so often. He also broke a steering rack. At Moab, Ford had people passing out cards that had a phone number on them to call if they broke down, and a tech would come out to help them. It's a serious issue and it's happening with all independent-front-suspension SUVs and trucks. I don't think the problem can be overstated.

The new Ford Bronco offers perfect examples of issues with rack-and-pinion steering even on new vehicles with few or no modifications. As previously stated, tie-rods and tie-rod ends are prone to bending and breaking under the heavy loads imposed by even moderate off-road terrain. The steering box on the Bronco uses nylon-type bushings to support the toothed rack as it travels laterally. If the steering is turned full lock and heavy loads are encountered, the bushings can become dislodged and allow the rack gear to disengage from the pinion gear, resulting in no steering. Similar problems are possible on any 4x4 with rack-and-pinion steering.

Solid-axle steering systems, while more sturdy, are also prone to failure. For example, take the Jeep Wrangler JK. The sector shaft inside the steering box works like the pinion gear in rack-and-pinion steering and turns rotational movement into lateral movement through the steering arm. The shafts wear over time. The free play between the shaft and bearings can cause death wobble. Even worse, the shaft can snap under impacts often encountered off-road. The break usually occurs where the sector shaft exits the steering box and joins to the steering arm. Death wobble is bad, but complete steering failure on the trail is worse.

The newer Jeep Wrangler JL models also have steering issues, especially the 2019 through 2020 models that came with aluminum steering boxes. The sector shaft, which is steel, expands much slower than the aluminum box as the box heats up. This creates free play in the steering system and creates possible death wobble. Near the end of the 2020 model run, Jeep began to use cast-iron steering boxes like those found on the JK. There's no more free play, but sector-shaft breakage is still a possibility.

Death Wobble

Death wobble strikes fear into the heart of Jeep owners, although death wobble can occur on any solid-front-axle vehicle. Death wobble happens when a bump is encountered, usually at moderate to higher speeds. The cause of death wobble is excessive free play in any of several components in the steering system or balance and wear issues of the tires.

Death wobble results in violent movement of the steering wheel. The vehicle will continue in a straight path during death wobble. Significant reduction in vehicle speed is the only method to stop death wobble. The rapid left-to-right shaking of the steering wheel is unnerving and can damage other components, including tires.

Free Play in Components

- Ball joints
- Tires out of balance or out of round
- Worn steering-box sector shaft
- Worn or loose tie-rod ends on the tie-rod or drag link
- Worn or loose idler arm
- Loose mounting bolts on the steering box
- Worn or loose wheel bearings

If death wobble occurs, components in the steering system beyond the offending part can be damaged, even tires, due to the extreme shaking.

Check for Free Play

Any style of steering system will experience wear that leads to free play. Checking for free play is easy. If the steering wheel is turned a few inches in either direction, the tires should also turn. If the steering wheel movement is more than 1/8- to 1/4-inch total, the free play is probably excessive, and all of the components should be checked. Any offending parts should be replaced.

Alignment

A good alignment shop can make a vehicle drive much better on the highway and off-road. All four wheels need to be aligned. In addition to caster, camber, and toe, axles must be centered in the chassis and square to the chassis. Modern alignment equipment makes this accurate when using a well-equipped alignment or tire shop. A competent shop can also determine free play and discover the problem parts.

Spare Parts and Tools

Any overlanding rig using stock steering components should carry spare tie-rods, tie-rod ends, and drag links (on solid axle vehicles) as well as the tools to replace bent, broken, and damaged steering-system parts.

Aftermarket Upgrades

Nearly every vehicle suitable for overlanding enjoys good aftermarket product support specific to its brand. Many companies offer upgraded steering components, especially tie-rods and tie-rod ends. Since any issue with steering creates a difficult repair or vehicle recovery, upgrading steering components is important. If you upgrade, it's wise to carry the old stock parts as spares—just in case.

On our Jeep 4x4 School Jeeps, we have upgraded the steering system completely. We use the PSC complete hydraulic-ram-assist system, which includes the hydraulic ram, a much beefier steering box, a heavy-duty power-steering pump, and all of the lines and hardware. Other steering upgrades include the full RockJock CurrectLync system, including strong tie-rods, drag link, and heavy-duty tie-rod ends (Johnny joints). While all of these steering components reduce the steering effort and improve steering feel, the primary reason for strong steering upgrades is to greatly reduce the chance of steering failures on the trail.

Brakes

Brake issues often result in catastrophic outcomes. Many problems can occur when driving off-road. The two most troublesome are steering failures and issues and failure of the brake system. Heavy overlanding rigs place increased stress and demands on the brakes. Even if the original brakes function perfectly, the additional load carried when overlanding can seriously diminish brake performance.

An additional factor that puts more stress on the brakes is larger, heavier tires. The rotational inertia increases stopping distances and the pressure applied to the brake pedal by the driver. Brake-system upgrades ranging from brake pads to complete brake setups can enhance performance off-road.

The stock braking system on most 4x4s can handle a load increase up to the maximum GVWR. GVWR is the total weight your vehicle can carry. It includes the curb weight, the actual weight of your vehicle unloaded (not including passengers), fuel, tools and gear, plus everything you carry in the vehicle. Many overlanding rigs exceed GVWR when loaded for overlanding adventures. When running near or over GVWR, the strain on the brakes can be considerable. If larger tires are added, the load and wear increases.

A stock 4x4 with a total weight well below the GVWR can handle tires up to 33 inches in diameter. When you add larger diameter tires

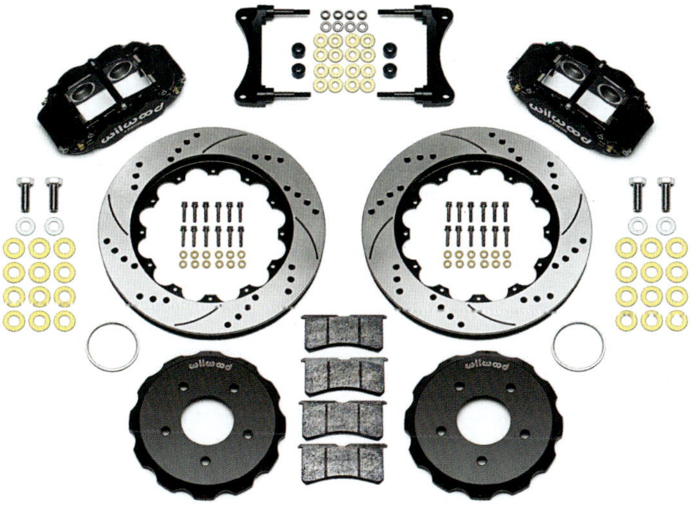

The most effective brake upgrade kits, such as this kit from Wilwood, provide rotors, calipers, and hats (if needed). (Photo Courtesy Wilwood)

Wilwood offers brake upgrades for many vehicles. The four-piston design has two pistons on each side of the caliper. This improves clamping force of the brake pads against the rotors for superior stopping power, especially on long, steep descents. (Photo Courtesy Wilwood)

that weigh a lot more than the stock tires, the rotational forces (inertia) increase dramatically. This is not only a factor on the highway, but it is critical when dropping off rocks or ledges off-road. The amount of pedal pressure to control a descent on a drop-off surprises most drivers. For this reason, brake upgrades provide much greater stopping force, which is the clamping force of the brake pads in the caliper against the rotor.

Most factory brake calipers are single-piston (left) or dual-piston (right). These calipers use a floating bridge with pistons on one side. Dual-piston designs spread the pressure on the brake pad more evenly than a single-piston caliper.

The diameter of the rotor is a key factor. The larger the diameter of the rotor, the more braking force the system can create. This occurs for the same reason that larger-diameter tires need more braking force to reduce speed. In many brake upgrade packages, the stock pedal and booster are used, but rotors, calipers, brake pads, and the master cylinder in some cases are changed for more stopping power at the optimal amount of pedal pressure (60 to 100 pounds) generated by the driver's leg muscles.

A good brake upgrade package, whether it has only rotors and pads or is a complete system, takes into account all of the factors needed to properly engineer the system. When properly designed, the improved performance when running larger tires and the heavier loads needed for most overlanding adventures is significant.

Brake Pads

A brake pad consists of a friction material that creates stopping power when pressed against the brake rotor by the caliper(s). Brake pads are available in various hardness compounds. Brake pads need heat to most effectively create stopping friction.

Softer compounds generate heat more quickly while harder compounds take longer to create heat. Harder compounds tend to wear longer. Most original equipment brake pads are on the soft side to allow quick heat build-up, especially for emergency-stopping situations. Harder compounds are used in extreme conditions, such as tow-

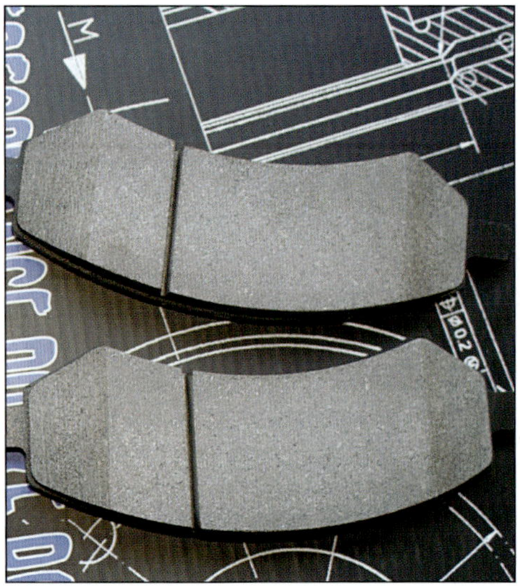

Many companies make high-performance brake pads. Hard-compound pads work best for high-speed, high-traction stops. Softer-compound pads heat up more quickly for better performance in the lower-traction off-road environment.

Large-diameter brake rotors not only have more surface area for more braking power, but the larger diameter also applies more torque to the wheel to add even more stopping power. Large-diameter rotors have more area for better heat dissipation.

ing heavy loads or driving on curvy mountain roads where hard braking occurs constantly. For off-road driving, while brake performance is critical in extreme rock crawling and steep hill descents, speeds are low. Maximum braking force is necessary at low speed, and low brake pad and rotor temperatures require a soft brake-pad compound. Stock original equipment brake pads do a good job off-road.

While several companies offer replacement brake pads in a variety of compounds, most companies offer brake pad and rotor packages so that the rotor materials and the brake pad compounds are compatible for optimal performance and wear. At a minimum, brake-pad upgrades should be part of an overlanding rig build.

Brake Rotors

Brake rotors are the heart of the braking system. With clamping force from the brake pads, the rotors reduce the rotation of the wheel and tire. The friction needed to accomplish this important job generates considerable heat. Brake rotors come in two styles: vented and solid. Vented rotors help dissipate heat for better braking performance in extreme conditions. Many companies offer brake-rotor upgrades for nearly every overlanding-capable vehicle. Most brake-rotor upgrades include brake pads that are compatible with the rotors.

Brake Calipers

Brake calipers turn hydraulic pressure from the master cylinder through the brake lines into clamping force. The clamping force squeezes the brake pads against the brake rotor. Brake calipers have pistons that are internally activated by the brake pedal. The pistons push the pads against the rotors to provide stopping power. Floating calipers have one or two pistons on one side of the caliper. The other side of the caliper "floats" to squeeze the pads against the rotor. Two-piston calipers can generate more clamping force. Rigid calipers feature pistons on each side of the caliper with two or three pistons per side. Rigid calipers can generate more clamping force. Larger calipers allow the use of larger brake pads. More brake-pad area translates into more braking force for a given amount of pedal pressure.

Stock-replacement calipers are available from several companies. Stock replacements will do little to improve stock braking performance. To gain significant braking performance improvements, a complete brake kit that includes calipers, pads, and rotors is needed.

Brake System Kits

Complete kits offer optimal performance and safety upgrades. Properly engineered kits handle larger tires, increased vehicle weight for improved stopping, and speed con-

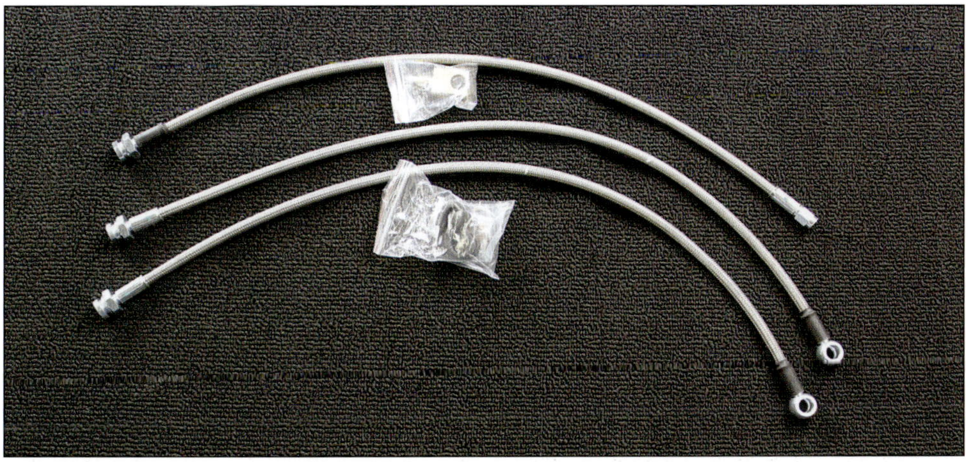

Braided stainless-steel brake lines reduce flex under the high pressures that are generated by the brake system. This allows for a firmer pedal and better brake feel. In many cases, the stock brake hoses are too short on a lifted vehicle and the hoses need to be upgraded to braided stainless-steel lines.

trol. Brake pad and rotor life generally improve over stock brakes or stock-brake replacements.

Brake Flex Lines

Brake hoses or flex lines are designed to move with the caliper during suspension travel. For optimal braking performance, steel-braided brake hoses should be used. They are more durable, and the braided steel does not expand like a rubber brake hose. If you upgrade to a big-brake system, replace the stock-brake flex lines with steel-braided lines. If you have lifted your overlanding rig, chances are good that extended (longer) steel-braided lines are already installed.

Brake Fluid

Brake fluid is hygroscopic, which means that the fluid absorbs water vapor from the air. For this reason, use small pint containers of brake fluid and keep them sealed tightly when not pouring fluid into the master-cylinder reservoir. Water vapor in the fluid will lower the boiling point of the fluid. This increases compressibility and can cause a spongy brake pedal or no pedal. Obviously, this is dangerous. Once contaminated, the brake fluid must be purged from the system and replaced with fresh fluid.

The US Department of Transportation specifies three common types of brake fluid: DOT 3, DOT 4, and DOT 5. DOT 3 and DOT 4 are the preferred types for high-performance, high-temperature use and are available in a wide range of formulations and performance characteristics. DOT 3 fluids are usually less expensive than DOT 4 fluids and are not as capable in extreme use. DOT 5 is a silicon-based fluid, which is not good for high-temperature use because it expands, becomes compressible, and makes the pedal soft and spongy.

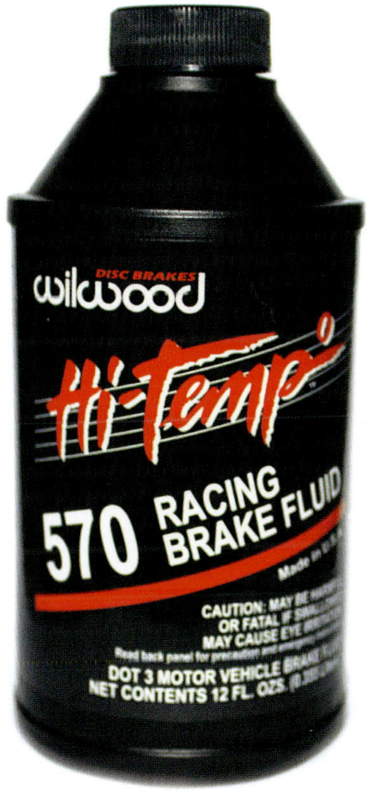

Brakes can get very hot. Much of the heat is transferred to the brake fluid. Use only DOT 3 fluid unless the vehicle or brake manufacturer recommends something else. Brake fluid can boil, but high-temperature fluid reduces this possibility. Brake fluid is hygroscopic, which means it absorbs water vapor from the atmosphere. The water vapor will contaminate the brake fluid and lower its boiling point. High-temperature fluid helps, as does keeping the cap on the bottle to minimize moisture absorption. Use small bottles for the same reason. If you notice a softer brake pedal, purging the brake lines and master cylinder with fresh brake fluid may cure the problem.

CHAPTER 7

TIRES AND WHEELS

Arguably the most important item to improved performance on an overlanding rig is tires. Most stock 4x4s, SUVs, and trucks come equipped with tires that lack the characteristics that are needed for a capable and reliable overlanding vehicle. Original-equipment tires generally lack the durability and traction needed to handle the conditions presented in the backcountry environment.

The tire industry offers a wide range of off-road tires from many manufacturers. Off-road tires are designed to improve traction and reliability. Quality tires are available at various price points to fit any budget, and fitment covers most vehicles that are suitable for overlanding.

Off-road tires are available in three general categories: mud-terrain, all-terrain, and hybrid. Mud-terrain tires are the most aggressive design. All-terrain tires feature a less-aggressive tread design. Hybrid tires fall somewhere in between the two categories.

Tire choice depends mostly on the type of driving you want to

Tires play a key role in helping overlanding rigs to successfully complete backcountry adventures. A good tire for overlanding must be able to perform in a variety of terrain and weather conditions and on a variety of surfaces. The more extensive and varied the overlanding trip, the more important it becomes to use a versatile and durable tire. The Nexen Roadian MTX tire offers great off-road performance while maintaining good manners on the pavement.

When purchasing a new overlanding rig, study the tire options carefully. Choose the best off-road-capable tire that is available. Ideally, the smallest-diameter wheel should be selected to allow for the tallest possible sidewall height.

All-terrain tires offer several advantages for overlanding: improved traction in wet and icy conditions, less road noise on the highway, and better wear characteristics.

The large lugs on a mud-terrain tire increase grip in most off-road situations. Mud-terrain tires are good off-road but are noisier, wear more quickly, and cost more than typical all-terrain tires.

do. You may select a less-aggressive design with better wear characteristics that is quieter on the highway if your rig is also a daily driver. If you travel through rough, muddy terrain, a mud-terrain or hybrid may suit your needs more effectively.

Quality off-road tires provide improved traction, a reduced chance of a puncture, and are less likely to have issues with getting stuck. Taller-than-stock tires offer more ground clearance, and wider tires increase traction and improve lateral stability. To fit larger tires requires additional tire clearance with a lift or fender modifications.

Taller tires, especially when a suspension lift is utilized, will raise the

Tire Load Capacity

Load capacity refers to the load-carrying capabilities of a tire. Most off-road tires have a fairly high load capacity. Load capacity requires careful consideration for overlanding vehicles. Heavier vehicles, such as fully loaded van conversions or full-size pickups with a large load of overlanding gear, need higher-load-capacity tires than a midsize SUV or pickup with a moderate load of gear and occupants.

For example, the Mickey Thompson Baja Boss A/T in the 33x11.50 R17 LT size has a load range E (10-ply equivalent) rating and a load capacity of 3,195 pounds at 80 psi, which is very high. The total load capacity of this tire is over 12,000 pounds at 80 psi. The load capacity drops considerably as tire pressures are reduced. The same tire in the 33x12.50 R17 LT size has a load range D rating (8 ply) with a load capacity of 2,600 pounds at 50 psi. This is the formula to calculate tire load capacity at a given tire pressure:

Tire Load Capacity ÷ Maximum Tire Pressure = Load Capacity (PSI)

For example, a tire with a 2,600-pound load capacity at 50 psi has a load capacity of 52 pounds per 1 psi. Working the formula backward to determine the lowest pressure for highway driving with a 6,000-pound vehicle (or 1,500 pounds per tire), 1,500 divided by 52 equals 29 psi. Most likely, the ideal pressure is around 31 to 33 psi for the highway.

At 15 psi, a common pressure for off-road driving, the load capacity drops to 780 pounds. While this load is nearly half of the ideal highway pressure, the low speeds and lower-friction terrain off-road makes this pressure acceptable for off-road driving at low speeds. I have utilized even lower pressures for rugged off-road terrain with no ill effects. ■

The load capacity for this tire is 3,195 pounds at 35 psi. Note that load capacity drops as tire pressure is reduced.

The load capacity for this tire is 3,195 pounds at 80 psi.

While this Jeep looks like it's in a precarious position, the tilt angle is about 33 degrees. A tilt angle up to 45 degrees should not cause a rollover. However, when most of the load is on the downhill tire and low tire pressure is being used, the ability of the vehicle to resist a rollover is reduced. Add a roof rack, rooftop tent, and other gear up high, and the rollover resistance is even less. Be aware and proceed cautiously.

height of the vehicle and raise the center of gravity. A higher center of gravity results in reduced stability. The vehicle becomes more tippy and prone to rollovers on side slopes and uneven, rutted terrain. The center of gravity becomes even higher with the addition of a heavy load on the roof, such as a roof rack, with a considerable amount of gear or a rooftop tent. A practical goal is to fit the largest tire possible without modifying the stock fenders unless the fenders are easily replaced (as is the case with Jeep Wranglers and Ford Broncos) and to use the smallest lift needed for clearance with the intended load of overlanding gear.

An additional consideration is the load rating of a tire compared to the load being carried by the tires. For small-to-midsize vehicles, the load, even with overlanding gear, will fall within the load capacity of good off-road tires. The area of most concern involves larger vehicles with the relatively small original-equipment tires that are found on van conversions. Vans typically have small tires and small fender openings that limit tire diameter without major modifications. Vans can also carry heavy loads. The high loads make load ratings of the tire a major consideration.

Selecting the Best Tire Type

Of the three types of off-road tire, which best suits your specific situation? There is no easy answer. The biggest factor beyond selecting a tire with adequate load-carrying capacity relates to the type of terrain that you will spend the most time exploring.

For example, if you travel off-road on the east coast or southern states of the US where mud is often encountered, a good mud-terrain tire is a great choice. If you off-road in Moab, Utah, an all-terrain or hybrid style off-road tire will work well on the slick rocks.

Over the years, my team and I have had the privilege to test many

Hybrid tires are now on the off-road tire scene. The hybrid tire offers some characteristics of an all-terrain tire but is more aggressive with a tread design closer to a mud-terrain tire. Wear and noise levels fall somewhere between an all-terrain and a mud-terrain. Great examples of the hybrid off-road tire are the Falken AT3W (left) and the Mickey Thompson Baja Boss A/T (right). The tread blocks on these tires are larger than a mud-terrain with less void, but they are more aggressive than an all-terrain tire. For many overlanding vehicles, the hybrid tire is a perfect compromise between highway performance, off-road capability, and overall durability.

The three types of tires feature varying tread designs. Mud-terrain tires, such as the Falken WildPeak M/T tire (left), work the best on extreme terrain and soft surfaces, including mud, sand, and snow. The large tread blocks and softer rubber compound increase grip. All-terrain tires, such as the BFG All Terrain TA tire (middle), are often the choice for overlanding. They provide better wear and a quieter ride on the highway. While the A/T tire may have a harder rubber compound, the increased tread area due to a smaller void ratio allows most A/T tires to perform similar to the equivalent M/T tire in most off-road conditions. The Mickey Thompson Baja ATZ03 (right) hybrid off-road tire features large tread blocks, a smaller void ratio, numerous sipes in the tread blocks, and a rubber compound that is softer than a typical A/T tire but harder than an M/T.

Softer rubber compounds provide more traction, while harder compounds wear better and last longer. The hardness of the rubber can be measured by a tire durometer. Tire rubber hardens over time.

types and brands of tires. The good news is that most off-road tires are high quality with good puncture resistance. Design differences include tread patterns, tread and sidewall construction, and tread compounds. Each of these design characteristics affect tire performance, tire life, and road noise. The differences can have a profound effect on how the specific tire performs in different circumstances. For example, the shape and design of tread blocks on the tread can affect how a tire performs on rocks, sand, mud, snow, and ice.

The tread design is also a factor in road noise. One tire may be exceptional on rocks but noisy on the highway. A quieter tire may work well in snow but lack good grip on rocks. One tread pattern may have good forward grip to climb up rock faces but not good lateral grip when the tire attempts to hold sideways on a slanted slab of granite.

Every tire that we tried has strong and weak points, so no tire is the perfect compromise. Make your choice based on specific needs. Personally, I feel that overall grip off-road is the most important, but that criteria leaves the door open to a wide range of tire brands and types.

Off-Road Tire Design Features

Several design elements affect the performance and durability of off-road tires.

Tread Compound

In the most basic terms, a softer tread compound offers more traction but wears more quickly. Many elements go into tire tread compounds. Materials such as silica can affect both wear and traction. Compounds can also affect wet weather and snow performance.

Sidewall Stiffness

Sidewall stiffness has a profound effect on off-road tire performance. Tire sidewalls flex under load. Stiffer tire sidewalls flex less at a given tire pressure. Less flex results in a stiffer, less-comfortable ride over rough terrain. This also affects traction by causing the tire contact patch to bounce over uneven surfaces rather than conform to the contours of the terrain. Stiffer tire sidewalls require lower tire pressures to achieve the same ability to wrap around rocks and conform to surface irregularities. Off-road tire pressures are covered in more detail later in this chapter.

A more flexible sidewall, such as the sidewall found on the Nexen Roadian MTX mud-terrain tire, allows the use of a higher tire pressure to achieve a good tire contact patch spread. Here, the tire is inflated to 15 psi.

At 10 psi, the Mickey Thompson Baja Boss mud-terrain tire provides great flex to wrap around rock surfaces and other types of uneven terrain. This tire features a fairly stiff sidewall with the capability of running at lower tire pressure with a beadlock wheel.

The Falken WildPeak MT01 uses a stiff sidewall construction. At the top, the tire pressure is 28 psi, and in the middle, the pressure is about 12 psi, which is about the lowest advisable for non-beadlock wheels. The lower tire is aired down to 6 psi. Extremely heavy overlanding rigs benefit from a stiffer tire sidewall.

Tire Diameter Versus Sidewall Height

Taller tires are desirable to increase ground clearance and improve traction. The goal for optimal off-road performance is to fit the tallest tire possible within reason on the smallest-diameter wheel possible. Wheel diameter is generally dictated by brake-rotor diameter. Many current off-road-capable vehicles have wheel diameters of 16 to 17 inches. The ideal situation is to have the tallest tire sidewall possible. Taller-tire sidewalls are generally more flexible than shorter-tire sidewalls.

Short tire sidewalls leave little room for running lower tire pressures. A tall sidewall allows much lower tire pressures for optimal off-road performance. Ideally, using the smallest-diameter wheel that will fit over the brake rotors and calipers allows the most flexibility when reducing tire pressures for off-road driving.

Wheel Diameter

Wheel diameter should be either the original-equipment diameter or as small as possible while providing adequate brake rotor and caliper clearance. This allows a tire with the tallest possible sidewall height.

Tread Design

Tread design affects tire traction and noise. The shape of the tread blocks determines how well the tire will grip in a variety of situations both on- and off-road. The shape, depth, and gaps between tread blocks contribute to noise. The tread blocks act like little air pumps. The more air that is pumped through the tire tread, the louder the tire will be on the highway. Additionally, the ability of the tread blocks to flex improves off-road traction but makes the tire feel squirmy on the highway. This is especially true with the large, deep tread blocks on mud-terrain tires.

Void Ratio

The void ratio is the ratio that compares the total area of the tire tread to the area of the gaps between the tread blocks or the voids in the tread surface. Larger void ratios allow the tread blocks to better conform to the road or trail surface. This improves traction in off-road situations. The reduction in surface area on the tread reduces traction on the highway and on hard, smoother surfaces off-road. The larger void ratios pump more air which makes the tire louder.

Siping

The little slices cut into treads are called sipes. Under load, especially on hard surfaces, such as rocks, the sipes spread to slightly increase grip. The lateral or cross-tread sipes improve grip while braking or applying power. Longitudinal siping, or sipes running parallel to the direction of the tire tread, increase grip laterally. These sipes are important when a tire is on a side slope where the tire can slip sideways.

The thin slices in the tread blocks are called sipes. On harder surfaces under load, the sipes spread to increase grip. The sipes across this tire improve forward traction, while the sipes running parallel to the tire tread improve its sideways bite.

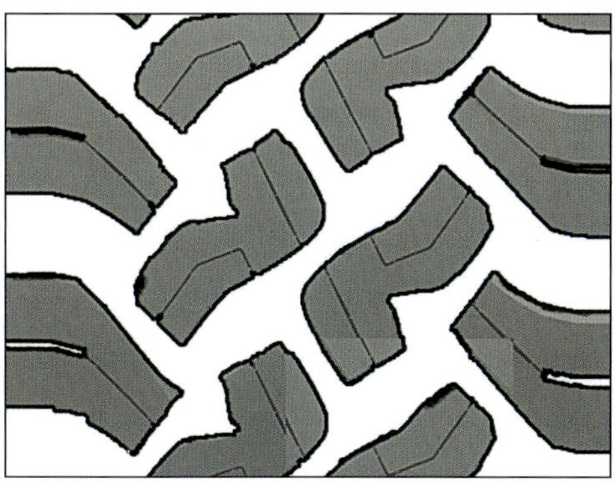

The void ratio compares the tread-block surface area to the total tread area. A high void ratio results in less rubber being on the ground. Large gaps between the tread blocks allow the tire tread to grip deeper into soft surfaces while a smaller void ratio puts more rubber on the road surface, which is a plus for highway driving or hard off-road surfaces.

What Type of Off-Road Tire Is Best for Your Specific Needs?

As mentioned earlier, off-road tires are available in three styles: all-terrain, mud-terrain, and a hybrid design that falls between the M/T and A/T designs. While all of the designs function well off-road, there are compromises that make significant differences in different types of terrain and on the highway.

All-Terrain Tires

All-terrain tires offer several advantages for overlanding:

Pros	Cons
• More tread surface area for better highway traction • Smaller void ratio for reduced highway noise • Tread compound designed for longer tread life • Generally improved performance on snow and ice	• Small void ratios create less grip on soft surfaces • Less grip in mud • Harder tread compounds reduce grip on hard surfaces off-road

Mud-Terrain Tires

Mud-terrain tires provide superior performance off-road in most conditions. However, mud-terrain tires are not ideal for highway and daily-driving scenarios.

All-terrain tires generally feature less-aggressive tread patterns with small void ratios and smaller tread blocks, but more rubber is in contact with the ground. The rubber compounds for the tread are generally harder, which increases tire life and reduces road noise. The sidewall designs of all-terrain tires tend to be less aggressive. For many overlanding applications, an all-terrain tire offers superior on-road performance with a minimal sacrifice off-road. For extreme off-road driving, a hybrid or mud-terrain tire may be a better choice.

Pros	Cons
• Large, deep tread blocks improve grip on soft surfaces and rocks • Larger void ratio for improves traction on soft surfaces off-road • Tread compound designed for increased grip off-road • Improved performance off-road	• Large void ratios create more noise • Less grip in wet conditions • Softer tread compounds reduce wear and tire life

The Kenda Klever M/T offers excellent off-road performance while maintaining good on-road characteristics. A moderate void ratio with medium-sized tread blocks and good siping allow this tire to provide excellent off-road handling while keeping on-road drivability, which is a good characteristic for overlanding vehicles.

An extreme off-road tire, such as the Maxxis Crawler LT, offers great performance in the rocks and mud. The large tread blocks and soft rubber compounds make this style of mud-terrain tire more suited to extreme conditions and limited highway use.

Hybrid or RT Off-Road Tires

Hybrid off-road tires combine most of the advantages of an all-terrain tire with a more aggressive tread pattern. For overlanders who spend considerable time off-road and travel for extended distances on the highway, a hybrid off-road tire may be the best compromise.

Pros	Cons
• More tread surface area for better highway traction but less than an A/T tire • Smaller void ratio for reduced highway noise but larger than an A/T tire • Tread compound designed for longer tread life but less than an A/T tire • Generally improved performance on snow and ice	• Smaller void ratios create less grip on soft surfaces • Less grip in mud than an M/T tire but better than an A/T • Medium-soft tread compounds offer better grip on hard surfaces off-road compared to an A/T tire.

The Kanati Terra Commander RTX hybrid or R/T (rugged-terrain or rough-terrain) tire offers a more aggressive tread design and sidewall pattern than a typical all-terrain tire. Many tires that are the R/T style are good options for overlanding.

Optimal Tire Size

Using the largest possible tires that fit on a rig may be the obvious optimal-tire-size choice. For the most part, that is true. When tire diameters are increased more than 10 percent, axle gear changes should be considered. Axle ratios allow the vehicle to maintain an RPM range close to stock for a given highway speed. If the stock axle ratios are retained with taller tires, acceleration will be adversely affected. Off-road performance on hillclimbs and descents in 4WD low range will suffer from degraded performance.

Suspension lifts allow the fitment of taller tires and reduce or eliminate tire clearance issues. Suspension lifts raise the center of gravity which reduces lateral stability when cornering on the highway and on more extreme off-road situations on side slopes, extreme ruts, and big rocks. For vehicles with independent front suspension, the lift height needs to be limited without the addition of spacers to keep the angles of the drive axles and steering tie-rods at a reasonable level.

Wider tires provide increased tire contact area with the ground to increase traction. Increasing tire tread width can cause tire rub with the fender and inner fender liners. Also, wider tires can protrude outside the cover of the fenders, which may be illegal in some states.

Less wheel backspacing means that the centerline of the wheel sits farther outboard and can increase clearance inside the fender well, but the tire will likely extend outside the fender line. If reduced backspacing moves the wheel/tire too far outboard, additional strain is placed on wheel bearings and hubs. In the front, steering geometry may be adversely affected. Aftermarket fenders or fender flares can be installed to increase coverage over the tires.

The Mickey Thompson Baja ATZ P3 was one of the first hybrid off-road tires. It leans towards the aggressive mud-terrain design but offers high performance and reduces road noise. The tire size is limited from 31 to 33 inches, which is a good fit for many overlanding rigs.

Tire Pressure

As vehicle loads increase, so should tire pressures. The optimal tire pressure is one that allows tire contact patches to remain in full contact with the road surface. If the outside edges are not in contact with the road surface, the tire is overinflated. If the center of the tire contact patch is not in contact with the road surface, the tire is underinflated.

Chalk Test

The easiest way to determine the optimal tire pressure for highway driving requires covering a portion of the tire tread with chalk across the entire width of the tire tread. Sidewalk chalk sticks make the job quicker and easier.

Once all four tires are chalked, drive the vehicle a short distance (a quarter to half mile) at moderate speed. Inspect the chalk marks. If the chalk is worn off across the surface of the tread, the tire pressure is optimal. Check the tire pressure and note for future reference. If the chalk is only worn from the center of the tire tread, the tire pressure is too high. Tire pressure that is too low will have the chalk worn off the edges of the tire. The amount of chalk remaining indicates how close the tire pressure is to optimal.

Adjust the tire pressure as needed and repeat the test. Once the tire pressure is optimized for highway driving and the entire contact patch connects to the road surface, maximum traction is available, and tire wear will be even across the tread surface.

Tire Pressure for Off-Road Driving

The most common question that people ask in our classes and at overlanding events is, "What tire pressure should I run off-road?"

This question is not easily answered. Many factors come into play including:

- Amount of weight resting on each tire
- Tire sidewall height
- Tire sidewall stiffness
- Type of wheel being used

Determining the optimal tire size requires the consideration of several factors. The largest tire on the smallest wheel diameter that offers adequate brake clearance is a good starting point. Tire clearance within the fender well is a critical parameter. The Chevy Colorado ZR2 takes a tire up to 33 inches in diameter without any suspension lift. The 33-inch tires on a 17-inch wheel provide plenty of clearance for the tires through full suspension travel and articulation. The Falken WildPeak A/T is a good overlanding tire with excellent manners for a daily driver.

Optimal tire pressures for off-roading are considerably lower than for highway driving. The process to get your tire to the optimal pressure for off-roading is called airing down. Tires are aired down for four important reasons:

- Increased tire traction by allowing the tire contact to grow as much as double over highway tire pressure contact patches. Some growth is lateral, but most of the size increase is longitudinal.
- Improved ride quality created by a reduction of the tire-sidewall spring rate or an increase in sidewall flex. Suspension springs can never be soft enough to allow for improved ride comfort on bumpy, rocky surfaces off-road.
- Less chance of a tire puncture. With the tire tread and sidewall more compliant, the tire can give more before a puncture occurs.
- Less damage to the road surface. With the increased tire contact area, the load on the tire is spread over a greater area. This increases traction and reduces the load on each square inch of tire contact. Wheelspin reduces, and less erosion occurs.

The chalk test is the optimal way to determine the proper tire pressure for a given load. Step 1: Use a chalk stick or crayon to mark a section of the tire all the way across the tread surface. Step 2: Drive the vehicle for a short distance and go around a few corners both to the left and to the right. Step 3: After stopping, check the chalk marks. If the chalk remains along the edges, the tire is overinflated. If the tire is underinflated, the chalk will be removed from the edges of the tire but will remain in the center of the tire contact patch. If the chalk is completely removed, the tire pressure is good for that tire and load. If the chalk is still showing, adjust the tire pressure and conduct the chalk test again. Step 4: Repeat as needed. If you add or remove a substantial amount of weight from the vehicle, such as a roof rack with a rooftop tent or other gear stowed onboard, the contact patch will change and the tires will require a different tire pressure. Retest with chalk to determine the new optimal tire pressure.

Tire pressure has a profound effect on tire compliance. The lower the pressure, the better the tire can conform to the shape of an obstacle. The ability of a tire to mold to the shape of a rock or other obstacle is critical for optimal traction and the ability to climb obstacles, especially in extreme terrain. This tire that is shown is a Nexen Roadian MTX, 27x12.50x17 at a variety of tire pressures on a Jeep Wrangler JLU. In Photo A, the pressure is 35 psi, which is the normal highway pressure. In Photo B, the pressure is 26 psi. In Photo C, the pressure is 18 psi. In Photo D, the pressure is 14 psi, which is what is normally used for off-road adventures. In Photo E, the pressure is 10 psi, which requires the use of beadlock wheels to keep the tire bead seated on the wheel rim.

The one downside to airing down tires is the reduction of ground clearance.

The lack of understanding for newcomers and many experienced off-roaders leads to running tire pressures too high for effective off-road driving. Many off-roaders feel that lower tire pressures are too low. In reality, modern tires are constructed to close tolerances. Tires that unseat from the wheel bead occurs only in exceptional circumstances with tire pressures over 10 psi. For most overlanding rigs, with the exception of heavy van conversions, tire pressure can be much lower than most believe to be safe.

I generally recommend tire pressures within a range from 16 psi down to 11 or 12 psi, depending on the tire. Some stiff-sidewall tires need to run at lower pressures compared to soft-sidewall tires. The softer sidewall allows more flex to achieve good contact spread at a higher pressure. Tire pressures below 10 to 11 psi require the use of beadlock wheels to ensure that the tire bead remains seated on the wheel.

An example that compares two tires on the same vehicle helps illustrate the difference in the effect of sidewall stiffness. We have tested many tires and found the sidewall height from the ground to the bottom of the wheel is a good indication of tire contact spread. This has proved to be true by measuring the tire-contact-patch areas of various tires at a variety of tire pressures.

Two of our favorite tires are the Nexen Roadian MTX and the Falken WildPeak M/T. Both mud-terrain tires work exceptionally well off-road. However, there are significant differences between these tires. When setting the tire pressure so that the measurements from the ground to the bottom of the wheel rim are the same, the Falken is at 10 psi while the Nexen comes in at 14 psi.

The difference is in sidewall flex. The Falken is close to needing a beadlock wheel for safe operation off-road, while the Nexen has a wide safety margin and does not need to use beadlock wheels. The comparison was done on 37-12.50x17 tires. The overall diameter was very close to identical.

Wheel and tire size are critical to determining proper tire pressure. Tall wheels and short tire sidewalls are not conducive to good off-road performance. For example, the Jeep Wrangler Sahara 4xe comes with 275/55 R20 tires. This tire is about 32 inches tall, as are many OEM off-road-capable vehicles. If we deduct the wheel diameter from the tire diameter, a sidewall height of 12 inches remains. Dividing the sidewall total by two (top and bottom are each about half the total sidewall height), there is 6 inches of sidewall. Given the loading on the tire, the sidewall height is closer to 5.5 inches, which is not much sidewall to work with. Airing down this tire more than 5 psi risks the tire getting pinched between hard obstacles, such as rocks and the wheel. The bottom line is that a short sidewall is far from optimal for off-road driving.

Most modern 4x4 trucks, crossovers, and SUVs are equipped with 17-inch-or-taller wheels. Brake clearance is one of the reasons that manufacturers use taller wheels. Reducing the ability to lower tire pressure to an optimal range due to a short tire sidewall is detrimental to off-road traction and comfort.

The ideal tire pressure for a given rig and trail conditions allows a tire to conform to obstacles. At high tire pressures, the tire will slide off the rock. The Hankook RF10 A/T tire offers excellent grip when properly inflated for off-road driving.

Getting caught between a rock and a hard spot happens often off-road. Extreme flex in a tire sidewall allows deformity such as this. The traction increase is dramatic. If the tire pressure was 3 to 4 psi lower on this Nexen Roadian MTX, the tire sidewall would become pinched between the wheel and the rock and cause possible damage.

A tire should wrap around obstacles, such as a small rock. In this case, high tire pressures may cause the tire to slip and dislodge the rock which can cause damage.

What Off-Road Tires Need to Do

Off-road tires provide grip in a broad range of road surface and weather conditions. Reducing tire pressure to an optimal level accommodates this. By airing down tires, the tire contact increases to make the tire footprint larger by as much as 100 percent.

Even more importantly, the reduced rigidity of the tire sidewall allows the tire to conform to rocks and uneven terrain. Why? In deep ruts and bumps, tires inflated to highway pressures can spin on soft soil. When the tire can flex, more of the tread remains in contact with the road surface to greatly increase traction. On rocks, even small ones, the tire must be able to wrap around the rock for maximum grip.

For example, a rock with a steep dome or point offers little traction with a tire at too high of a pressure. Very little of tire tread is in contact with the rock surface. When the pressure is reduced to optimal levels, the increased flex of the tire sidewall allows the tire to wrap around the rock, which greatly increases tire traction.

The ability of the tire to wrap around obstacles like rocks and ledges is critical in rugged terrain. An extreme example of this occurs when an undercut rock ledge is encountered. If the upper portion of the ledge is higher than the middle of

The right front and left rear tires show high levels of sidewall grip. The sidewall grip helps in the rocks but is even more important in heavily rutted terrain and on side slopes. The Nexen Roadian MTX has an aggressive sidewall design that provides a high level of sidewall traction.

the tire or axle height, the tire must move backward to climb over the rock ledge. This can only occur if the tire can flex enough for the tread to wrap around the obstacle. Optimal tire pressures allow this to happen.

How to Measure for Optimal Sidewall Heights and Tire Pressures

In essence, the tire pressure is irrelevant. What *does* matter is the spread of the tire contact patch on the ground. While the tire pressure is ultimately an important factor, finding the optimal pressure requires a few simple measurements. This

Inflate the tire to the maximum pressure noted on the tire sidewall or to about 50 psi, whichever is less. Tire sidewall heights change very little above 50 psi.

Measure the distance from the ground to the bottom of the wheel. We use 85 percent of this measurement as a guide for off-road tire pressure. If the sidewall is short, use 90 percent. In some cases, such as sand, mud, and deep snow, use 80 percent.

Multiply the measurement in Step 2 by 0.85 or by the amount that you feel is correct for your situation. Install a deflator. Using a 35-inch-tall tire on a 17-inch wheel, the distance from the ground to the bottom of the wheel is about 8.5 inches. It is less than 9 inches because the tire is slightly smaller than 35 inches in diameter. The measurement is taken at the bottom of the wheel and not the top of the tire sidewall.

Reduce the tire pressure to the new ideal sidewall height. The 85-percent measurement works off-road in most cases. The goal is to keep the tire sidewall from becoming pinched between the wheel and a hard surface or rock. Be sure to reinflate the tires to the normal highway pressure before heading home or to your next destination.

applies mostly to tires with a reasonable tire sidewall height. Here is the procedure:

1. Inflate the tires to a high pressure but below the maximum pressure listed on the sidewall. In most cases, a pressure around 50 psi is adequate.
2. Carefully measure the distance from the bottom of the wheel to the ground. Make sure that your measurement is perpendicular to the ground and at the lowest point on the wheel.
3. Multiply the distance measured in the step above by 0.85 for normal off-road conditions, 0.90 for higher speeds on smooth dirt roads, and 0.80 for low speeds on soft surfaces, such as snow, mud, and sand.
4. Reduce the tire pressure until the new measurement is reached.

Examples

With a 35-inch-diameter tire on a 17-inch wheel, the fully inflated measurement from the rim bottom to the sidewall is about 8.5 inches, and 8.5 multiplied by 0.85 equals 7.225 inches. For higher speeds on smooth dirt surfaces, 8.5 is multiplied by 0.90 for a final measurement of 7.65 inches. For low speeds on soft surfaces, the 8.5-inch measurement is multiplied by 0.80 for a final sidewall height of 6.8 inches. At this sidewall height, the tire contact patch nearly doubles in area on the ground.

Keep in mind that different weights on the tire and different sidewall structures yield different results. Technically, each tire may have different measurements and could benefit from different tire pressures for each tire.

With a 37-inch-diameter tire on a 17-inch wheel, the fully inflated measurement from the rim bottom to the sidewall is about 9.5 inches, and 9.5 multiplied by 0.85 equals just over 8 inches. For higher speeds on smooth dirt surfaces, 9.5 is multiplied by 0.90 for a final measurement of 8.55 inches. For low speeds on soft surfaces, the 9.5-inch measurement is multiplied by 0.80 for a final sidewall height of 7.6 inches. The same criteria listed in this example apply here as well.

A final example uses the previous Jeep Wrangler Sahara 4xe example. With a 32-inch-diameter tire on a 20-inch wheel, the fully inflated measurement from the rim bottom to the sidewall is about 5.5 inches, and 5.5 multiplied by 0.85 equals 4.7 inches. At this low sidewall height, the tire is susceptible to tire damage if the sidewall is pinched between a rock or other hard surface and the wheel. I would not use this measurement but would use no more than the 90-percent measurement. The 5.5 is multiplied by 0.90 for a final measurement just under 5 inches. This is not much of reduction and offers a minimal increase in the tire contact patch on the ground. It also doesn't offer much improvement in ride quality. This example highlights why tall wheels with short tire sidewalls are not ideal for off-road performance.

Off-Road Tire Pressures

Many off-roaders run a tire pressure that is too high. Misinformation concerning off-road tire pressure is widespread. One comment often heard from those preparing for an off-road adventure goes something like, "I don't need to air down. This is an easy trail." or, "I'll air down to 25 psi since the conditions are dry and there are no major obstacles." The idea that reducing tire pressure or airing down to the optimal pressure for off-road driving is not always necessary is misguided. Here are three reasons why to always air down tires even when conditions are ideal for good traction:

- Ride quality and comfort is an important consideration for vehicle occupants, the suspension and chassis, and the contents inside the vehicle.
- Significantly reduced tire pressure reduces the chance of a puncture or tread damage by allowing the tire to flex more.
- Aired-down tires spread the load on the tire over a greater area on the ground. The reduced load per square inch of tire contact reduces damage to the surface. The reduced disturbance of the road surface reduces erosion and dust, which is better for the environment.

Options for Airing Down Tires

Reducing tire pressure is a simple and straightforward job. The valve stem mounted in the wheel has a spring-loaded valve core that allows air to enter and exit the tire when it is depressed. A valve-stem cap screws onto the valve stem to keep dirt and debris out of the valve stem. Pressurized air will depress the valve core to allow the tire to be inflated. By depressing the valve core without a pressurized air source, air will escape from the tire.

Air pressure is measured with a tire-pressure gauge. Many tire-pressure gauges have a relief valve to allow air pressure to be reduced by depressing the button on the gauge while the hose is engaged on the tire's valve stem. Pressure can

The RockJock Deflator removes the valve core from the valve stem on the wheel. This allows rapid deflation to get to the desired tire pressure. To use the RockJock Deflator, screw the fitting onto the valve stem, depress the plunger and rotate until it captures the valve core, unscrew the valve core, and pull the plunger out. Open the air valve to deflate, and close the air valve to check the pressure. When the desired pressure is reached, keep the valve closed, push in the plunger and screw in the valve core until it is snug, and pull the plunger out so that the valve core cannot be unscrewed while unscrewing the fitting from the valve stem. Unscrew the fitting from the valve stem and replace the valve cap.

also be released by depressing the valve within the valve stem with the tip of a key or other pointed object. While this method will work, it is slow and inconvenient.

Tire deflators provide quick and more convenient ways to deflate tires. A valve-core-removal tool can be used to rapidly deflate tires by unscrewing the valve core from the valve stem. However, there is no way to easily monitor tire pressure with this method.

The RockJock deflator removes the valve core from the valve stem on the wheel. This allows rapid deflation to the desired tire pressure. To use the RockJock Deflator, screw the fitting onto the valve stem, depress the plunger, and rotate until it captures the valve core. Unscrew the valve core and pull the plunger out. Open the air valve to deflate, and close the air valve to check the pressure. When the desired pressure is reached, keep the valve closed, push in the plunger, and screw in the valve core until snug. Pull the plunger out so the valve core cannot be unscrewed while unscrewing the fitting from the valve stem. Unscrew the fitting from the valve stem and replace the valve cap.

Tire-Pressure Deflators

Tire-pressure deflators allow rapid deflation using three different methods:

- Deflators that screw onto the valve stem and depress the spring-loaded valve core
- Deflators that screw onto the valve stem and have an additional internal tool to allow the valve core to be removed while being captured within the tool
- Replacement or additional valve stems with ports to allow rapid deflation

Screw-on deflators depress the valve core to release air from the tire. These deflators use a spring-loaded valve that can be adjusted to a preset pressure. Once that pressure is reached, the valve is closed and airflow ceases. Screw-on deflators are usually sold in sets of four, although they sometimes come in pairs. Once it is set to the desired pressure, the deflator can be screwed on to the valve stem of each tire and left to shut off when the set pressure is reached.

While it is convenient, this style of deflator is on the slow side, which is counteracted by deflating all four tires at once. Screw-on deflators also require regular adjustment for ideal pressure. The internal adjustment springs are affected by atmospheric pressure, and the spring can weaken over time. Several styles of screw-on deflators are offered by a wide range of manufacturers. Some of the popular screw-on deflators are available from Coyote, Staun, Smittybilt, Boulder Tools, real 4x4, and several other companies. Coyote and Staun deflators were the first on the market and are high quality.

Tire-pressure deflators that screw onto the valve stem and utilize a tool to remove and capture the valve core release air pressure much more quickly. These deflators have a built-in pressure gauge so that setting tire pressure is more accurate. The downside of this style of deflator is the need to monitor deflation progress rather than relying on the automatic shut-off on other deflators. On the other hand, this type of deflator is much faster and allow all four tires to be individually deflated in about the same time period as automatic shut-off deflators. These deflators come in both analog and digital styles, and one is available with a liquid-filled gauge.

The price range of the deflators that remove the valve core is roughly half the cost of the automatic screw-on style. The first companies to offer this style of deflator were RockJock 4x4 and ARB. Many other companies now offer similar deflators.

The procedure for these deflators is as follows:

1. Remove the valve-stem cap from the valve stem
2. Completely screw the deflator body onto the valve stem
3. Fully depress the knurled knob plunger and rotate to engage the valve core
4. Completely unscrew the valve core. Then, disengage the plunger by pulling it up. If it's not fully disengaged, the noise from the release of pressure will be fairly quiet. If it's fully disengaged, the airflow noise will be loud.
5. Pull up the pressure-relief knurled knob to allow air to flow from the valve. Push down to stop the flow and check tire pressure. Tire pressure readings are only accurate when the pressure valve is closed.
6. Once the desired pressure is reached, close the valve, depress the plunger, and screw the valve core back into the valve stem by rotating the knurled knob on the plunger clockwise until the valve core is seated and snug but not overtightened.
7. Once the core is seated, pull the plunger out before unscrewing the tool from the valve stem. Failure to pull up the plunger may cause the valve core to be removed and cause a rapid deflation of the tire, which usually means it will go flat. I speak from experience! This issue is why it is wise to carry spare valve cores and a core removal tool.

Deflators, Replacing Valve Stems, or Adding a Second Valve Stem

Additional valve stems, such as the Power Tank Monster valve, and replacement valve stems, such as the Apex Designs RPV Rapid deflator, are by far the fastest way to reduce tire pressure to an optimal level for off-road driving. This style of deflator uses ports that are uncovered by a sliding valve or a more standard valve stem with a core but larger opening to allow air to evacuate more quickly. These valves typically air down a tire in 30 seconds or less. We have tested both styles. With a 40-inch-diameter by 13.50-inch-wide tire, we can air down from 26 psi to 9 psi in about 25 seconds. All four tires can be deflated in about 2 minutes and 30 seconds.

Tire-Pressure Gauges

Tire-pressure gauges are rarely accurate. We have tested many, and the accuracy can vary by up to 20 percent from one gauge to another. We finally invested in a high-quality certified gauge and compared other gauges to the baseline. Some of the gauges that are part of the deflators that remove valve stems are off by up to 4 psi. While not ideal, as long as you measure tire-sidewall heights with one gauge and always use that gauge for deflating tires, you should have accurate deflation levels. This is one important reason to take sidewall measurements to ensure accuracy.

Reinflating (Airing up) Tires

Two options exist for reinflating tires at the end of an off-road adventure. Onboard compressors are the first option. Second, tanks containing compressed air, CO_2, or nitrogen can be used to air up tires. The most common compound for airing up from a tank is CO_2. The Power Tank is the most common product that uses CO_2.

One additional alternative exists. When an adventure ends in close proximity to a public compressor, such as those found at many gas stations, it is acceptable to drive a short distance (5 miles maximum) at low speeds (45 mph maximum) to air up tires. Tire failures from low tire pressures occur mostly due to heat buildup in the tire tread and sidewalls. Heat buildup is caused by excessive flex in the tire due to low tire pressures, high speeds, and high ambient temperatures. Low speeds, short distances, and cooler road surface temperatures allow you to drive to a source of compressed air. Exercise extreme caution when using this option.

Onboard Air Compressors

A wide variety of portable 12-volt air compressors and onboard air systems are readily available. Inexpensive compressors for less than $100 from many sources will get the job done. However, these compressors take a significant amount of time to air up four tires, often in excess of 30 minutes. Additionally, the duty cycle of an inexpensive compressor is far less than 100 percent, which means the compressor will overheat if not shut off to cool down.

High-quality portable compressors have higher duty cycles, often up to 100 percent. Onboard compressor systems, such as those from Viair and ARB, are mounted within the vehicle and hard-wired for quick and easy operation. Both companies offer dual compressor systems to allow even faster inflation. Viair also offers a system with a tank to store enough compressed air to get a head start on the airing-up process. Many other companies offer good compressors.

Compressed CO_2 Systems

An alternative to onboard air systems and portable compressors is the compressed CO_2 tank system. A CO_2 system offers several advantages:

- Faster airing-up time
- Quieter operation
- Easy portability
- Ability to operate air tools

Disadvantages include needing to refill the tank and limited capacity. Tanks from Power Tank come in 5-, 10-, and 15-pound sizes to suit a variety of needs. A 15-pound tank can refill all four tires 15 to 30 psi about 10 times. The Power Tank system uses a flow regulator to adjust airflow rates. Power Tank offers

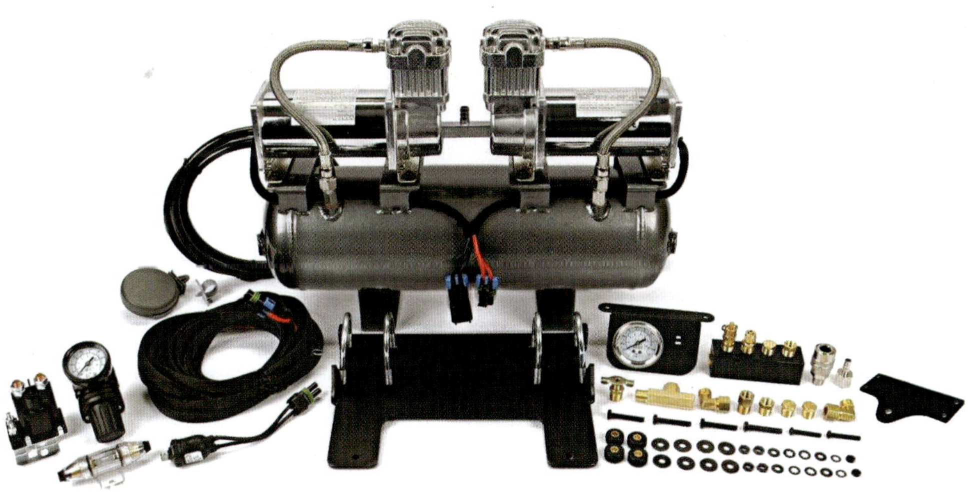

The Viair compressor systems offer a range of options, including a compressor with an air tank. The company also offers a dual-compressor system to make airing up faster.

Power Tank offers a wide range of CO_2 tanks, regulators, mounts, hoses, gauges, and accessories. The Power Tank inflator is the fastest way to air up tires. It uses compressed CO_2 to inflate tires or drive air tools. We inflate all four 37-inch tires from 14 psi to 30 psi in about 3 minutes, including moving from tire to tire. This compares to about 20 minutes with an onboard air compressor. The Power Tank is also quieter and more reliable than an electric air compressor. The downside is the need to refill the tank with CO_2. CO_2 is available from paintball shops, some welding supply shops, and beverage-dispensing equipment stores.

Viair makes a range of portable air compressors in a variety of outputs and duty cycles.

complete systems that include the tank, regulator, hose, pressure gauge, mounting brackets, and handles that protect the fragile pressure regulator.

Multi-Tire Inflation/Deflation Systems

Tire inflation/deflation systems utilize connectors, valves, and hoses to allow the inflation or deflation of all four tires simultaneously. These systems allow the use of a single tire-pressure gauge to alter tire pressure on all tires at once. The system functions with compressors and tank systems like the Power Tank. SpeedFlate and ARB offer multi-tire systems. Other similar products are coming into the marketplace.

The central valve on the Speedflate system allows all four tires to be deflated at once. Plug in an air source (a compressor or a Power Tank) at the valve fitting to air up the tires. The pressure equalizes on all four tires. (Photo Courtesy Speedflate)

The Speedflate air system is a convenient way to inflate and deflate tires. The system uses a series of hoses that connects all four tire valves to a central valve. (Photo Courtesy Speedflate)

Beadlock wheels provide great durability and strength, but they require some maintenance. They allow very low tire pressures without the risk of unseating the tire bead from the wheel. The Grid beadlock design is attractive and is available in a variety of diameters, backspacing, and widths.

Wheel Specifications

Wheel dimensions play a critical role in affecting off-road tire performance. The wheel diameter affects tire options and sidewall height. Wheel width affects how the tire contact patch interacts with the road surface. Wheel offset/backspacing affects tire clearance with the fender well and loads on wheel bearings.

Raceline Wheels manufactures a wide range of off-road wheels, including beadlocks and simulated beadlocks, such as the Clutch aluminum alloy simulated beadlock.

Diameter

Large-diameter wheels reduce the potential tire sidewall height. Smaller-diameter wheels allow greater tire sidewall heights. More tire sidewall height translates to greater tire flex and increased traction. The largest-diameter wheel should be no more than the original-equipment wheel diameter.

In some cases where the brake rotors and calipers can be cleared by a smaller-diameter wheel, it is a good idea to go smaller when upgrading. The Jeep Wrangler Sahara models are a good example of this. The Sahara is equipped with 18-inch-diameter wheels, and in one case, 20-inch

The 17-inch diameter Raceline Defender wheel mounts a 37-inch-diameter tire to leave considerable sidewall height for effective tire-pressure reduction.

Tire Test No. 1: Toyo Tire Open Country RT Trail

Specifications

- Size: 37x12050 R17 LT
- Load Range: E
- Max Load: 3,970 pounds at 65 psi
- Plies: Tread: 2 steel, 3 polyester, and 2 nylon; Sidewall: 3 polyester
- Durometer (rubber compound hardness): 68 (medium)

Features

- Optimized pattern arrangement
- Reduced noise for improved driving comfort.
- Stone and mud ejectors
- Aggressive sidewall designs with durable sidewall compound
- Enhanced traction and side-impact protection
- Offers customization with a distinct look on each side of the tire
- Open, scalloped shoulder blocks
- Improved off-road traction
- Enhanced grip in muddy, sandy, or snowy off-road conditions

Optimal Tire Pressures

- Vehicle: 2020 Jeep Wrangler Unlimited
- Weight: 5,500 pounds
- Highway Pressure (chalk test) 32 psi
- All-Purpose Off-Road: 15 psi
- Soft Surface Off-Road (sand, snow, and mud): 11 psi (lowest pressure without beadlock wheels). Heavier vehicles run higher pressure and lighter vehicles run lower pressure.

Impressions

The Toyo Tire Open Country RT Trail features an E-load rating, but the sidewalls are relatively flexible to allow a higher-than-average tire pressure to achieve optimal tire-contact-patch spread for off-road driving. The flexible sidewall is ideal for overlanding since beadlock wheels are unnecessary for most off-road driving situations.

While driving the Open Country RT Trail on our standard off-road test loop that includes climbs, descents, large ruts, and some rock-crawling sections, we encountered no wheelspin even on loose dirt and steep climbs. Traction was excellent, sidewall grip (even in muddy conditions) was very good, and the tire contact patches conformed to rocks to offer excellent grip. Overall, the Open Country RT Trail is an impressive off-road tire and ideal for overlanding.

On the highway, the Open Country RT Trail provides a surprising level of cornering grip on the twisty sections. Noise levels at 50 mph are a low 68 decibels, which means that the tire noise is unnoticed over the wind noise of the Jeep Wrangler. ■

Tire Test No. 2: Toyo Tire Open Country MT

Specifications

- Size: 37x12050 R17 LT
- Load Range: D
- Max Load: 3,525 pounds at 50 psi
- Plies: Tread: 2 steel, 3 polyester, and 2 nylon; Sidewall: 3 polyester
- Durometer (rubber compound hardness): 60 (soft)

Features

- High turn-up, tough polyester construction
- Excellent durability, impact resistance, and handling
- Aggressive tread design with hook-shaped blocks
- Excellent off-road traction while maintaining great on-road performance
- Deep siping in the tread blocks
- Maintains grip on wet surfaces
- Open, scalloped shoulder blocks
- Improved off-road traction
- Enhanced grip in muddy, sandy, or snowy off-road conditions
- Ejects mud and snow through the open channels.
- Over-the-shoulder tread
- Provided traction in deep mud and snow
- Improved off-road handling in hard turns

Optimal Tire Pressures

- Vehicle: 2020 Jeep Wrangler Unlimited
- Weight: 5,500 pounds
- Highway Pressure (chalk test) 30 psi
- All-Purpose Off-Road: 12 psi
- Soft Surface Off-Road (sand, snow, mud): 9 psi (bead-lock wheels should be used)
- Heavier vehicles run higher pressure and lighter vehicles run lower pressure

Impressions

The Toyo Tire Open Country MT has a great reputation as an excellent all-around off-road performer with good on-road manners. Off-road, the Toyo Open Country MT provides great grip on loose rock climbs and descents.

On side slopes, the large sidewall lugs keep the vehicle from slipping sideways. The sidewall design is moderately soft to allow great contact patch spread at higher tire pressures. For vehicles over 4,500 pounds, beadlock wheels are unnecessary. The softer sidewall construction allows improved grip on uneven surfaces where considerable grip is needed. They work exceptionally well climbing up steep, near vertical rock faces and dropping down ledges.

On the highway, traction is good with a positive feel to the steering. Compared to the Toyo RT Trail, grip is somewhat lower and feel is less positive, mostly due to the large tread blocks and large void ratio. Noise is on the quiet side for a mud-terrain tire. ■

The Toyo Tire Open Country RT Trail tire features large tread blocks with siping and a low void ratio, which keeps noise to a minimum. The large sidewall lugs protect the tire sidewall while offering great traction from the sidewall on side slopes in steeply slanted rock situations.

The Open Country RT wraps around rocks to provide good traction for crawling up rocks. Here, the tire pressure is 15 psi on a 5,500-pound Jeep Gladiator Rubicon.

The hybrid nature of the Toyo Tire Open Country RT Trail offers a more aggressive tread design than an all-terrain tire to allow good traction in mud and other slippery surfaces.

A good mud-terrain tire conforms to uneven road and rock surfaces to improve traction. The Toyo Tire Open Country MT wraps around the rock surface and allows the sidewall to add extra traction.

The Toyo Tire Open Country MT offers excellent grip, especially on rocks. The aggressive tread design utilizes a relatively large void ratio, large tread blocks, and sidewall lugs that hold on side slopes and near vertical rock faces and ruts. (Photo Courtesy Paul Crawford)

By wrapping around the rock, the tire can lift the vehicle up the face of the rock. The tire pressure on the Toyo Tire Open Country MT is 12 psi. Sidewall flex is excellent. While the Raceline beadlocks are nice to have, the tire contact patch spread at 12 psi means that beadlock wheels are not necessary.

Tire Test No. 3: Nexen Roadian MTX

The Nexen Roadian MTX is an extreme mud-terrain tire with excellent highway manners, reasonable noise levels, and great wear characteristics. The Nexen Roadian MTX is priced in the mid-level price range of comparable mud-terrain tires.

Off-road, the Nexen Roadian MTX really shines. Our team was fortunate enough to conduct extensive tire testing for Nexen to compare the Nexen Roadian MTX to other competitive brands before the final design went into production. We conducted more than 20 different tests that ranged from hillclimbs and descents to rock crawling on a variety of surfaces. We used one Jeep Wrangler Rubicon for all tests that required an insane number of tire and wheel changes in the field. We used three drivers who rated performance separately. Ratings were averaged at the end of testing to generate a final tally.

The Nexen Roadian MTX was the highest-ranked tire in most of the tests, often by a small margin compared to some formidable competition. One characteristic of the Nexen Roadian MTX is the sidewall construction. While the Nexen Roadian MTX is an F-rated (12-ply rating) sidewall, it is very flexible. This means the Nexen Roadian MTX can operate at a higher tire pressure with the optimal tire-contact-patch spread when compared with other tires.

Optimal pressure for the Nexen Roadian MTX is in the 13-to-14-psi range, where similar mud-terrain tires, such as the BFG MT and Falken MT01, require a pressure 3 to 4 psi lower to achieve the optimal tire-contact-patch spread. This difference can determine whether beadlock wheels are necessary.

While the Nexen Roadian MTX tires performed well on all tests, the tires seemed to be at their best on rocks, especially with loose grit and sand. In part, this is due to the longitudinal siping that improves lateral grip. The edges of the sipes flex and grab the surface to improve grip on slanted rocks and side slopes. The Nexen Roadian MTX held tight where other tires slipped off the rocks and required a change of lines to navigate over the hard obstacles.

At the optimal tire pressure, which was 14 psi on the test rig, the Nexen Roadian MTX tires were able to wrap around rocks and other obstacles. This allows the tire contact patch to provide maximum traction, even on undercut rocks over 20 inches high. Our team has been running the Nexen Roadian MTX tires on several vehicles for more than four years. The tires perform exceptionally, and the wear characteristics are outstanding. ■

The Nexen Roadian MTX tires feature a dual sidewall design. Each side uses a unique sidewall pattern. On the left is the claw pattern, and on the right is the machine pattern. Both patterns are fairly aggressive. During our extensive testing on the Roadian MTX, we found that both designs work well in situations where sidewall traction is critical.

The tire tread design on the Nexen Roadian MTX tire uses tread blocks with good lateral and longitudinal siping to improve grip on most surfaces, especially granite slabs and slick rock.

Tire Review: Mickey Thompson Baja Boss M/T

The Mickey Thompson Baja Boss A/T and M/T tread pattern designs offer aggressive features for the type of tire. The M/T tire (left) uses a fairly small void ratio for an M/T tire. This reduces road noise and aids traction on hard surfaces. The A/T tire (right) is closer to an R/T style than an A/T tread pattern. The A/T tread pattern uses extensive siping for improved grip.

The Mickey Thompson Baja Boss M/T tire utilizes a fairly stiff sidewall construction. To get optimal performance on most rigs, low tire pressures are necessary. We run this tire on a 5,500-pound Jeep at 8 to 10 psi which necessitates using beadlock wheels.

wheels. All other current Wrangler models use 17-inch-diameter wheels. We always recommend that Sahara owners upgrade to 17-inch wheels to allow more tire sidewall height.

Width

Every tire manufacturer provides data on the range of wheel widths that are suitable for a given tire. Ideally, the optimal wheel width is slightly to the larger side of the manufacturer's list wheel width range. If a wheel is too narrow, it will cause the tire to bulge slightly. This will cause the tire contact patch to be smaller than ideal on the highway.

Accelerated tire wear in the center of the tread can occur. If the wheel is too wide, the tire bead is more likely to become unseated from the wheel rim at lower pressures over rough and rocky terrain. Generally, the optimal range is about 1 inch within the manufacturer's recommended range. For example, a 35 x 12.50-inch tire will best seat on a rim of 8.5 to 9.0 inches wide.

Offset

Wheel offset, which is similar to backspacing, refers to the distance that the centerline of the wheel is offset from the mounting face where the wheel bolts to the hub of the wheel. Zero offset means that the wheel mounting flange is on the exact centerline of the wheel. A negative offset refers to the mounting flange being positioned toward the inside of the wheel, which positions the wheel outward toward the fender. A positive offset refers to the mounting flange of the wheel being positioned toward the inside of the vehicle. This reduces clearance to the inner fender, frame, steering, and suspension, especially at the front of a vehicle.

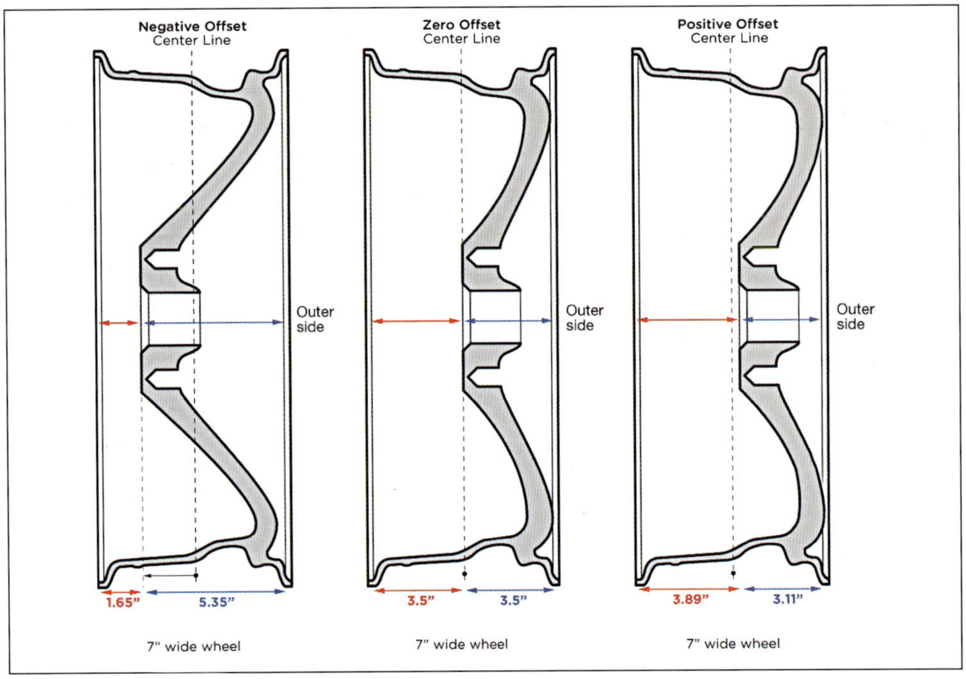

Wheel offset is measured from the centerline of the wheel, as is shown in the illustration.

Backspacing

Similar to wheel offset, wheel backspacing accomplishes the same goal, which is to determine the location of the wheel-mounting surface compared to the centerline of the wheel. Instead of measuring from the exact centerline of the wheel, backspacing is measured from the inside edge of the wheel rim, which is the part of the wheel facing the inside of the vehicle. A wheel with less backspacing will move the wheel outboard to make the vehicle track width wider. More backspacing moves the wheel/tire inboard. An 8-inch-wide wheel with zero offset has the wheel mounting flange in the exact center of the wheel. The same wheel has 4 inches of backspacing.

It is important to minimize offset or backspacing changes from stock. Excessive offsets place more loads on the wheel bearings and ball joints and can adversely affect steering geometry at the front. Keeping near stock backspacing on wheels offers the best option for optimal performance and reliability.

Backspacing is measured from the inside of the wheel-to-hub mounting surface to the outer edge of the back of the wheel. This wheel has 4 inches of backspacing.

Bolt Pattern

Wheel lug bolt patterns are most often left stock. Exceptions are when axle assemblies are upgraded. Aftermarket axle assemblies from companies such as Currie and Dynatrac often use 6- and 8-lug bolt patterns that require matching wheels. These aftermarket axles are generally utilized for rock crawling and run large tires (40- to 44-inch tire diameters) on extreme terrain. Wheel studs are also larger in diameter.

Wheel lug nuts must be tightened in a crisscross-pattern sequence. Wheel lug nuts should always be tightened to the recommended torque specification from the wheel manufacturer using a torque wrench. An impact wrench can be used to spin the lug nuts on the studs but not to tighten the nuts. Impact wrenches can easily overtighten the lug nuts and stretch the wheel studs.

Materials

The two most common materials for off-road wheels are aluminum alloys and steel. Steel wheels are heavier, cheaper, and durable. A bent steel wheel can often be repaired.

Aluminum alloy wheels are offered in a huge range of styles.

Two manufacturing processes are used: casting and forging. Forged wheels are expensive. They are usually machined from blocks or billets of aluminum alloys. Cast wheels use forms that are usually made from sand. Molten alloys are poured into the sand forms. After casting, the wheels are machined for a finished look. Most aluminum alloy wheels are hard-anodize finished for additional strength and scratch resistance. Wheels can also be powder-coated in a wide variety of colors. If an aluminum alloy wheel is damaged or cracked, it cannot be easily repaired.

Lug Nuts and Studs

For most applications, the stock wheel studs are adequate, but the wheel lug nuts many not be compatible with aftermarket wheels. For extreme builds, especially when axles are upgraded, larger-diameter wheel studs and compatible lug nuts add strength and reliability.

It is dangerous when wheel studs break. Even if you carry spares, it can be difficult to replace them in the field. Overtightening lug nuts weakens the studs and is a primary cause of wheel-stud failure. Always tighten lug nuts to the proper torque settings recommended by the wheel manufacturer. Be aware that using an impact wrench, especially an electric impact, often results in overtightened lug nuts. It is fine if an impact wrench is used to snug down the lug nuts, but the nuts should be tightened by hand with a torque wrench. Be sure to tighten lug nuts using a crisscross pattern to make sure that the wheel is seated squarely on the hub flange. To protect the large investment in nice wheels, use locking or splined lug nuts to make theft more difficult. Splined nuts use a special socket for removing or replacing the lug nuts.

Spacers and Adapters

Thin wheel spacers can help with tire clearance, but if the spacer is more than 1/4-inch-thick, steering geometry and wheel-bearing loads may be compromised. If the wheel bolt pattern is not compatible with the desired wheel, wheel adapters can be used to change the bolt pattern. The adapter bolts to the hub with the existing wheel studs. The adapter has studs with the new bolt pattern. Quality wheel adapters are expensive. Purchasing new wheels with the correct bolt pattern and backspacing may be a better alternative.

Standard versus Beadlock

Modern manufacturing processes for tires and wheels ensure a close tolerance fit between the wheel rim bead and the tire bead. The tight fit reduces the chance of the tire bead becoming unseated from the wheel. As long as tire pressures are high enough, the tire will remain seated under all but the most extreme conditions. We have found over the years that tire pressures as low as 10 psi will keep the tire seated to the wheel. With the size of most overlanding vehicles, generally smaller tire sizes,

Lug nuts can take a beating. Quality lug nuts hold up to the rigors of overlanding. Splined lug nuts come with a special socket for installation and removal and are a theft deterrent. Be sure to carry the splined socket in your vehicle.

While wheel spacers are not ideal, bolt-on wheel adapters provide excellent strength. Wheel adapters are used primarily to adapt the lug bolt pattern of the hub to a different bolt-pattern wheel.

and heavy loads from overlanding gear, tire pressures as low as 10 psi are unusual. Non-beadlock wheels work well in nearly all applications.

If rock crawling, snowy and icy conditions, and sand are on the agenda, beadlock wheels may be desirable. Beadlocks use a removable circular ring on the outside of the wheel to replace the wheel bead. When the tire is mounted, the ring is removed for tire installation. When the tire is in place, the ring is installed using a series of bolts around the perimeter.

Most beadlock wheels use 32 bolts to secure the ring to the wheel. The bolts must be installed in a crisscross pattern to ensure proper seating of the ring on the wheel. After the bolts are secured, they are tightened in three steps to reach the proper torque specifications. Final torque for the wheel-ring bolts is usually between 15 and 18 ft-lbs. Too much torque can lead to early bolt failure. Be sure to consult with the wheel manufacturer for proper ring bolt torque specs.

After driving for a few miles, re-torque the ring bolts. Ring-bolt torque should be checked every two to three months. Check for broken or missing ring bolts. We have run tire pressures as low as 3 psi with beadlock wheels with no issues. Normally, extremely low tire pressures are only used in mud, snow, ice, or sand where extra traction is needed and speeds are low. One note of caution: beadlock wheels are only legal in some states. Check your local vehicle code to ensure compliance.

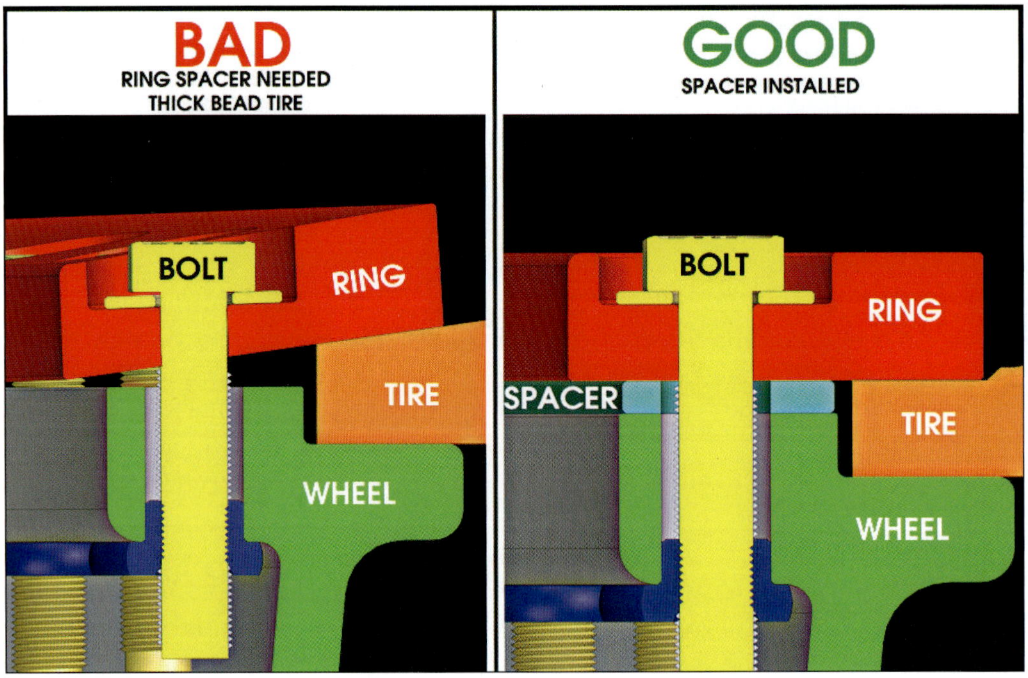

Raceline Wheels use a spacer between the wheel and beadlock ring to ensure proper alignment of the ring, tire, and wheel.

After the beadlock ring bolts are snug (not tight), torque them in two stages. Refer to the torque specifications of the wheel manufacturer for the correct torque settings. The first round of torquing should be about 5 to 6 pounds below the final torque setting. After torquing all bolts to the lower torque, go around all the bolts and re-torque them to the final torque value.

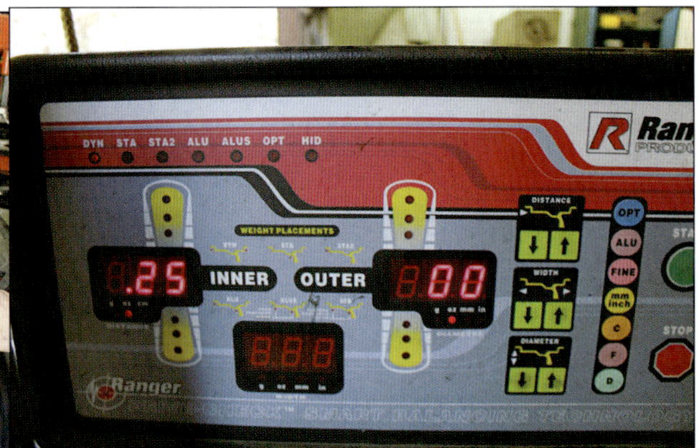

The heavier the tire, the more important it is to have the tire properly balanced. Dynamic balancing is the most effective form of tire balancing. Dynamic balancing requires a balancing machine that measures the necessary balance weights on both the inner and outer wheel surfaces.

CHAPTER 8

Vehicle Protection

Traveling backcountry roads offers exceptional scenery, breathtaking views, and many opportunities for adventure. The same roads, even the easily navigated ones, also present a wide range of hazards. Off-road rigs are susceptible to damage. Most damage requires expensive repairs, and some can end an overlanding trip in a heartbeat. Protecting your overlanding rig with skid plates, bumpers, and rock sliders reduces the risk of costly repairs or adventure-ending damage.

Many overlanding-capable vehicles come equipped with some protection, and others offer protection as an option. The overlanding and off-road aftermarket offers many effective armor and protection options.

Overlanding rigs such as the Toyota Tacoma, Tundra, and 4Runner TRD Pro; Jeep Wrangler, Cherokee TrailHawk, and Gladiator; Dodge Ram Power Wagon, Ram 1500 Rebel, and Ram 1500 TRX; Rivian R1T; Nissan Titan and Frontier 4ProX; Ford Raptor, Ranger, and Bronco; Chevy Silverado 1500 Trail Boss and Colorado ZR2; and some AWD crossover vehicles feature some armor and protection.

Driving in rough, rocky terrain can easily damage critical underside components, such as rock guards and front and rear bumpers. While many overlanding-capable vehicles are equipped with skidplates, nearly all vehicles can benefit from additional protection. The Jeep Gladiator Rubicon has some skidplates, good rocker-panel protection, and steel bumpers. (Photo Courtesy Stellantis)

In many cases, while some protection is provided, the degree of protection is minimal, and some critical components are not protected. For example, Jeep Wranglers and Gladiators come equipped with underside skid plates made of sheet metal. The skid plates cover some key components, including the fuel tank and transfer case, but leave the engine and transmission oil pans exposed. Steel bumpers are optional on some models, and rock sliders are only offered on Rubicon models.

In all cases, the overlanding aftermarket offers more choices and superior protection over stock armor. Even if you plan to stick to easy to moderate roads and trails, hazards will present themselves. Given the inadequate budgets that public land managers have for road and trail maintenance, erosion, and traffic, ground movement (rock slides or minor earthquakes) makes travel more perilous and vehicles more likely to sustain damage.

Potential Hazards

- Ruts and bumps can damage underside components when unseen and speeds are too fast
- Fallen rocks can damage critical underside items, such as oil pans or plastic bumpers
- Downed tree limbs can get under a vehicle and cause damage
- Large rocks, tree trunks, and other obstacles can damage rocker panels, especially in tight quarters
- Plastic bumpers and bumper covers can be torn off when steep ruts and bumps cause the covers to drag

Dozens of 4WD vehicles and some AWD rigs work well for overlanding adventures but have a wide range of protection. Many companies offer products for enhanced protection. There are far too many vehicles and aftermarket options to cover here, but each type of protection is covered and easily found for specific vehicles.

Skid Plates

When driving off-road, even moderate conditions can cause issues that can damage the underside of your overlanding rig. Loose rocks, ruts and bumps, and downed tree branches and shrubs can reach unprotected underside parts, such as the oil pan, transmission, and other critical components. Even the areas protected by stock skid plates can still be damaged, given a hard enough impact. Additional and stronger underside protection enhances the reduction of possible damage.

The cost to repair unprotected underside components can be major. Damage to the engine oil pan and transmission pan can be extensive. The sheet-metal gas tank skid plate offers some protection, but a sharp rock or branch can penetrate the sheet metal and cause the plastic fuel tank on some vehicles to leak. Not only is this a hazardous materials issue but it could also cause a fire with extreme consequences.

Many stock skid plates are made of sheet metal that offers some protection. Aftermarket skid plates are most often made from plate steel or aluminum. Metal-plate skid plates offer greater protection.

While adding skid plates to unprotected areas, such as the engine oil pan, is important, consider that many skid-plate manufactures make skid-plate packages that cover all important items. They are normally designed to work together for improved fit and appearance.

Skid plates will get damaged. That is why they are there in the first place. Most skid plates are painted, and some are powder coated. Because they will get scraped and dinged, painting is adequate protection, and it is easier to touch-up painted skid plates.

Lifted rigs are less susceptible to damage. A stubby front bumper improves the approach angle on rocks but eliminates protection of the tires in many situations that are encountered while overlanding.

Ironman 4x4 has a heavy-duty skid-plate kit for the 2005-and-newer Toyota Tacoma that offers excellent protection for the radiator, engine and transmission oil pans, and steering. (Photo Courtesy Ironman 4x4)

A full-coverage belly-pan skidplate offers the ultimate underside protection, such as this Artec aluminum system for the Gladiator. Note the recessed hole for the chamfered allen bolts.

Rock sliders protect rocker panels that can be costly to repair if damaged. The Toyota Tacoma sliders are from Relations Race Wheels (RRW).

Rockslide Engineering makes a rock slider with a retractable step for most Jeep Wrangler models and the new Ford Bronco in both two- and four-door versions. The step is well protected, and the sliders are extremely strong. We have tested and abused these steps on several vehicles, and wc love the ease of entry with the steps and the high level of protection that they provide.

Muffler Skid Plates

Tail pipes and mufflers take a beating even with moderate off-road driving on many vehicles. While they are not critical components, such as a gas tank or oil pan, skid plates are available to protect the muffler for some vehicles. A solution for many vehicles is to use an aftermarket cat-back exhaust system that often moves the muffler to a location where it is protected from damage. These exhausts often have a shorter, more compact tail pipe that is out of harm's way.

Rock Sliders

Rock sliders, which are also called rocker slides, protect the vulnerable rocker panels below the doors. Damage to the rocker panels can be difficult and expensive to repair. Most rigs that are suitable for overlanding lack rock-slider protection. For more extensive off-road activities, more-robust sliders are a great idea. Rock sliders can take a real beating even in relatively easy off-road situations. For this reason, they need to be made from durable, heavy-duty materials. Sliders can be made from formed steel plate or heavy-wall steel tubing. Additionally, sliders should bolt to the frame rails whenever possible.

Stock rock sliders offer minimal protection, especially concerning their width. Most stock rock sliders are nearly flush with the body. They offer good vertical protection but little lateral protection. Lateral protection is best provided by sliders that protrude 3 or 4 inches from the body. This design provides protection if the rig slides sideways, potentially off a steep rock or ledge. This allows the slider to strike another rock or tree. The stock sliders offer virtually no protection in these instances, but protruding sliders will protect the body in many cases.

Bumpers

While stock front and rear bumpers can be used for overlanding, they lack good protection and offer

The classic off-road bumper for the 2014-and-newer Lexus GX 460 and Toyota Prado 150 from Ironman 4x4 provides added protection for fenders and front tires with the full-width design. (Photo Courtesy Ironman 4x4)

little or no utility. Aftermarket bumpers made from steel or aluminum increase protection for the body panels and provide mounting locations for winches and lights on the front and tire carriers and racks on the rear.

Front

Front bumpers are available in a wide range of styles but fall into two general categories: full-width and narrow (stubby) bumpers. Recently, modular bumpers have become popular. These allow a stubby bumper to become a full-width bumper or something in between by adding bolt-on sections to the narrow bumper. Some of these bumpers are designed with a locking storage compartment. Most easily accommodate winches, lights, and D-rings for recovery. Bumpers can be made from fabricated steel, aluminum, or formed under extreme pressure from either material.

Front bumpers with a bull bar, winch, light bars, and other accessories can interfere with airflow to the radiator. In hot conditions, this can cause the engine and transmission to overheat. Vented hoods help alleviate this problem.

Full-Width

As the name implies, a full-width bumper is about as wide as the front of most vehicles. They offer tire protection, but when encountering single large rocks, the approach angle is not as great as the stubby bumper. For overlanding, a full-width front bumper is preferred for most rigs unless more-extreme rock crawling is planned.

Stubby

Stubby or narrow front bumpers have two distinct advantages. First, they weigh less. When you add a winch and winch line, this can be an important consideration. Second,

The Ironman 4x4 Ram 1500 DS Raid bumper provides great protection with a lightweight tubing design. It also has space for lights and a winch mount. (Photo Courtesy Ironman 4x4)

Stubby front bumpers offer no protection for the tires but maximize approach angles when climbing rocks with only one front tire.

they have a much better approach angle when crawling over single large rocks.

Materials

Both front and rear bumpers are made from steel or aluminum. They can be fabricated from a plate or pressure formed. The big advantage to aluminum is its light weight. Steel offers superior strength. For optimal strength on either aluminum or steel, the welds must have excellent penetration. This is especially important on aluminum, as the loads on the bumper can cause poor welds to fail.

Winch Mounts

Most aftermarket front bumpers feature mounts for winches. Some need additional plates to mount a winch. Be aware that not all winches have the same mounting bolt pattern, so be sure to check. Some winches will not fit on some bumpers.

D-ring mounts that are directly welded to the bumper provide strong mounting points for winching and other vehicle recovery operations. We use D-ring shackles, such as this one from Gear America, to attach soft shackles for recovery operations. Shackle mounts often have a sharp edge that can wear a soft shackle and create a failure point.

Winches place extremely heavy loads on the bumper and frame. Be sure that mounting points are strong for the bumper and winch mounts.

D-Ring Mounts

D-rings or shackles are a critical component for winching and vehicle recovery. Many front bumpers have D-ring mounts. Most are welded in place and are strong. Some are bolted in place. Bolt-on mounts should be a metal plate with four mounting holes because the load from winching puts the bolts in tension.

Rear Bumpers

As with front bumpers, rear bumpers are available in many styles. The most important feature on a rear bumper when running larger tires is a spare-tire carrier. The stock spare-tire carrier on most vehicles will not handle oversized tires without an auxiliary mounting plate to

The ideal aftermarket steel rear bumper has a trailer hitch, tow points, light receptacles, and will wrap around the rear quarter panel behind the rear tires for additional protection. The Raid Series rear bumper kit from Ironman 4x4 fits the 2010-and-newer Toyota 4Runner. (Photo Courtesy Ironman 4x4)

gain clearance. More importantly, the extra weight of a tire and wheel over the stock-size diameter puts a large load on the stock spare-tire mount.

Rear bumpers need to be sturdy, especially for rock crawling, because they often impact large rocks when dropping off a rock or ledge or they can scrape when climbing. Most rear bumpers are designed to provide better departure angles than stock. Stock bumpers are rarely suitable for more extreme trail conditions. As with front bumpers, rear bumpers are made from steel and aluminum and can be fabricated or formed. Light mounts and D-ring mounts are included in some bumpers and are optional on others.

Tire Mounts

Most rear bumpers include a tire carrier, but not all bumpers do. Tire carriers come in two styles. Some swing out with the tailgate door, and others swing out separately. Those that swing with the door are more convenient but cost more. Both work well as long as the tire carrier mount to the bumper is strong enough to handle the heavy load of a larger wheel and tire.

Other Mounts

Many rear bumpers have mounts (built-in and optional) for Hi-Lift jacks, Pull Pal ground anchors, fuel/water cans/tanks, shovels and axes, and antenna mounts for General Mobile Radio Service (GMRS) or ham radios. These mounts can be convenient for quick access and keep some large, heavy items outside the passenger compartment, which enhances safety.

Rugged Ridge makes a replacement tailgate hinge assembly for the Jeep Wrangler JL. The setup, which is much stronger than stock, allows the use of a heavy-duty tire carrier to mount into the square tube bracket in the center of the photo. Larger tires are easily accommodated with this setup.

Rigid Supply makes a rear tire carrier with an attached fold-down table and a carrier for RotopaX fuel cans.

Electrical Accessories, Electronics, and Lighting

Modern 4WD vehicles equipped with a wide range of electronic and electrical components place a major strain on the electrical system. Adding more electronics and electrical components for overlanding requires some upgrades to the system to ensure the power needs are met without overstressing the electrical capacity of the vehicle.

Electrical power demands from auxiliary lighting, refrigerators, radios, electronics, power tools, and appliances require high-capacity charging sources and switches and controllers that protect critical electronics and computers. Short overlanding adventures may require minimal upgrades, but any extended overland trips need resources to keep electricity flowing and components protected.

Modern vehicles use extensive electronics. With even more lights and electronics added to a rig, power demands soar. Running out of daylight occurs often, so good lights are important. Ironman 4x4 offers the Rally Innovations front rally light bar mount kit with LEDs for the 2021-and-newer Subaru Crosstrek along with the Night Saber LED single-row, curved 28.5-inch light bar. (Photo Courtesy Ironman 4x4)

Auxiliary Switch Solutions

Overlanders and more serious off-roaders will most likely need additional auxiliary switches for lights, radio communication, compressors, and lockers. Auxiliary switching systems allow the addition of switches that provide additional options and isolate power from the computers to eliminate possible damage to the stock electrical system. Rather than tie into the hot wires that are already present in the vehicle, the switch relay box is powered directly from the battery. Auxiliary components are wired to the relay box. The box then connects to the switches with wires or by Bluetooth.

Several auxiliary-switch options are available from the aftermarket. sPOD was among the first to offer switching solutions for the Jeep Wrangler. Its product line has grown and includes an eight-switch Bantam

Power supplies, controllers, and switch panels are a necessity to safely operate all of the electronics and electrical components for overlanding. The Trigger 4 Plus power distribution system controls electrical devices, such as lights, wirelessly from a cab-mounted switch panel or through the Trigger smartphone application. A Trigger 6 Plus system is also available.

Lights mounted to a roof rack have the advantage of being set back a few inches from the windshield. This reduces glare on the hood. Ironman 4x4 makes both alloy and steel roof racks with mounts for its Eclipse driving lights.

with highly sophisticated programming and smartphone applications. Several other companies offer a variety of switch panels. At the other end of the price scale is the Rough Country MLC-6 multiple-light controller. The MLC-6 features six switches and two interior mounting options. The layout is similar to the original SPOD six-switch panel. All of the switching products share a direct connection to the vehicle battery and a control module. Auxiliary electrical components, such as lights, wire into the control module. A wiring harness runs to the switch panel mounted in the interior. One of the newest switch panels is the Trigger controller that uses wireless switches to activate relays in the control box.

Auxiliary Lighting

As with many automotive electronic and electrical products, the lighting market has evolved with some sophisticated lighting products that are nearly all LED based in today's market. Even Jeep offers a nice LED package. Many companies offer LED packages that vary considerably in price. Premium LED lights are available from many aftermarket resources and are less expensive.

While the factory LED option works well, additional auxiliary lights improve visibility at night, especially on difficult trails. The latest LEDs can be programmed to create a variety of lighting effects and even light shows. Some lights can be controlled by a user with a smartphone application. Auxiliary lights come in several designs that include light bars of different sizes, driving lights, cube A-pillar-mount lights, fog lights, flush-mounted lights, and rock lights. LEDs are available in a variety of lighting patterns, including narrow, long range, and wide. Some light bars use LEDs of different light patterns so that you have the benefit of both wide and narrow patterns. High- and low-beam functions are also found on some lights.

Light Bars

Light bars can put out tremendous amounts of light, especially the large 48-inch roof-mounted light bars. Smaller light bars can be mounted on the hood or bumper. Roof-mounted light bars have several issues. The first is the reflection off the hood. It can be distracting. Wind noise is another issue. Light bar covers can help reduce wind noise. Some states have laws that limit the height of light bars or any auxiliary lighting to at or below the level of the headlights. Some states require the light bar to be covered when operated on the highway or streets.

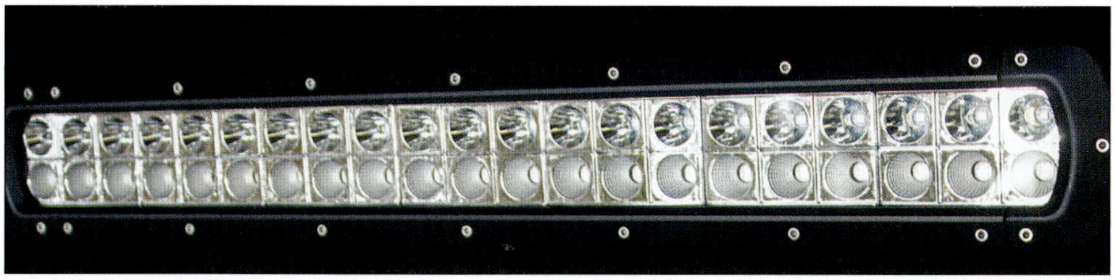

Light bars provide considerable light for navigating dark roads. Light bars are most often mounted on the roof, but mounting to a front bumper reduces glare on the hood. The Type S application-controlled 24-inch light bar provides control from a smartphone or tablet.

Driving Lights

One advantage to driving lights is that the compact size allows them to be mounted to the bumper. A pair of bumper-mounted driving lights can be angled outward slightly to improve coverage. Driving lights are available in different lighting patterns and light temperatures.

Driving lights, such as the Ultra Vision Max, provide great lighting capacity with the added advantage of altering the mounting angle slightly to illuminate the edges of the road or trail more effectively. This helps in situations where a tight turn is needed.

Fog Lights

Several companies offer fog lights that fit in the stock fog-light receptacles. Fog lights provide lighting at a low level in front of the vehicle. Fog lights are ideal for low speed on trails especially when following other rigs. Headlights and light bars can be blinding to other vehicles, especially to spotters. Many aftermarket bumpers feature openings and mounts for stock or aftermarket replacement fog lights.

Cube Cowl Lights

Cowl lights can also be angled outward, usually at a greater angle than driving lights, to help illuminate the sides of a trail. This is especially helpful when navigating tight

Cowl-mounted cube lights can be angled a few degrees outboard to light up the edges of the trail and make turning around in tight corners easier. The unique cowl mounts from Rockslide Engineering hold Rigid cube lights.

Good lighting makes tackling difficult terrain much easier at night. The spotter's view (left) and the driver's view (right) show excellent illumination on the rocks.

turns that are lined with obstacles. Several companies offer a wide range of cube lights and cowl mounts for all overlanding vehicles.

Camp lights provide good visibility when working at night. Ironman 4x4 makes several camp-light kits. (Photo Courtesy Ironman 4x4)

Rock Lights

Rock lights, when first introduced, were seen as a mall-crawler fad. In reality, rock lights can be a great aid for navigating difficult terrain at night. The underside lights make it easy for a spotter to see obstacles under the vehicle. Most rock-light kits use six to eight lights mounted in various locations under the body but are protected from damage from rocks and other obstacles.

White-colored lights are the most effective. As a side note, it is often best to minimize using bright headlights and light bars when a spotter is trying to see a rig. The bright lights can be blinding and cause misdirection.

Camp/Work Lights

Having good lighting when stationary on the trail or in camp allows setup, cooking, or trail repairs when the sun sets early or you arrive at a campsite after dark due to the inevitable delays. Camp lights can be mounted to the vehicle to provide lighting around the vehicle. Other designs are portable and allow lights to be used in specific locations away from the rig. The portable lights are often battery-powered with rechargeable batteries. Many choices provide good area lighting from rack lights, recessed lights, and portable lights. Some lights are battery powered, while others can be mounted on the vehicle to operate from the vehicle power or an auxiliary power supply.

Auxiliary lights are available from many sources. US-based companies, including Baja Designs, Rigid, JW Speaker, and KC HiLites, all make premium lighting in a wide range of designs. Type S Automotive offers some innovative lights that can be operated and programmed with a smartphone application.

Daylight Driving on Dusty Trails

Dust can make visibility difficult during the day, especially to oncoming traffic. Run all lights during dusty conditions, even in daylight. Another tip when overlanding in a group is that unless you are the run leader, be careful how you use the auxiliary lights. The drivers in front can be easily blinded by bright lights from behind.

Radio Communication

Citizens band (CB) radios were the go-to form of radio communication for many years. In recent years, ham radios have become popular. Dual-band (UHF and VHF) radios with ham and commercial channels offer more frequency choices including non-ham channels that do not require a ham license.

Using LEDs on all trails, especially on dusty trails in the daylight, improves safety and allows others to see you more easily.

The Midland Radio's MXT-115 general mobile radio service (GMRS) provides maximum power for this radio category, which is now the most common radio type used for overlanding. GMRS radios require a license, but there is no test and just a $35 fee for 10 years. GMRS radios also operate on family radio service (FRS) frequencies that require no license. (Photo Courtesy Midland Radio)

Due to their short range, CB radios are becoming much less popular. General Mobile Radio Service (GMRS) radios are rapidly gaining popularity, especially with overlanders. GMRS radios operate on several different frequency ranges, including the Family Radio Service (FRS) frequencies.

GMRS radios require a license, but no test is involved as with a ham radio license. A license costs $35 for 10 years. No license is needed to operate on the FRS frequencies. Midland Radios is on the leading edge of GMRS radios with a 40-watt version that has a line-of-sight range of 40 miles. The Midland MXT400 is loaded with features, including 8 repeater channels and 15 high-power channels. Many other companies offer a wide range of GMRS and FRS radios.

Satellite Messengers

Satellite messengers provide satellite communications via text message and emergency contacts with first responders. While it is always best to travel the backcountry in groups, satellite messengers, such as Garmin inReach and SpotX, make solo travel much more viable.

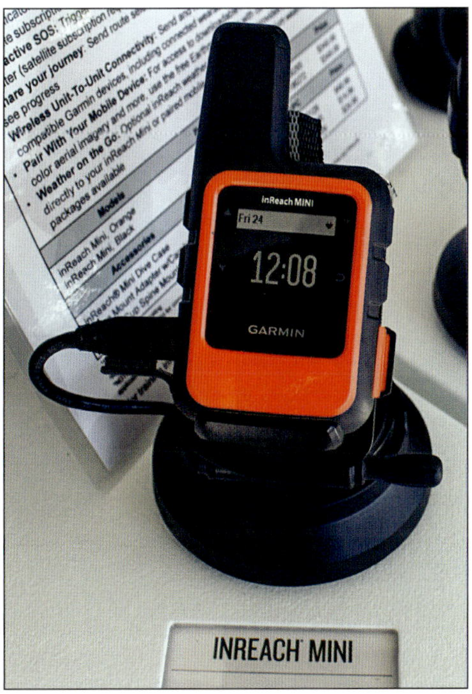

Satellite locators, such as the Garmin inReach, allow text messaging and an emergency SOS button to transmit your location to authorities in case of an extreme emergency that requires a rescue operation.

GPS and Smartphone GPS Applications

Aftermarket GPS systems and smartphone applications designed for off-road travel generally provide more accurate and up to date information. The Magellan TRX7 GPS unit allows advanced trip planning and trip tracking. Several GPS apps

The Magellan TRX7 GPS provides thousands of off-road trail maps for the TRX7, including many crowd-sourced maps. You can also record trails that you drive to save them for future use or share on the TRX7 website. Creating a route is easy on the TRX7 app.

The onX off-road GPS map smartphone application offers a wide range of features, including offline map capabilities, tracking and saving routes, trail difficulty ratings, and compatibility with Apple CarPlay and Android Auto.

use both iOS and Android operating systems for use on tablets and smartphones. GAIA, onX, and AllTrails are designed for backcountry use.

As reliable as modern GPS systems are, carrying a paper map as a backup is advised. One flaw with most GPS systems is the use of old US Geological Survey (USGS) maps as a base map. The old maps show many roads and trails that are decommissioned and no longer passable.

The electrical needs of overlanding place large loads on batteries. High-capacity, high-quality batteries are a must. Deep-cycle lithium-ion batteries, such as the AG-DC-100-V2 from Antigravity Battery, offers plenty of power and great reliability but at a high cost.

One way to ensure adequate electrical power is with a dual 12-volt battery system. Genesis Off-Road makes systems for most off-road vehicles. Combined with a pair of ultra-strong Odyssey batteries, this setup offers power and durability in an off-road environment.

Electronic-Calibration Modules

Electronic-calibration modules allow the vehicle's computer to be reprogrammed to change a wide range of parameters, such as tire diameter, gear ratio, and transfer-case ratio. The modules plug into the vehicle's OBD-II port to access the onboard computer system. Some systems use an external screen with a variety of menu options that allow changes to many parameters and the ability to monitor vehicle system outputs, such as temperature and pressure. Other systems use the onboard data screen and require a series of operations that use steering-wheel-control buttons and other vehicle controls.

Batteries and Jumper Batteries

The addition of auxiliary lights, a winch, and other electronic devices puts a strain on the battery. Aftermarket batteries from Odyssey, Antigravity, and Optima are designed to handle the additional electrical power requirements and rigors of off-road driving. Lithium-based batteries are becoming more popular and offer more power for a given package size. Dual-battery setups and auxiliary systems allow more electrical components to be used or recharged while at camp. Considering the potential for battery overload or failure, carrying a jumper battery is a sound practice. Type S Automotive offers a compact jump starter and power bank.

Inverters

Inverters transform DC electrical current from a battery source to 110-volt AC current to operate household appliances or charge electronic devices. The capacity (amp-hours) of the battery combined with the current draw of the device or appliance determines how long the battery will last.

Sine-wave inverters operate appliances where square-wave inverters are intended to operate electric motors. Stand-alone inverters can be used to charge electronic device batteries or power small appliances. Many modern overlanding-capable vehicles feature some form of connectivity for charging or operating applications from smartphones and tablets. Some vehicles feature 110-volt outlets to power 110-volt chargers and devices. Many low-amperage devices can be operated from a USB port or a 12-volt power port.

Jumper batteries can save the day if the main vehicle battery loses power from overuse. The Type S auto jumper battery is compact, holds a charge well, and offers plenty of cranking power. Electronics can also be charged through the USB port. While jumper batteries hold a charge quite well, make sure the battery is fully charged before embarking on an overlanding adventure.

Ironman 4x4's DC to DC dual-battery charger uses the vehicle alternator for charging while the vehicle is running and uses solar panels when the rig is parked. (Photo Courtesy Ironman 4x4)

The heart of Rough Country's electronic calibration module is powered directly from the battery. Wires run to the desired electrical components. Power is controlled by the interior-mounted switch panel through relays.

Power Sources/Power Stations

In an era when electronic devices and portable electrical appliances offer unmatched convenience for overlanding adventures, especially long-term trips, carrying an electric power source is nearly a requirement. Electric power sources using batteries, usually lithium-ion, provide a compact and quiet source of electricity. However, these battery-based sources require charging. Most lithium portable power stations can be charged with solar panels, 110-volt house outlets, 9-volt automotive power ports, and gas-, diesel-, or propane-powered generators.

Most portable electric power sources offer several forms of power output. Most provide USB charging ports for electronics, 12-volt DC outlets, and 110-volt AC outlets. Power sources use built-in sine-wave inverters to convert DC power to AC power.

Portable power stations are available in watt ratings up to 6,000 watts, which are big, heavy, and expensive, with the most common watt storage capacity of 500 to 2,000 watts.

Battery Isolators and Monitoring Systems

Battery isolators prioritize battery charging so that the alternator only charges the main battery when the engine is running to prevent the electrical load from other devices from draining the primary battery that is used for starting the vehicle. A battery management system can take electricity from the primary (starting)

The Jeep Wrangler JL and Gladiator Rubicon models feature a four-switch auxiliary panel for add-on electrical accessories. (Photo Courtesy Stellantis)

Ironman 4x4's portable 200-watt solar panel kit generates electricity to charge a wide array of batteries and battery-powered electronics and appliances. The awning is also from Ironman 4x4. (Photo Courtesy Ironman 4x4)

battery and solar panels to charge the auxiliary battery. Battery-monitoring systems can monitor and maintain the auxiliary battery at optimal charge and monitor batteries with a display that shows the battery charge levels and usage.

Generators

Electrical generators have provided electrical power for many decades. Fuel-powered generators offer reliable, consistent electricity. Disadvantages of generators include the need to carry a fuel supply, weight and bulk, and high noise levels. However, many modern generators are quiet, especially the Alp propane-powered generator. Fuel for generators include gasoline, diesel, and propane.

Portable generators that are suitable for overlanding range from 500 watts to 4,000 watts of output. The higher the wattage output, the more devices and appliances can be used. Powerful generators use more fuel.

Solar Panels

Solar panels, either portable or roof-mounted, offer an efficient and simple way to charge storage

For extended stays at base camp, solar panels are a great resource for keeping the electricity flowing. Zamp Solar makes a range of solar panels for a variety of charging needs, including the Obsidian-series 45-watt portable kit with regulator.

batteries. Solar panels are available in watt ratings from 50 watts to 400 watts. The wattage output is directly proportional to the area of the panels. In addition to the solar panels, a solar-charging system requires a storage battery (lithium-ion preferred), a solar-charge controller, and a sine-wave inverter.

High-Output Alternators

Alternators provide electrical power to charge batteries and run electrical systems on a vehicle. Modern overlanding-capable rigs generally have alternator power outputs that will easily handle the need of the original-equipment electrical components. But when winches, stereo systems, lights, and other components, including auxiliary batteries, are added, it places a higher demand on the charging system. High-output alternators are a worthwhile investment when additional electrical components are used. Stock alternator output is in the range of 100 to 200 amps. High-output alternators range up to 300 amps. Higher-amp outputs also use more fuel. Higher-output alternators are available for most overlanding rigs.

A heavy-duty alternator is a must-have item to keep up with charging needs for serious overlanding setups. Many overlanding vehicles come with heavy-duty alternators or are offered as an option. For existing rigs, several suppliers offer high-capacity alternators for most pickups and SUVs capable of overlanding.

Estimating Electrical Power Needs

Electrical power is calculated in watts. Watts are determined by multiplying amps by volts. For example, a typical light bar will range from 90 watts to more than 400 watts. With a 12-volt battery system, the amperage range is 10 to 33 amps when the lights are in use. Using several off-road lights, standard lights, a winch, and other accessories simultaneously can require high amperage from the battery and alternator. A 10,000-pound winch that pulls 10,000 pounds uses as much as 500 amps. Even a 5,000-pound winch pull can use nearly 250 amps. Add lights and other components, and an alternator cannot keep up with the amp draw from the night winching operation. Battery voltage will drop. Dual-battery setups can be a big help in these circumstances.

When in camp, most electrical needs can be calculated by determining the watt-hours of electrical storage available in batteries and compare that to the total wattage of components, tools, and appliances being used. Then, multiply the total watts by the amount of time that each item is used. That is the watt-hour number.

For example, if you use a coffee maker at 10 watts for 15 minutes, charge a laptop battery at 100 watts for one hour, and a 200-watt heater for two hours, the total watt-hour amount is just over 500 watt-hours. A 1,000-watt power source or generator can easily handle this load. The more electrical components used over a period in camp, the more watt capacity is needed from a battery power source or the more fuel is needed for a generator.

Vehicle Recovery Gear, Winches, and Trail Tools

Getting stuck sucks. Helping someone get unstuck is much more enjoyable, but getting stuck is part of having off-roading adventures. Recovery gear provides many ways to get yourself unstuck with or without the assistance of another vehicle. Keep in mind that vehicle recoveries can be very dangerous. Exercise extreme caution.

Before delving into vehicle recovery and the important tools available to overlanders, let's take a quick look at common ways that off-roaders can become stuck. Sooner or later, everyone gets stuck. Only one reason is at the crux of all situations where a vehicle becomes stuck (as opposed to having a breakdown): lack of traction.

Getting stuck happens to everyone at some point. Having the proper recovery gear to get unstuck is critical for overlanders—even more so if you travel as a single vehicle. You can't count on someone coming by to help when you are far out in the backcountry. (Photo Courtesy Ironman 4x4)

Traction loss that results in the inability to move forward or backward comes in two varieties: 1) loss of tire traction due to slippery surface conditions or steep inclines, and 2) loss of tire traction due to the vehicle becoming high-centered, which creates drag and requires more traction to move forward. This takes weight off of one or more tires, thus reducing traction even more. Most vehicles become stuck due to getting high-centered on bumps and rocks and when exiting ruts.

The first agenda item in our vehicle recovery class is the most important: how to avoid getting stuck. This book is not a driving guide, but here are a few principles to consider:

- When encountering slippery surfaces, such as sand, mud, snow (a little momentum helps), or ice (drive very slowly), look for the path that offers the most traction, such as rocks or brush, that may be protruding through the surface.
- Avoid wheelspin. A little wheelspin is okay if the vehicle is moving forward. If momentum

is lost, wheelspin will only make the situation worse. The exception is when crawling on rock surfaces that are wet, muddy, sandy, or snow-covered. Wheelspin can burn through the slippery surfaces and traction can improve. This can also increase the temperature on the tire treads, which will also increase traction.

- Pick lines in ruts and bumps that will keep the vehicle as level as possible.
- Approaching ruts and bumps at an angle (as opposed to a 90-degree head-on approach) will maximize ground clearance and reduce the risk of getting stuck. The best approach is to tackle a bump, ledge, or rut one tire at a time.
- If your vehicle feels tippy, steer downhill. This can be on a side slope or when dropping down steep ledges or off rocks. Steering uphill, which is a natural reaction, turns the downhill front tire into a fulcrum that makes a rollover more likely. Turn downhill or at least keep the steering wheel straight ahead to allow the downhill front tire to act as a stabilizer.
- When steering, the rear tires do not follow the tracks of the front tires. In a tight, full-steering lock turn on a four-door vehicle, the rear tires track a full half-width of the vehicle inside the front tires.
- When planning a line through rutted or rocky terrain where steering is involved, it is just as important, maybe more, to plan a line for the rear tires. Most drivers and spotters ignore the rear tires when planning a line through obstacles.
- Use a spotter (or at least get out of the vehicle to survey the situation) when the terrain becomes challenging, especially when the driver's visibility is limited to the sky and treetops.

The second agenda item in our vehicle recovery class relates to taking inventory. First, analyze the situation. Then, look at recovery gear options and decide what tool will be the most efficient and safest for the job.

Recovery Tools

Nine important recovery tools include a tow strap, shackles (soft and hard), a kinetic (yanker) strap, extraction (traction) boards, a shovel, off-road jack, winch, tree-saver strap, and winching anchor points.

Tow Strap

Tow straps are used for towing but can also be used for pulling a stuck vehicle out of a moderately stuck situation. Pulling out a stuck vehicle should be done with no slack in the strap, unlike a kinetic yanker strap. Tow straps have very little stretch. Use only tow straps with stitched-material loops on the ends. Metal hooks tend to break under higher loads. The most common straps are 20 to 30 feet long by 3 inches wide. For towing, the strap should be fairly short (no more than 20 feet) especially when towing in close quarters and tight turns. Longer straps can get hung up in tight turns or pull the towed vehicle on an undesirable path, such as into a rock, tree, or soft shoulder.

Shackles

Shackles are used for attaching a winch line or tow straps to a vehicle. Shackles must be rated to be stronger than the strap or winch line to which they are attached. Two types of shackles are commonly used. The most common is the D-ring shackle made of high-strength steel. The soft shackle is becoming more popular and is made from the same synthetic materials that are used for synthetic winch line. If a D-ring shackle fails,

Tow straps are used for towing or minor pulls to extract a stuck vehicle. Never use a tow strap to yank a vehicle out of a stuck situation. Straps including the Factor 55 tow strap, which is rated at 31,000 pounds of breaking strength, are incredibly durable and strong. They should only be used for a no-slack pull.

Metal shackles are strong, but a soft shackle can handle just as much load. Soft shackles are quick and easy to use, offer great versatility, and are much safer to use. We often use a soft shackle in a D-ring shackle for convenience and to keep the soft shackle from chafing on the hard edge of a metal shackle mount.

Kinetic, or yanker, straps are used to yank stuck vehicles out of mud, sand, snow, or slightly high-centered situations. Some slack is used in the strap so that the pulling vehicle can get a running start to gain momentum. As the slack is taken up, the kinetic strap will stretch. The energy from the stretching will snap the strap back and help move the stuck vehicle. Never use a kinetic strap over a trailer hitch ball or hitch receiver. The load can snap the ball or the hitch, especially a drop hitch. People have died when the hitch or ball breaks and is launched with great force through a windshield. If someone is within the vehicle being pulled, the hood should be open to add an extra layer of protection just in case. Vehicle recoveries can be very dangerous. Exercise extreme caution.

it can cause damage or serious injury. Soft shackles are safer, easier to use, and lighter.

Many aftermarket bumpers have shackle-attachment points. Many of the attachment holes have a sharp edge that can accelerate wear on soft shackles. We use hard shackles on bumpers and then attach the soft shackle to the hard shackle.

Kinetic (Yanker) Strap

A kinetic strap functions like a large bungee cord. When stretched, it stores energy. Unlike chain, cable, or a nylon tow strap, which do not stretch much when a pulling force is applied, the kinetic strap is designed to store energy as it is stretched. When snapped back, the effective pulling force is increased because the strap snaps back faster than it was stretched.

Kinetic yanker straps are used to yank a stuck rig off of a dirt obstacle or out of mud, snow, or sand. Kinetic straps are not ideal for yanking a stuck vehicle out of a rocky situation. The forces are substantial, even though the kinetic-shock-absorption characteristics of the kinetic strap soften the blow. Attach the yanker strap with shackles to a secure point on each rig.

Extraction Boards

Extraction boards are best used when stuck in soft surfaces, such as snow, mud, and sand. The lugs on the board are designed to engage with the tire tread. When the tires begin to rotate, the tire tread pulls on the lugs on the board. The board then elevates the vehicle as it moves forward or backward and provides a solid surface to get unstuck. They

No gear says "overlander" quite like the MaxTrax extraction boards. They work great in soft surfaces when stuck.

are easy to use and often the quickest way to get unstuck. They do not work on hard surfaces or rocks.

Most traction boards, such as the MaxTrax, are solid boards that use molded lugs to grip the tire tread.

GoTread extraction boards work remarkably well in many circumstances. They have distinct advantages over many extraction boards. They are inexpensive, high quality, fold for easy storage, conform to the terrain better, and can be used as blocks to help level a rig.

Bridging ladders (as the name implies) are used to bridge gaps where a vehicle can get stuck. Extruded aluminum bridging ladders are strong and can support considerable weight—more than extraction boards. In the early days of expedition off-roading, bridging ladders were a common recovery tool. However, they are rarely seen today.

The newer MaxTrax designs feature metal lugs that are much more durable. A new-to-us extraction board is the GoTread. The GoTreads are hinged so that they easily conform to a rough surface, and they can be folded for easy storage. The GoTread is also much less expensive, and they work.

Shovel

Shovels are most often used to dig a vehicle out of snow, mud, or sand when stuck. They are also used for digging holes to place ground anchors for winching. Folding shovels are inexpensive and compact. More useful options include multi-tool kits, such as the Hi-Lift Handle-All, that use a telescoping handle and shovel, pick, sledgehammer, and axe head attachments. The Max Ax is a similar took kit with interchangeable attachments.

Off-Road Jack

An off-road jack provides a means to change a flat tire and gain clearance under a tire when stuck. The Hi-Lift jack is the gold standard of off-road jacks. The Hi-Lift jack can be used in a variety of vehicle recovery situations as well as tire changing. Hi-Lift offers many accessories.

In recent years, other off-road jacks have flooded the market. Many copy the Hi-Lift design, while others offer innovative jacking solutions. ARB offers a hydraulic hand-cranked vertical jack that is easy to use, expensive, and a little bulky. Pro Eagle makes a traditional-looking floor jack with off-road-type wheels and tires. These jacks make lifting a Jeep really easy, but the cost is high, and storage can be an issue.

While the vertical jacks work great for lifting, changing a tire is problematic due the distance the body/frame must be raised to get the tire free from the road surface. Hi-Lift sells the Lift-Mate, which is designed to directly lift the vehicle from a wheel, greatly reducing the amount of travel upward that the jack bar is needed to lift the wheel off the ground. The Lift-Mate is also the quickest way to lift a vehicle that is high-centered on rocks, humps, or logs. For changing a tire, a jack stand is needed to support the axle and tire off the ground so the Hi-Lift jack can be removed to change the tire. The process is reversed to lift the vehicle off the jack stand.

Another option for tire changing is a compact, inexpensive bottle jack. A bottle jack can be placed under the axle housing near the offending tire to quickly lift the tire off the ground. We use a jack stand with a built-in bottle jack. The stand has a solid-plate base to minimize sinking into the surface under load.

The Hi-Lift jack is great for many recovery jobs, even winching in a pinch, but it's not so great for changing a tire. We purchased a Powerbuilt 3-ton "bottle jack and jack stand in one" from Amazon for less than $100. The jack stand even has a plate base so that it doesn't sink into the ground. It's great for easy and safe tire changes.

Winches

Winches usually provide the easiest way to get unstuck in many situations. With the ever-increasing popularity of overlanding, many companies have entered the winch market. It can be difficult to know which winch will get the job done safely and over the long haul. Quality is important.

The last issue that anyone wants is a winch failure during a critical recovery process. We have seen several winches fail during our vehicle recovery classes. The failure points are most often related to electrical wiring that shorts out. We always recommend quality winches we have used by companies including Warn, Novawinch, Trekker from Rugged Ridge, Ramsey, Superwinch, and Viking. There are many economy brands available.

For the economical winches, we recommend using the winch at about half the maximum pull capacity. For a 10,000-pound economy winch, any pull estimated to exceed 5,000 pounds is fine. We suggest using a snatch block to keep the load as light as possible to reduce strain on the winch.

This Novawinch 12,500-pound-capacity electric winch with synthetic winch line has seen considerable duty for vehicle recoveries and moving downed trees and rocks from trails. The winch has performed flawlessly.

Most overlanding rigs weigh between 5,000 and 8,000 pounds. The minimum winch pull rating should be 9,500 pounds, but a 12,500-pound pull rating is more desirable. With heavily loaded van conversions and overlanding trailers, winch load needs can be very high. Only a few manufacturers, such as Warn, offer winch capacities over 15,000 pounds.

Keep in mind that the load on the winch is more than just the vehicle weight. The terrain is a significant factor. A pull on a flat, level, hard surface requires only about 100 to 200 pounds. The power needed to pull up a 45-degree slope with a smooth, hard surface is equal to the weight of vehicle. If that surface happens to be deep sand, snow, or soft dirt, you can double the pulling power necessary. With a 10,000-pound-rated winch, a snatch block pulley can be added to double the pulling power of the winch.

The maximum pulling power of a winch occurs when the winch line is nearly fully unspooled with only one layer around the winch spool. When the winch line is fully wound, most winch lines will have four layers around the spool. The least pulling power occurs with the most layers of winch line on the spool. With four layers on the spool, pulling power is reduced nearly 50 percent or about 12 percent per layer.

Wire Rope versus Synthetic

Wire rope has a singular advantage: cost. Synthetic winch line is light and considerably safer. Synthetic line absorbs shock load better and softens the abrupt loads as slack is taken up. The synthetic line is much easier to handle, especially when rewinding the winch drum.

If you use synthetic winch line, you need a hawse fairlead so that the winch line does not get frayed or stuck in the rollers of a roller fairlead that was intended for a steel winch line. The Factor 55 flat link allows closed-system winching. The oblong opening allows for easy use of a soft shackle.

The Factor 55 winch line end links are strong and allow the use of closed-system winching to reduce failures and increase safety during winching operation.

Wire rope stands can break and cause potential gashes on unprotected hands. Synthetic line will not cause cuts when frayed. Synthetic line is thicker for a given tensile strength, so the length of line on the winch spool will be shorter than on wire cable.

Winch Controllers

Two types of winch controllers are commonly used. The most common is the plug-in remote that attaches to the winch for operation. Wireless-remote winch controllers use a signal from a handheld controller to operate the winch. The advantage to the remote winch controller is the ability to use it away from the vehicle and out of harm's way. Be sure the controller's battery is working before heading out on an off-road adventure.

Winch Accessories

Winch-line end links connect the winch line to a strap or another vehicle. Most end links are hooks with a spring-loaded latch to retain the hook to its attachment point. Other end links accommodate closed winching system rigging. A closed winching system features connections with no openings like those found on hooks. Hooks with sheet metal and spring-loaded safety latches are not closed-system connections. End links for closed-system winching are available in several designs. Factor 55 is a leader in closed-winching-system recovery hardware. Closed-winching-system rigging is more secure and safer.

Winch fairleads help control the direction and smooth flow of the winch line when it's being unspooled. Two types of fairleads are used. The roller fairlead features four rollers around the perimeter of the fairlead mount and is used for wire-rope winch line. A hawse fairlead is generally made from machined aluminum with a smooth radius on the opening. Hawse fairleads are used with synthetic winch line.

Shackles are critical and have previously been covered in this book.

Another critical accessory is the snatch block. A snatch block, or pulley, increases the pulling power of a winch. Snatch blocks can also alter the direction of the winch line, if necessary, when a straight-line pull is not possible. A new style of snatch block (called a retention ring, or pulley) is much lighter and easier to use

A wireless remote allows winch operation from a safe distance to increase safety margins. Warn winches are high quality and most have a wireless remote as an option.

Snatch blocks allow the winch line to go around corners for difficult pulls and double the pulling power of the winch when used as a pulley. Metal snatch blocks are heavy. Ring snatch blocks are lightweight, attach to a strap or shackle with a soft shackle, and make the use of the snatch block arrangement much easier. The Factor 55 ring snatch block features rubber nubs in the groove walls to hold the synthetic winch line in place when slack is present in the line.

Tree-saver straps protect the tree bark from damage that can kill a tree. The wider the strap, the more the load is distributed over a larger area of the tree trunk, which reduces the risk of damage. The wider strap is also stronger and safer.

compared to a traditional snatch block. Retention rings look like a metal wheel with a groove for the synthetic winch line and a smooth center bore for a soft shackle. The soft shackle anchors to a tree saver or a second vehicle while the winch line runs back to the winching vehicle for attachment to the shackle mount on a bumper.

Other important winching accessories include gloves to protect your hands and a winch-line damper. Winch-line dampers keep a winch line from flying if the loaded line breaks. Dampers are important on any winch line but are critical on steel winch rope. Winch manufacturers offer both weighted dampers and dampers with pockets for weights, such as rocks or sand. An alternative to commercial winch-line dampers is the use of a blanket, towel, or jacket on the winch line when the line is under load.

Tree-Saver Strap

Attachment points away from a vehicle, like a tree, large rock, another rig, or other object, require strength and stability. Use care when selecting a winching point. The most common attachment point in the backcountry is a tree or rock. Never loop a winch line around a tree trunk or rock. You will damage and often destroy the tree, and a winch line can pull under a rock, dislodge it, and cause a serious problem.

In either case, use a strap (not a chain or cable) around the tree trunk or rock. If you really care about the environment, use a 3- or 4-inch-wide tree-saver strap. Wide tree-saver straps increase strength and spread the load over a larger area to protect the tree bark and reduce chafing on large rocks. Many companies make wide tree-saver straps, such as Gear America, Factor 55, Hi-Lift, and Warn. A bow shackle or soft shackle is then threaded through the loops at the ends of the tree-saver strap. The winch line link or hook attaches onto the shackle.

Multi-Use Tool Kits

The Max Ax Tool kit is extremely versatile for a wide variety of trail needs. This includes digging out of sand, snow, and mud as well as chopping large fallen trees for removal from a trail. The axe head is permanently mounted to a stout fiberglass handle that has a spud for mounting the other accessories, including a shovel, rake, and a variety of pick heads. This is not a recovery tool that is needed often, but when it is needed, it's worth its weight in gold.

The Max Ax features a selection of tool heads that attach to the ax handle. The Max Ax can be used for chopping wood, shoveling, and several other jobs. The rake attachment makes campfire cleanup easier by allowing coals and ashes to be spread out to extinguish the fire.

The Hi-Lift Handle-All kit uses a telescoping, pinned handle to hold several attachments, including a shovel head, axe head, pick, and sledgehammer.

The Hi-Lift Handle-All is a multi-functional tool with a telescoping handle and four full-sized implements, including a full-sized shovel head, sledgehammer head, axe head, and pick-axe head.

While flat tires do occur off-road, they are unusual with off-road tires rated at D-, E-, or F-ply ratings, especially when the tires have been aired down. If a tire goes down, two options are possible: change the tire or plug the puncture with a tire-puncture repair kit.

Extreme Outback and Safety Seal make comprehensive tire-repair kits. Simple kits are available from auto parts stores. A flat tire in a convenient location is contrary to Murphy's law—it is extremely unusual.

A 35-inch-diameter M/T or A/T tire mounted on the spare tire carrier can weigh more than 100 pounds. Even on flat, stable ground, that weight creates a difficult task. Imagine changing that tire on a loose dirt hill with an off-camber slope. Just jacking up the vehicle to remove the flat becomes dangerous. A tire-repair kit can be used to plug a tire without jacking or removing the tire. It can be done in any location as long as the puncture is exposed. Plugging the tire is easier, usually quicker, and much safer than trying to change the tire.

Occasionally, a flat is caused when the valve stem is damaged by a rock or a shrub branch. There is a new product available to replace the valve stem from the outside of the rim. The Colby valve uses a unique design that secures the valve stem to the rim from the outside without removing the tire from the rim.

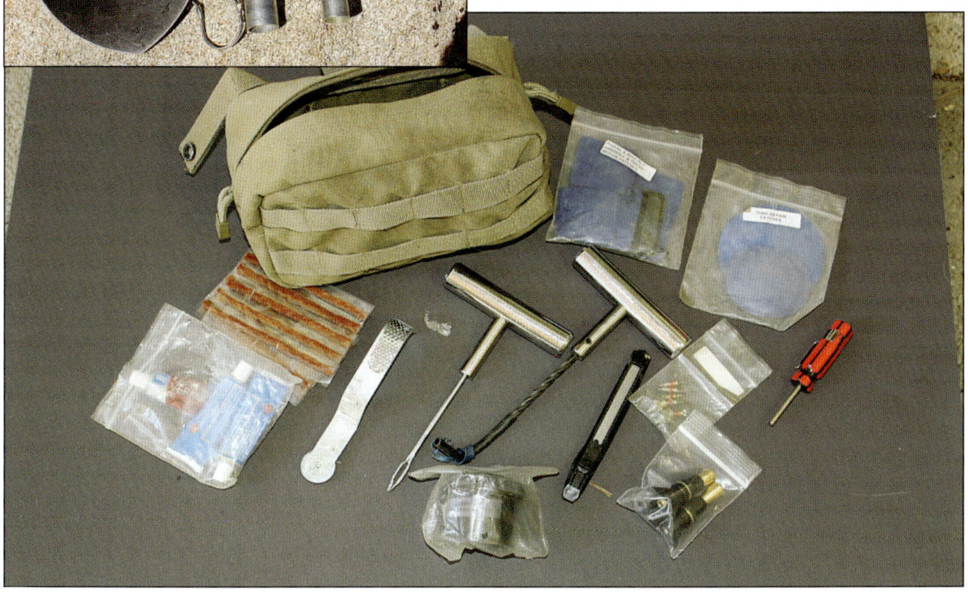

An absolute must for any overlanding gear kit is a good tire repair kit, such as this one from Extreme Outback. Plugging a tire puncture is much easier and often safer than trying to change a tire on a trail.

Winching Tips, Tricks, and Techniques

Winches are designed to pull in a straight line perpendicular to the centerline of the winch spool drum. Any variation from a straight pull places a greater load on the winch, the winch line, and other components, as well as increases the risk of a problem. If the winch line is being bent to either side by the fairlead (if it is rubbing or rolling on the side of the winch fairlead) the angle of the winch line is too great. This puts a lateral, or sideways, load on the winching vehicle. Lateral loads will pull the rig sideways. Realign either the winching rig or the anchor point to get a straight pull. Ideally, the winch line should clear the side of the fairlead or hawse by at least 1 inch.

Angles too large can cause all sorts of nasty problems beyond accelerated wear and tear on the winch, fairleads, and winch lines. The side load creates a large additional drag component. Think of trying to pull a rig from the side and furrows that the tires would try to dig. Any angle that is not straight adds a sideways pull and increases resistance, and that sideways load puts a strain on the suspension, tires, wheels, and wheel bearings.

We have seen tires begin to unseat from the wheel bead with a nominal side load while winching up a steep incline. In a wide-open area, either sloped or flat, you may simply need to steer the rig that is being winched in the first few feet of pulling so that everything aligns properly. Be careful if you are on a steep slope. If the steering causes the winched rig to traverse the slope at even a small angle, the probability of a rollover becomes greater. It is wiser to find an anchor point that better aligns with the winching process. The winch will try to align everything naturally anyway, but the real issues occur on narrow trails where there is no room to maneuver or steer.

Next, select an anchor point that will use most but not all of the winch line. Remember that a winch makes the most power with the fewest layers of winch line on the drum. As layers are added, the drum diameter increases, which changes the gear ratio of the winch and reduces its effective pulling torque.

The greater the load that you think the winch will be pulling, the more important it is to start with the fewest layers on the winch drum. There needs to be at least four wraps of winch line on the winch drum. Never allow the winch to pull without several wraps on the drum. If need be, use a snatch or pulley block to allow more winch line to be unspooled from the winch drum. The key is to always survey the situation before you begin. Take your time. Haste in the beginning almost always costs much more time than having patience. Plus, it is much safer to take stock before you take action.

Estimating the Winch Pull Load

Different situations, such as the slope grade and surface condition, affect the pulling load on a rig. Naturally, the weight of a fully loaded rig is the most obvious, and having a good idea of your rig's laden weight is important. For example, overlanding rigs weigh about 5,000 to 7,000 pounds, depending on the number of occupants and the amount of gear being carried. The weight of a trailer or van conversion increases loads considerably.

The surface condition is also a major factor. Smooth asphalt or concrete offer little resistance and, therefore, little pulling load. In fact, the resistance is only about 2 to 3 percent of the rig's weight, or about 100 to 210 pounds using our rig as an example. That's not much load, to be sure. When you get into soft surfaces and rolling, resistance goes up as high as 50 percent of the rig's weight (or up to 3,500 pounds in our case). That does not take in to account a rig stuck in snow or mud. The pull needed to free one of our rigs stuck up to the axles or frame may be as high as 120 percent of the rig's weight.

The hardest pull that we have encountered was a 4x4 pickup that was stuck in soft, slushy snow up to the frame. A straight winch pull with only a single layer of winch line on the drum did not budge the rig, even after an hour of digging snow away to reduce drag. After using a snatch block, the 9,000-pound winch was able to pull the rig free with an estimated load over 15,000 pounds.

For most soft surfaces, such as sand, snow, mud, gravel, and soft dirt, figure that the load will be about 25 to 30 percent of the rig's weight. That's about 1,250 to 2,000 pounds in our example. This is a pretty close estimate for most backcountry trail situations. That is, until you're winching up a slope.

Intuitively, the steeper the slope angle, the more the load will increase. At 30 degrees, it is about 60 percent of the total weight of the rig, but at 45 degrees (a 1:1 grade), the load is 100 percent of the rig's weight. It goes up from there but at a slower rate. Don't try to winch up a 60-plus-degree slope. Take an alternate route. Remember that you need to add the rolling-resistance factor to the equation along with the slope. It's a tough pull to go up a 60-percent slope with soft surface conditions and a 5,000-pound rig using a 9,000-pound-rated winch.

Finally, most 4x4 electric winches are rated for an intermittent duty cycle, so if you have a long, hard pull, give your winch and battery a break once in a while. Let the motor and battery cool for a few minutes. Then, resume the winching process.

Using a Tree-Saver Strap

A 3-inch-or-larger tree-saver strap is stronger and less likely to damage sensitive tree bark. Straps can be used around trees or rocks and even posts, although not many posts are found in the backcountry. Make sure that the tree or rock is substantial. Small trees can become uprooted, and rocks can become dislodged. Unless you are trying to down a tree or move a rock, this is not a good thing. You really want to move the rig, not the anchor.

Place the tree-saver strap around the bottom of a tree trunk as close to the ground as possible. This is the strongest spot on a tree. The exception to this is if the tree is over the brow of a slope, where placing the strap higher will keep the winch line off the ground. Watch the tree closely as the load increases. If the trunk begins to bend a lot, you may need to move the strap lower on the trunk.

Another exception occurs when the vehicle being winched sits higher than the ground where the anchor point is located. The winch will pull down on the suspension greatly and increase drag. Placing the anchor point higher on a tree (assuming the tree is stout enough) can lift the front of the vehicle slightly and help pull the vehicle, especially if the winched vehicle is in mud or snow.

Use a towel or piece of carpet under the winch line where it rubs on the ground to protect the line, especially if it is synthetic rope. If you are pulling your own rig, the line will be stationary as the vehicle moves. If you pull another rig, the winch line will move since the since the winching vehicle is stationary.

On a rock, attempt to place the strap below the waistline of the rock, so that if the strap slips under load, it will slide down towards the ground and not up where it can slip off the rock.

After placing the strap around the object, make sure that no twists are in the strap to reduce wear on the strap and minimize tree damage. Next, place the looped ends together and align the ends in line with the winch's direction of pull.

Finally, insert the loops onto the bowed section of a bow shackle. Then, insert the pin. Remember to tighten the pin until it bottoms. Then, back off about a quarter to a half turn so that the pin is easy to unscrew when removing it. A soft shackle can also be used.

Anchor to Another Rig

While other rigs can be good anchor points, they should not be your first choice. Since another rig may also be traction-limited, it can easily slide toward the rig being winched, even when in gear and with the brakes applied. This applies to a stationary rig attempting to winch out another vehicle.

We have had a rig chained to the back of the winching rig in muddy and icy trail conditions. Instead of pulling the stuck rig, both stationary rigs moved across the slippery surface. Ultimately, we had to use a tree-saver strap around a tree down the road. Then, we secure the winching rig to the strap with a length of heavy-duty chain.

If a stationary rig with an automatic transmission is used, the driver should be in place, holding the brakes

When winching another vehicle, the stationary vehicle doing the pulling has the winch line moving relative to the stationary vehicle. The winch line can drag on the ground, so use some form of ground cover to protect the winch line, especially if it is a synthetic line.

with the rig in gear and the engine running. Place wheel chocks to help keep the rig stationary. If the rig that is intended to remain stationary does not, cease winching immediately and try something different.

Using a Pull Pal Ground Anchor

The Pull Pal is a great tool. If you have nothing to pull against with a winch, the winch is useless. The Pull Pal provides an anchor point when no trees, large rocks, or other rigs are available. This happens more often than you might expect. If you drive in snow, sand, or desert areas, there are often no trees or rocks for an anchor. If you are on a narrow trail with a steep climb with other rigs, they may not be in a position to provide an anchor.

Many times, finding a suitable anchor that lines up adequately with your winch so that the pull angle is within an acceptable range can be impossible. The one thing that is always available is ground, and it is unusual to find solid rock trails with no rock outcropping to anchor to. We have used the Pull Pal in snow, ice, sand, dirt, loose dirt from mine tailings, gravel, and loose small rocks. It has always dug in enough to easily pull from, and it is easy to use. The only potential drawback is that it is somewhat bulky by necessity.

Using a Deadman Off-Road Winching Anchor

The Deadman off-road winching anchor works as an anchor point in a wide range of winching situations. The Deadman anchor is a large tarp that measures 28x48 inches. Each line has a breaking strength of 19,600 pounds in a straight-pull configuration and 39,200 pounds in a basket configuration.

Most often used in soft surfaces, the Deadman Anchor works by being buried in the soft dirt, sand, or snow from 2 to 3 feet deep, depending on the softness of the material. Harder, more-dense surfaces require a shallower hole than softer surfaces. Most

The Pull Pal ground anchor is a must-have tool for the overlander, especially when traveling solo. Often when you are stuck, there is no convenient anchor point. The Pull Pal can be used on nearly any surface, except large boulders. The Pull Pal has saved our bacon many times.

The Deadman off-road winching anchor is designed to be used on soft surfaces, such as sand, snow, and mud, although we are not eager to try it in mud. The force that the Deadman provides when buried is nothing short of amazing. It takes some work to set the Deadman, but it works extremely well. The Deadman can also be used on large rocks and as a tree-saver strap. The Deadman is relatively light and packs into a compact carrying case for storage.

assume that the weight of the material covering the Deadman anchor basket provides resistance to winch against. However, the resistance is provided by the dirt, sand, or snow from the full depth that the anchor is buried all the way to the winching point. In other words, the Deadman anchor is attempting to compress many cubic yards of material.

The Deadman anchor has been tested with pulls exceeding 7,000 pounds in soft surfaces. Due to the strength of the vinyl rip-stop tarp (basket), the Deadman anchor can be used around rock for an anchor. The Deadman also works great as a tree saver.

Winching Rules

Never use a winch that has been designed for off-road use as a hoist for lifting a vertical load, and never use a winch to lift a person. Always wear gloves, especially when working with wire rope. They fray and cause nasty cuts.

Pull the winch line from the spool by hand with the clutch lock released just in case the line was doubled over when rewinding. When doubled over, the line suddenly reverses direction and gives the person pulling out the line quite a tug. The exception to this may be on a steep slope where the winch being used for recovery is on the rig stuck on the slope. The driver should stay in the rig if possible to hold the brake and make sure that the rig remains stationary while someone else pulls out the winch line. After the line is pulled out, the slope must be descended again to engage the clutch lock. In this case, it may be easier and safer to slowly ascend the slope as the winch operator runs the line out with the winch control.

Keep everyone away from the swing zone of the winch rope. This is the radius that the winch line could swing in if the connection were to break at either end. This zone actually has two radii: one at each end. The safest place to be is to the side of either the rig being pulled or the anchor point, whether it's a tree, rock, or another rig. Anyone within the winch line swing zone is at great risk if the winch line or any attached component fails. Synthetic winch rope is much safer than the more common steel winch rope, which, when under tension, can act like a powerful sling shot. Be very careful.

After putting a little tension on the winch line, place a line damper on the winch line. This is important when using steel winching rope, as it is not self-damping like synthetic winch rope. A winch-line damper is any fabric that weighs at least 4 to 5 pounds and is draped over the winch line. Should the line snap, the damper will minimize the snapping effect of the broken line and reduce the flinging of the line itself or items that are attached to it. A damper can be a large towel, jacket, blanket, sleeping bag, or a special winch-line damper designed for this purpose. While synthetic winch line is much less dangerous, it can't hurt to use a damper on it.

Assign tasks to all who are available. Make sure that someone is positioned to watch the vehicle being winched to make sure there are no binds or other potential problems. Someone else can watch the anchor point, especially if it is another rig. Make sure that everyone is on the same page for communication both verbally and with hand signals. Keep it simple, such as a thumbs up and verbal "okay" for pulling and a verbal "stop" with a balled fist thrust into the air to stop winching. The driver of the rig with the winch doing the pulling should be responsible for organizing this. Make sure that any observers are out of harm's way before beginning the winching operation.

Always have at least four wraps of winch line around the drum before winching. This is the minimum to ensure there is no slippage of the line on the drum. Synthetic winch line can slip on the winch drum. Bubba Rope makes an inexpensive attachment for the drum to eliminate this problem.

As layers of winch line accumulate on the winch drum, pulling power decreases. Winch power can be reduced nearly 50 percent from maximum when the line is five layers thick versus the single layer with a starting point of four or five wraps on the drum. If you have a difficult pull, pull out the winch line as much as possible to maximize the pulling power. If necessary, use a snatch block to pull out more line. The pulley will also double the pulling power while reducing line speed to half.

If the winch line is dragging on the ground over a slope breakover, use a piece of carpet or a towel to minimize wear on the line as it drags on the dirt or rocks.

After checking all connections, lightly tension the winch line. Then, recheck every connection and make sure everyone is in a safe location and ready to start the pull. ■

Road Building

If you get stuck on a trail due to a high-centered situation or when you are trying to crawl over a steep rock and lose traction, road building is the best solution 9 times out of 10 for getting beyond the difficult spot. Most often, road building is altering the contour of the trail to gain ground clearance under your rig or to build a ramp up a steep boulder to reduce the angle of attack. This is done by using trailside rocks, tree limbs, or extraction boards.

There are three distinct scenarios. First, the underside of your rig will get hit without altering the line or increasing ground clearance. If you continue, you will likely become high-centered, which is the second scenario. Third, you encounter a large rock you must crawl over to continue forward, but the combination of traction, or more specifically the lack of traction and the steepness of the boulder, halts forward progress.

In the first case, either alter your path or back up and build up the trail so there is more clearance when the obstruction is approached. Doing this before getting high-centered is easier and reduces the chance of rig damage. Position rocks or limbs so the tires can drive over them in a way that allows increased ground clearance.

If you do get high-centered, try reversing off the obstacle. This can cause damage, so first analyze the situation carefully. If available traction is too little for this, your first inclination will be to pull the stuck rig with a tow strap or a winch to free it from the obstacle. This will often work but the damage risk is much higher. It is almost always best to use a Hi-Lift jack to raise one or more tires. Then, build up the trail under the tires to gain the needed ground clearance. Make sure that the new section of road is stable.

If you come to a boulder that you must crawl across, but it is too steep or there isn't adequate traction to ascend it, try building a ramp with rocks to reduce the angle of attack up the rock face. Extraction boards can be used if you have them. You will not usually need to use a jack for this process.

Here are some tips:

- Always wear gloves when road building
- Have someone assist you when moving large, heavy rocks
- Be aware of the potential of crushing your fingers when moving rocks
- A spotter should communicate to the driver when crossing the new section of road that was just built
- Keep clear of the new road buildup when the driver takes off because rocks can move or be thrown and cause injury

Be creative in your problem solving, but also think through what can happen before you take action. It almost always pays to take the most conservative action that will get you going again, even if it takes a few minutes longer.

Winter Recovery

Recovering a stuck rig in the winter is more difficult and more likely to happen. Snow is the perfect medium for getting stuck, and it comes in so many forms that it's impossible to describe them all. A rule of thumb for snow depth is to avoid roads where snow depth or the tracks in the snow from previous travelers is so deep that the frame, bumpers, or any part of the vehicle drags on the snow. In short-distance sections, a depth of few feet is okay if it's only a few inches deeper. Long distances through chassis-deep snow will cause build up under the rig and you will get high-centered on the accumulation. It can be a real pain to get out of, even if you have a winch.

Snow surfaces change, especially on warmer days. The hard crust in the morning or late evening can soften. What supported you earlier may cause you to sink in and possibly become trapped. It's good to know the area where you're driving, the slope of the trail, which can be much more problematic than flatter trails, the snow conditions, and the weather forecast.

Then, there's ice. Iced-over trails can be nearly impossible to navigate, especially on climbs, and they are treacherous on descents. Take extreme caution and drive slowly when it gets icy. Look for a path along the trail where traction may be better, such as the edges of the trail where there might be rocks or brush.

Finally, slippery, gooey mud is also likely in the winter. Like snow, it comes in many varieties.

Always carry plenty of provisions, water, clothes, blankets, and other survival gear just in case.

Travel with another rig. The more difficult the trail and conditions, the more important this is. Be well equipped. Four-wheeling in the winter is great fun, beautiful, and challenging, but it can turn disastrous quickly, so be prepared. Remember that a lack of preparation can open the door for Murphy to implement his annoying law.

What equipment do you need to carry? We have used every piece of gear we have on winter recoveries, sometimes on a single recovery. Here is what's mandatory:

Carry a set of chains, preferably two sets so that you can chain up all four tires. You'd be amazed at how well you can climb icy slopes with all four tires chained up. We've even towed disabled rigs up icy slopes with chains.

Take along the standard gear that you should always have, such as a Hi-Lift jack and accessories, a tow strap, shackles, and a shovel. Don't forget the shovel. Digging out of snow with your hands is no fun!

In winter, a winch is invaluable. It is by far the easiest and quickest way to get unstuck. Make sure you have a tree-saver strap and a snatch block. Pulling a rig out of deep snow can create huge loads, so be ready and be very careful. Winch line loads can easily exceed 10,000 pounds when pulling out of deep snow. A ground anchor, such as the Pull Pal, is invaluable.

Even in the mountains with lots of trees and rocks, I got stuck on a road in snow with nothing to pull against. We bought a Pull Pal the day before, and I loaded it almost as an afterthought. Including figuring out how to use the Pull Pal, which was pretty simple, I was out in less than 20 minutes. The Pull Pal dug in so solidly that I had to position the winch over the end of the Pull Pal to pry it free, which turned out to be easy and effective.

An axe and pick can be handy for breaking up ice, which can happen in fresh snow when the hot driveline melts snow and it refreezes into a much nastier ice or hard pack.

We have also found extraction boards to be helpful for ramping up out of snow or crossing narrow gullies from spring-melt runoff. We don't use them often, but when you need them, they are invaluable. This, like a Pull Pal and other big-ticket items, can be shared by a group. Not every rig on a backcountry adventure needs every item, but always carry the basics yourself so that you are prepared for most situations, including being stranded overnight.

Watch out for Murphy and be prepared so that you can enjoy the beauty and challenge of winter backcountry adventures. Remember the shovel!

CHAPTER 11

Engine and Driveline Upgrades

Some vehicles, such as the Jeep Wrangler Rubicon Hemi, don't need engine or driveline enhancements. Other vehicles may find some improved performance with engine and driveline upgrades. (Photo Courtesy Stellantis)

Overlanding is blessed with a wide selection of vehicles. In this chapter, we explore two distinct categories of overlanding modifications and upgrades. In the engine and driveline sections, we consider general modifications and upgrades because there are too many vehicles to get into the specifics. Other categories are more generic with products suitable for any overlanding rig. Lights, electronics, and many electrical accessories can be used on most vehicles.

Engine Upgrades

Cold-air intakes and cat-back exhaust systems are available for most overlanding-capable rigs. The cold-air intakes and the cat-back exhaust systems add small power increases and are relatively easy to install. Banks Power, Airaid, aFe, Rough Country, K&N, and several other companies offer cold-air intakes. Borla, aFe, JBA, Magnaflow, Flowmaster, MBRP, and others offer cat-back exhaust systems.

Banks Power offers a range of Ram-Air cold-air intakes for several overlanding trucks and SUVs.

Cold-air intakes improve airflow into the induction system and add a little power. Airaid makes systems for some trucks and SUVs.

Air-intake snorkels provide cleaner air in dusty environments and allow passage through water crossings. AEV makes snorkels for Jeep Wranglers and Gladiators, the Dodge Ram, and Chevy Colorado trucks.

Engine-tuning programmers can change the factory tune for the engine and add some power and/or improve fuel economy. Tuners can help improve items such as throttle response with the Banks Power Pedal Monster. A wide range of tuning and programming products are available from several manufacturers.

Automatic Transmission Coolers

The automatic transmission coolers in most overlanding rigs can handle the heat build-up of normal driving, but the more extreme conditions off-road, such as steep, long climbs, heavier loads, more drag, and trailer towing, can overheat the transmission. Towing, hot desert environments, and slow rock crawling can cause the transmission to overheat. Overheating will accelerate wear considerably. An auxiliary automatic transmission cooler improves transmission-fluid cooling and reduces stress and wear to the transmission. Mopar, Derale, Mishimoto, and Flex-A-Lite make coolers for several vehicles.

Cooling System

For normal highway driving and moderate off-roading, the stock cooling system in most rigs is adequate. Overheating can become an issue when towing or driving on steep grades. When larger tires, armor, bumpers, overlanding gear, and other accessories are added, overheating becomes more likely. Part of the problem is evacuating hot air from the engine compartment. Vented hoods can help with cooling issues.

Removing hot air is not the only issue. Adding weight is a factor, but so is blocking airflow through the grille into the radiator. Bull bars, winches, and light bars are often installed in front of the radiator opening. This reduces flow to the radiator and creates turbulence that disturbs airflow.

Keeping an engine cool is all about getting heat out of the water. Two factors contribute to this: 1) airflow through the radiator fins and 2) water flow through the radiator tubes. Too little airflow leads to overheating, as does water that is inadequately cooled. This can happen due to too little volume of water in the system but also when the water flow occurs too quickly through the radiator cooling tubes. Bent or clogged cooling fins on the radiator can also restrict airflow, which is a problem when wheeling in deep mud. Heavy mud and small stones can clog and bend the cooling fins.

High-Flow Radiators

The efficiency of a radiator depends upon the coolant capacity or volume and the ability of the coolant to extract heat from the engine. Large-capacity radiators improve cooling. Cooling also improves when the flow of coolant stays in the radiator core longer. Aftermarket radiators use larger tubes or additional rows of cooling tubes to create more volume. The radiator core is thicker to accommodate the increased capacity. Companies that offer high-flow radiators include C&R Racing, Flex-A-Lite, and Mishimoto.

The extra weight of many overlanding rigs and harsh conditions strain the cooling system. Make sure to keep the cooling system, including the radiator, hoses, water pump, belts, and fan, in good working order. If the stock radiator is not up to the cooling demands of your rig, consider a higher-capacity aluminum radiator. Always carry spare hoses and belts.

Cooling fans make a difference. Many stock cooling fans operate at low cubic feet per minute (CFM) volume. Higher-flow-rate fans enhance cooling and lower operating temperatures.

Drivelines

Questions regarding gear ratios are among the most asked online and at our Jeep 4x4 school. Gear-ratio selection must account for several factors. The optimal gear ratio for a given overlanding rig depends on the tire size, transmission and transfer-case gear ratios, and the intended use of the vehicle. Optimal gearing for on-road driving at highway speeds is in the 1,800- to 2,500-rpm range on level ground. If engine RPM is too low, the engine strains and the automatic transmission will downshift to keep the engine speed at optimal levels. Wear to both the engine and transmission accelerate under these conditions.

Ideally, the engine RPM at 60 mph with the stock tires and gearing is close to the same when re-gearing for larger tires. For example, on a rig with a standard 3.7:1 axle ratio, 32-inch-diameter tires, and in fifth (or the highest) gear, the engine RPM at highway speeds is similar to running 35-inch-diameter tires with a re-gearing to a 4.56:1 axle ratio. If 35-inch tires are used with the stock 3.70 axle ratio, the engine RPM drops below the ideal RPM for highway cruising. A taller tire acts like having a taller gear ratio.

The ideal gearing for off-road driving depends on the terrain. Low gear ratios are necessary for steep descents (25 degrees or more). Hillclimbs with most modern engines on overlanding-capable vehicles have sufficient torque to handle hillclimbs and rock crawling with higher gearing. Descents require gearing that allows minimal use of the brakes, especially on long, steep descents. When descending a 25-degree slope, speeds should be kept at or below 3 mph in first gear low range without needing to use the brakes.

Example 1: Speeds in Gears

Vehicle	2016 Toyota Tacoma
Tire Diameter	32 inches
Axle Ratio	3.111:1, 3.60 in 1st gear
Transmission	6-speed automatic
4x4 Transfer-Case Ratio (High/Low)	1.00:1/2.57:1

Gear	Transmission Ratio x Axle Ratio	Engine RPM	High-Range Speed (MPH)	Low-Range Speed (MPH)
1st	14.08:1	2,000	13	5
2nd	8.17:1	2,000	22	11
3rd	5.83:1	2,000	31	12
4th	3.111:1	2,000	46	18
5th	2.70:1	2,000	67	26
6th	2.27:1	2,000	80	31

Example 2: Speeds in Gears

Vehicle	2016 Chevrolet Colorado
Tire Diameter	30.6 inches
Axle Ratio	axle ratio 3.42, 4.06 in 1st gear
Transmission	6-speed automatic
4x4 Transfer-Case Ratio (High/Low)	1.00:1/2.72:1

Gear	Transmission Ratio x Axle Ratio	Engine RPM	High-Range Speed (MPH)	Low-Range Speed (MPH)
1st	13.811:1	2,000	13	5
2nd	8.11:1	2,000	22	8
3rd	5.30:1	2,000	34	13
4th	3.117:1	2,000	46	17
5th	2.911:1	2,000	62	23
6th	2.497:1	2,000	71	27

Speed at 2,000 rpm in Top Gear 2WD (Stock Configuration)

Year	Make	Model	Tire Size	Speed (MPH)
2016	Chevy	Colorado	32 inches	71
2016	Toyota	Tacoma	32 inches	80
2022	Ford	Bronco (Badlands Sasquatch)	35 inches	67
2022	Jeep	Wrangler (Rubicon Extreme Recon)	35 inches	65

Speed at 700 rpm in First Gear 4WD Low-Range (Stock Configuration)

Year	Make	Model	Tire Size	Speed (MPH)
2016	Chevy	Colorado	32 inches	2
2016	Toyota	Tacoma	32 inches	2
2022	Ford	Bronco (Badlands Sasquatch)	35 inches	3
2022	Jeep	Wrangler (Rubicon Extreme Recon)	35 inches	3

What do all of these ratios mean? There are two ratios that are critical for off-roading. The first is the final-drive ratio which determines the speed of the vehicle at a given engine RPM. A numerically higher ratio means the vehicle will travel at a slower speed for a given engine RPM with all else being equal.

The second important ratio is the crawl ratio. In 2WD and in drive (1.0:1 transmission ratio), the crawl ratio is the same as the axle ratio. In 4WD low range with a 4.0:1 transfer-case ratio also in drive, the crawl ratio is 16.0:1. This is calculated by multiplying the transmission gear ratio times the axle ratio and then multiplying the result times the transfer-case ratio. A vehicle with a 2.72 low-range transfer-case ratio, a 4.10 axle ratio, and an automatic transmission with a first-gear ratio of 4.71 has a crawl ratio of 52.3. The higher the numerical crawl ratio number, the slower the vehicle speed will be at a given engine RPM. The higher number also translates into more torque multiplication which is important when climbing hills and rock crawling. The higher crawl ratio number also helps keep the speed lower when descending steep hills.

The table below shows OEM and aftermarket axle ratios and standard transfer-case ratio combinations and the overall crawl ratio. The calculations use a 4.71:1 first-gear transmission ratio, which is common on several overlanding vehicles.

Make/Model	Low-Range Transfer Case	Axle	Crawl Ratio
Jeep/Wrangler (Rubicon)	4.00	4.10	77.2
Common on many overland rigs	2.72	3.45	44.2
Optional 3.73 final-drive ratio	2.72	3.73	47.8
Optional 3.73 final-drive ratio	4.00	3.73	70.3
Aftermarket rear-axle ratio	4.00	4.56	85.11
Aftermarket rear-axle ratio	4.00	4.88	111.11
Aftermarket rear-axle ratio	4.00	5.13	116.6
Aftermarket rear-axle ratio	4.00	5.38	101.4
Aftermarket rear-axle ratio	2.72	4.88	62.5
Aftermarket rear-axle ratio	2.72	5.13	65.7
Aftermarket rear-axle ratio	2.72	5.38	68.11

Crawl Ratios First Gear 4WD Low-Range (Stock Configuration)

Year	Make	Model	Ratio
2016	Chevy	Colorado	37.8
2016	Toyota	Tacoma	36.2
2022	Ford	Bronco (Badlands Sasquatch)	60.3
2022	Jeep	Wrangler (Rubicon Extreme Recon)	85.11

Crawl Ratios First Gear 4WD Low-Range (4.88:1 Axle Ratios)

Year	Make	Model	Ratio
2016	Chevy	Colorado	53.11
2016	Toyota	Tacoma	45.2
2022	Ford	Bronco (Badlands Sasquatch)	62.4
2022	Jeep	Wrangler (Rubicon Extreme Recon)	111.11

The crawl ratio does not take the tire diameter into account. By dividing the crawl ratio by the tire diameter, another ratio tells a more complete story. The table below shows the crawl ratio divided by tire-diameter ratios for a variety of axle ratios, tire diameters, and transfer-case ratios. The higher that the crawl ratio divided by the tire-diameter ratio is, the higher the engine RPM will be for a given speed. Increasing tire diameter reduces the ratio. Increasing tire diameter generally requires a lower axle ratio (numerically higher number) to achieve optimal performance.

Crawl Ratio and Tire Diameter

Axle Ratio	Crawl Ratio	Tire Diameter	Crawl Ratio/Tire Diameter Ratio
With 4.00:1 Transfer Case			
4.56	85.11	35	2.45
4.88	111.11	35	2.62
5.13	116.11	35	2.77
5.38	101.4	35	2.110
4.56	85.11	37	2.32
4.88	111.11	37	2.48
5.13	116.11	37	2.62
5.38	101.4	37	2.74
4.56	85.11	40	2.15
4.88	111.11	40	2.30
5.13	116.11	40	2.42
5.38	101.4	40	2.54
With 2.72:1 Transfer Case			
4.88	62.5	35	1.711
5.13	65.7	35	1.88
5.38	68.11	35	1.117
4.88	62.5	37	1.611
5.13	65.7	37	1.78
5.38	68.11	37	1.86
4.88	62.5	40	1.56
5.13	65.7	40	1.64
5.38	68.11	40	1.73

*The optimal ratio is 1.7 to 2.4

Crawl Ratio Divided by Tire Diameter on Factory Specification Vehicles

Year	Make	Model	Tire Size	Ratio
2016	Chevy	Colorado	32 inches	1.18
2016	Toyota	Tacoma	32 inches	1.13
2022	Ford	Bronco (Badlands Sasquatch)	35 inches	1.74
2022	Jeep	Wrangler (Rubicon Extreme Recon)	35 inches	2.45

Ring-and-Pinion Gear Upgrades

Ring-and-pinion swaps are made to maintain optimal engine RPM on the highway and a good crawl ratio off-road. Aftermarket ring-and-pinion upgrades are often more durable than factory gears. Several companies offer ring-and-pinion gearsets and installation kits, including Yukon Gear & Axle, Alloy USA, Mopar, Revolution, Motive Gear, G2, and Dana Spicer. Every brand and model of overlanding vehicle may use a different design. Not all companies that offer ring-and-pinion gears have gearsets for all vehicles.

Earlier vehicles relied on gears in the transmission to operate the speedometer. Modern vehicles use electronics. When changing axle ratios or tire diameter, the computer must be flashed or reprogrammed for the speedometer to read correctly. This can usually be done at the dealership. Aftermarket programmers are available on some vehicles.

Front Axle Shafts

Front axle shafts can easily break under more severe conditions on both solid-axle-equipped and independent-front-suspension-equipped vehicles. A major cause of axle failure is excessive wheelspin followed by a sudden increase of traction that can occur when the spinning tires burn through moisture or dirt/sand and grab traction. This places enormous loads on the axle shafts. Spinning tires and too much throttle application causes the suspension to bounce, which changes traction on the tires. The sudden increase in traction can break and axle or twist a driveshaft in solid-front-axle rigs.

Chrome-moly axle shafts with the correct spline ends for specific solid-front-axle applications are more durable and less prone to break. Axles on independent front suspension rigs are often more vulnerable to failure. Aftermarket replacement axles for the front-axle assemblies on both independent and solid-axle applications are available from Yukon Gear & Axle, Motive Gear, Alloy USA, Dana Spicer, and RCV Performance.

Rear Axle Shafts

Rear axle shafts tend to be more durable than front axle shafts because they do not provide steering. Ironically, rear axle shafts can break as often as front shafts. Wheelspin on hillclimbs and climbing large rocks where the weight has shifted to the rear tires can heat tires, increase traction, and allow the tires to grab, which sometimes leads to twisting or breakage. Chrome-moly axle shafts still offer superior strength and reliability. Yukon Gear & Axle, Alloy USA, Dana Spicer, Crown, and Motive Gear offer rear axle-shaft upgrades.

Selectable Axle Lockers

Differential or axle lockers physically lock the left- and right-side axles together so that the axles rotate at the same speed. Differentials are designed so that one wheel on an axle can freewheel. While cornering,

Axle lockers provide enhanced traction when driving on slippery surfaces, climbing rocks, and ascending steep grades. Having both front and rear axle lockers is ideal, but only the rear locker is a significant aid for traction. Lockers are operated by air compressors or electric servos. Lockers are available for most differentials that are found on overlanding rigs.

the inside tire will rotate slower than the outside tire. The differential allows this to occur without tire scrub. A differential locker locks the left- and right-side wheels together. This increases traction, tire scrub, and steering effort when cornering. Differential lockers are usually associated with extreme four-wheeling situations. If you drive in sand, mud, snow, or ice, having at least one diff locker will make life much easier in adverse conditions. Selectable lockers allow the driver to select when the locker engages by using a switch that activates a solenoid which engages the locker with an electrified magnet or compressed air.

Some overlanding-capable models come equipped with electric lockers on either both front and rear axles or just the rear axles. While electric lockers work quite well, they are prone to failure in extreme conditions, often due to electrical issues and actuator failure. Aftermarket e-lockers tend to be more durable and are a good choice if you are upgrading on a model with no lockers. Air lockers use compressed air from a compressor or a compressed gas source, such as the CO_2 in a Power Tank. Air lockers are more durable and activate more quickly.

Limited-Slip Differentials and Detroit Lockers

Limited-slip differentials, like the Eaton Detroit TruTrac, operate automatically and work well to improve traction. These traction aids are fine for easy-to-moderate off-road driving. Other types of traction aids, such as the Detroit locker, are more aggressive and work great in a straight line but can be difficult to drive in adverse conditions on the highway. For more aggressive off-roading, selectable lockers, such as e-lockers or air lockers are preferred.

Driveshafts, Yokes, CV Joints, and U-Joints

When lifting a 4x4 rig, stock driveshafts may be too short depending on the amount of suspension

Driveshafts and U-joints take a beating off-road. Upgrades reduce the risk of failure. Additionally, when lifting a vehicle, the stock driveshafts may be too short and require modifications or new driveshafts.

lift. In extreme off-road conditions, some (if not most) stock driveshafts are prone to damage from rocks, twisting, and U-joint failure. Clearance issues with the exhaust pipe can be an issue on some vehicles. The solution to these issues is to upgrade the driveshafts to aftermarket products that handle lifts and extreme conditions more effectively. Make sure that the yokes are compatible with the transfer case and axle pinion shafts. JE Reel Drivelines, Tom Woods, and Adams Driveshaft & Off-Road offer custom and off-the-shelf driveshafts. Some companies offer only off-the-shelf driveshafts, including Yukon Driveshafts from Randy's Worldwide, Teraflex, Metalcloak, and Rough Country.

Full Axle Assembly Swaps for Solid-Axle-Housing-Equipped Vehicles

Upgrading to complete axle assemblies solves several problems. Axle housings are stronger, axles are bigger with more splines, big brakes are generally included, brackets are installed for a true bolt-in swap, and lockers and gear-ratio options allow for complete customization. These aftermarket housings typically use larger-diameter, thicker-wall axle tubes, heavy-duty brackets with gussets for added strength, and the ability to accommodate a large range of axles and diff lockers.

Some of these assemblies are designed as a bolt-in replacement for the stock Dana 30, 35, and 44 axle assemblies. Aftermarket axle assemblies are also designed to retain the factory ESP, ABS, and speedometer sensors as well as the rear parking brake cables. Currie Enterprises, Dynatrac, G2, and Dana Spicer offer upgraded Dana 44 and 60 axle assemblies.

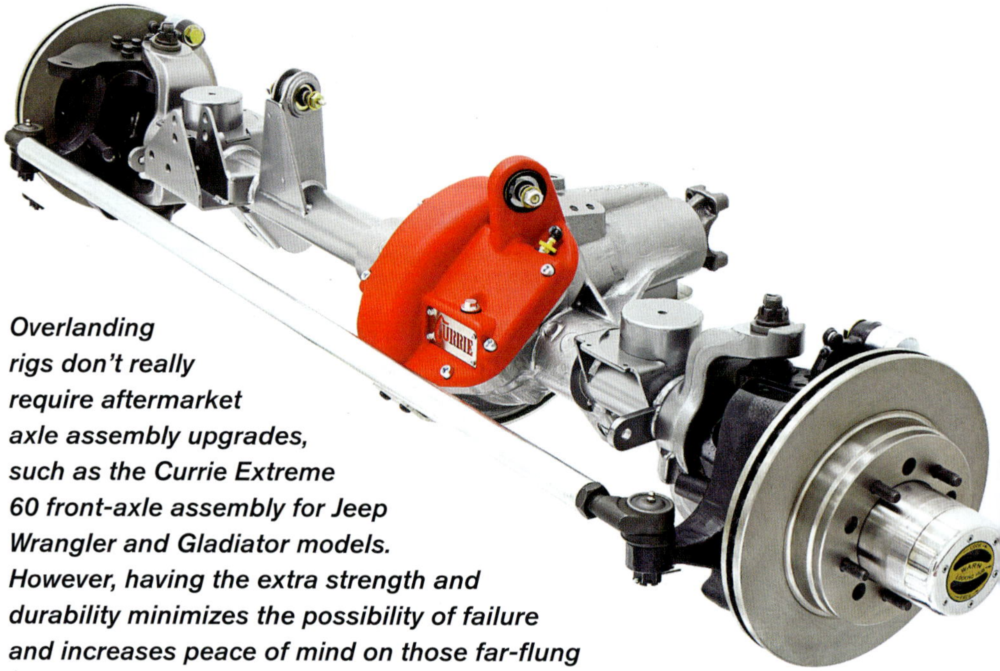

Overlanding rigs don't really require aftermarket axle assembly upgrades, such as the Currie Extreme 60 front-axle assembly for Jeep Wrangler and Gladiator models. However, having the extra strength and durability minimizes the possibility of failure and increases peace of mind on those far-flung adventures.

CHAPTER 12

Overlanding Adventure Accommodations

The combination of a folding canopy and rooftop tent provide good shelter and sleeping accommodations for overlanding trips.

Overlanding adventures can encompass multiple days. You are not overlanding if you are not spending at least one night in the backcountry. Some say overlanding requires much longer periods of roughing it, but a single night is necessary.

In Chapter 4, we looked at more luxurious accommodations, such as camper vans, trailers, and massive expedition-style behemoths. Here we will look at simpler, more practical, traditional, and cost-effective forms of accommodations for overlanding: tents. Ground tents (swag is a commonly used Australian term that means a ground tent), rooftop tents, and even sleeping on the ground on a pad in a sleeping bag will be addressed. We also look at a variety of shelters, such as awnings, privacy shelters for showering and toilets, annex rooms, portable toilets, sleeping bags, and ground covers.

Rooftop Tents

Rooftop tents are immensely popular. More than 100 companies manufacture rooftop tents. They come in a wide range of styles, sizes, and price points. Rooftop tents require a ladder to access the tent—even those that are mounted to truck beds or small overlanding trailers.

Dynamic and Static Roof Load Limitations

Dynamic roof load is the maximum permissible loads (total weight) allowed on a vehicle while the vehicle is in motion. Static maximum load refers to weight limit while the vehicle is stationary. The static load can be much higher. The static load includes the weight of occupants in a rooftop tent and any supplies, such as a change of clothing stored in the tent while in camp but removed before travel.

Dynamic roof load limits for most overlanding vehicles are a maximum of 165 pounds. This includes the weight of a roof rack, gear, and/or a rooftop tent. Some vehicle

Hard-shell rooftop tents, such as those from iKamper, offer better protection, a lower profile, and improved aerodynamics. The 270-degree swing-out canopy attaches to the roof rack and offers quick and easy shade.

The Ironman 4x4 Nomad 1300 hard-shell rooftop tent features a slim-line shell made from ABS and a queen-size mattress. The weight is 150 pounds which allows it to be used on smaller SUVs and crossover vehicles. (Photo Courtesy Ironman 4x4)

Pros	Cons
• Cool factor • Above-ground isolation from water puddles	• Cost, especially compared to ground tents • Weight (roof dynamic load) • Storage when not in use • Increased aerodynamic drag hurts fuel economy • Raised center of gravity increases sway on the highway when cornering or in crosswinds • Raised center of gravity increases rollover potential in rough, rutted, and rocky terrain • Overhead clearance issues • Requires a ladder to access the tent • Wind noise and sway from wind • The need to break camp and stow gear when leaving for a day adventure from base camp

manufacturers specify that there should be no weight on the roof at all. The Jeep Wrangler JL Unlimited is one model with this restriction, although it has been tested with a roof load of 150 pounds with no known ill effects. Reasons for the low roof-weight carrying capacity include higher aerodynamic drag from the wind, a higher center of gravity (increasing the possibility of a rollover in difficult terrain), and stress on the roof-rack mounting points from wind drag and wind gusts. The factors affecting dynamic roof loads do not apply to static roof loads. However, roof mounting points, such as rain gutters do have limitations on weight-bearing capacity.

Hard-Shell

A hard-shell tent offers the most convenience for setup and takedown. They require the least amount of time for use and offer more protection from the elements. Hard-shell tents generally have soft sides with access doors and windows. The sides easily fold up within the hard-shell when stowed.

Some hard-shell tent tops raise completely around the perimeter of the tent. Others, like clam-shell-style rooftop tents are hinged at one end. Hard-shell tents generally offer more room inside for sleeping, relaxing, and some storage for clothes and shoes. Most hard-shell tents offer

The ARB Touring hard-shell rooftop tent offers sturdy construction and a spacious interior. One issue with rooftop tents is the mounting gap between the tent bottom and roof. A fairing to force wind over the tent instead of under reduces drag and improves fuel efficiency.

A soft-shell rooftop tent offers a few important advantages. First, they cost considerably less. In addition, they are generally lighter but are more difficult to set up and take down compared to most solid-shell tents. This Raptor Series Voyager rooftop tent has many features for comfort and ease of operation and is reasonably priced.

The Tuff Stuff Overland Alpha hard-shell rooftop tent offers a large, comfortable sleeping area. The shell is tall when collapsed at 14 inches and heavy at 176 pounds, which exceeds the safe roof load limits for most vehicles. This tent is best installed on a pickup bed to handle the weight and aerodynamic drag.

Keeping in mind the downsides of a rooftop tent, one of our facilitators developed a clever system that uses a Billie Bars rack system to install a plywood slide-out platform using the tracks in the Billie Bar rack. He then attached a ground tent to that elevated platform for sleeping. It is easy to use and inexpensive. (Photo Courtesy Paul Crawford)

a lower profile for reduced wind resistance, but they tend to weigh more. Some hard-shell tents feature extruded aluminum rails to allow for some storage or racks for use when the tent is in the closed position.

Soft-Shell

A soft-shell tent, as the name implies, is made from fabric on the sides and top. The floor is made from a hard material, such as fiberglass, plywood, or aluminum. Soft-shell rooftop tents are less costly. Be aware of low-cost tents. Look at material specifications, window materials, and especially zippers. The weight and ease of opening and stowing are also things to consider.

Ground Tents

A wide range of ground (swag) tents are available to suit a variety of needs and accommodations. As with the fabric on rooftop tents, pay attention to quality of materials in the tent structure, rain fly, windows, and zippers. Many tent designs can be set up in less than a minute, and

Thule is a premier maker of rooftop tents and offers a wide range of designs. The rain fly that covers the tent is a great addition in rain, snow, and damp conditions.

Roam Adventure Company offers a range of rooftop tents with many features, including the Vagabond. The bed area is large while overall weight is low at about 130 pounds, which is suitable for most roof-load ratings. A rain fly is standard. The package includes a cover for highway use that protects the tent and reduces wind noise. A large annex is a worthwhile option.

The classic rooftop tent from Ironman 4x4 offers exceptional room and remains relatively lightweight. (Photo Courtesy Ironman 4x4)

The inside of the classic rooftop tent from Ironman 4x4 provides plenty of light and ventilation with the window covers unzipped. (Photo Courtesy Ironman 4x4)

takedown takes only a little longer. Be sure to use a ground cover, such as a tarp, under the tent to stop moisture from entering the tent. If possible, pitch the tent on higher ground to avoid flooding if a thunderstorm hits.

One argument against ground tents is the threat of attack by wild animals. While there is a threat, it is surprisingly small and nearly nonexistent. Here are some facts:

- Between 2000 and 2016, there were 664 bear attacks worldwide
- In that same period, there were 23 fatal bear attacks in the US
- The last wolf attack on a person occurred in the late 1800s
- On average, sharks kill six humans annually
- Mosquitoes cause 750,000 human deaths each year

A rollover on the trails is far more likely than a wild animal attack—except for mosquitoes. Carry bug repellent.

Napier offers two styles of tents for pickup beds and SUVs. The SUV tents can be used as a stand-alone ground tent, or they can be attached to the back of an SUV to access the SUV's interior for sleeping or gear access.

The Ironman 4x4 ridge-pole Double Swag tent is large enough for two people. This tent is compact and reasonably priced. Setup time is about 5 minutes for this compact two-person design. (Photo Courtesy Ironman 4x4)

Gazelle Tents makes a unique hub-design ground tent that offers considerable room and 6 feet, 6 inches of headroom in the T4 model, which is shown here. Setup and takedown time are only 90 seconds which makes this ground tent quick and easy.

23ZERO makes a wide range of swag tents for a variety of needs. The durability and compact design make these tents ideal for overlanding in smaller SUVs and crossovers.

Awnings

Awnings provide protection from the sun and wind. Many manufacturers offer a wide range of awning options. Inexpensive awning options generally strap to the vehicle or spare tire and uses poles to support the awning. Higher-quality awnings use a pullout retractable design with the housing mounted to the side of the vehicle roof line or roof rack. Some awnings swing out to cover up to 270 degrees, which is a nice feature for a respite from the sun and while preparing meals.

Awnings provide shade and shelter. The Rhino-Rack Batwing awning covers 270 degrees, folds into a compact receptacle, and requires only two vertical supports.

The 270 Gull Wing awning from the Bush Company swings out from a roof-rack receptacle on aluminum arms. No vertical supports are required. The design is quick and easy to deploy, and the awning covers a large area.

Privacy Shelters

As the name implies, privacy shelters provide a place to change, shower, and use a portable toilet. Several designs are available in a wide range of prices and a wide range of ease of setup and takedown.

The large annex on the Turtleback trailer includes an awning and attaches to the canvas-style camper shell on the trailer roof.

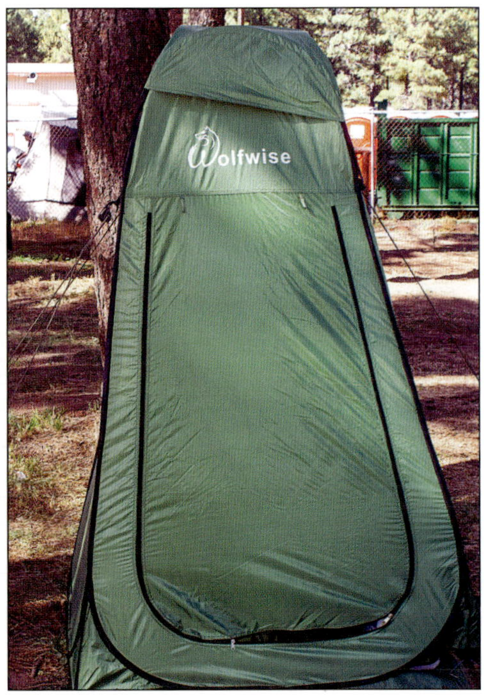

Privacy shelters, such as the Wolfwise shower/restroom/changing room, provide privacy and are simple to set up.

This shelter hangs from an aluminum frame. The entire shelter folds into a container that is attached to the side of the rig.

Annex Rooms

Annex rooms provide shelter from the elements and bugs. Annexes are great for relaxing, avoiding the elements, and meal preparation. Annex rooms can be attached to rooftop tents or ground tents, or they can stand alone—usually attached to a vehicle to provide additional stability.

Portable Toilets

A portable toilet is a must-have item when overlanding with a tent or rooftop tent, especially during nighttime hours. Combined with a privacy shelter, portable toilets add a touch of convenience and privacy that many folks appreciate. Capture bags with chemicals turn waste into a solid odor-free, mess free, easily disposable package. Be sure to dispose of all trash in a proper receptacle. Don't leave it behind for others to deal with.

Awnings with side walls can be used as an annex room.

The tapered design and small footprint base make the EverShower great for showering, but space is limited for a toilet or use as a changing room.

Annex rooms are generally stand-alone units, such as this gazebo from Gazelle.

Flushable marine-style toilets are generally found in large overlanding trailers and van conversions.

Folding toilet seats use a waterproof bag with added chemicals to solidify waste, eliminate odor, and make disposal easy.

Portable Showers

If you are overlanding for more than a day or two, a shower can be a necessity. A warm shower is even better. A simple solar shower consists of vinyl bags, usually black, that sit in the sun to heat. They are then hung in a privacy shelter or on a tree limb to allow gravity to create a shower stream. Some are available with water pumps, either foot-operated or electric. Shower heads are standard on most models.

Sleeping Bags

Sleeping bags range widely in price. Most bags have temperature ratings that indicate the lowest temperature at which occupants will stay comfortably warm. Sleeping bag shells are available in several materials and fills. High-quality bags, especially those with low temperature ratings, are more expensive. Investing in a good sleeping bag is worthwhile. Keep in mind that nighttime temperatures, even in summer months, can drop into the 30°F range in mountain areas and around 40°F in desert environments.

Ironman 4x4 makes a 3-gallon portable camping pressure solar shower that allows outdoor showers with warm water.

Ground Covers and Cots

Ground covers, such as tarps, can prevent moisture from wicking up into a tent or sleeping bag. A variety of mattresses that range from inflatable air mattresses to egg-crate-style pads can improve comfort while fending off cold or moist ground. Folding cots are a great way to get off the ground in or outside of a tent. They are comfortable and make getting in and out of a sleeping bag a little easier.

The Ironman 4x4 3-gallon portable camping shower uses a foot pump to pressurize the water-storage container.

The InstaPrivy portable toilet kit is a unique shelter for privacy when nature calls. The hands-free shelter is "worn" rather than entered. A folding plastic toilet seat is lightweight and easy to use. The shelter uses a vent screen for outward visibility and odor removal, and the kit includes a storage pack with disposal bags, toilet paper, seat covers, chemicals, and hand wipes. The compact kit weighs only 7 pounds.

CHAPTER 13

Gear Storage, Food Storage, and Preparation Gear

Packing your gear for overlanding adventures is an art form. A lot of gear is required even for short-term adventures. Finding space for all the gear is a challenge. Dozens of storage solutions are available for overlanding gear and food. While soft storage bags work for anything, storing non-perishable food in a hard-shell, latching case provides better protection from the elements and critter theft. Perishable food should be stored in refrigerators or a hard-shell ice chest. Canned or bottled drinks can be kept in soft-sided coolers. This chapter focuses on gear used in rigs that are set up for rooftop-tent or ground-tent camping.

Refrigerators

Keeping food cold is both a necessity and a luxury when overlanding. Having a consistent temperature ensures that the food will not spoil too quickly. Portable 12-volt refrigerators have exploded in popularity with the growth of overlanding and so has the number of refrigerators that are currently available. Storage capacities range from a small 12-quart size up to about 100 quarts. Prices are proportional to size. Power needs range from a low of about

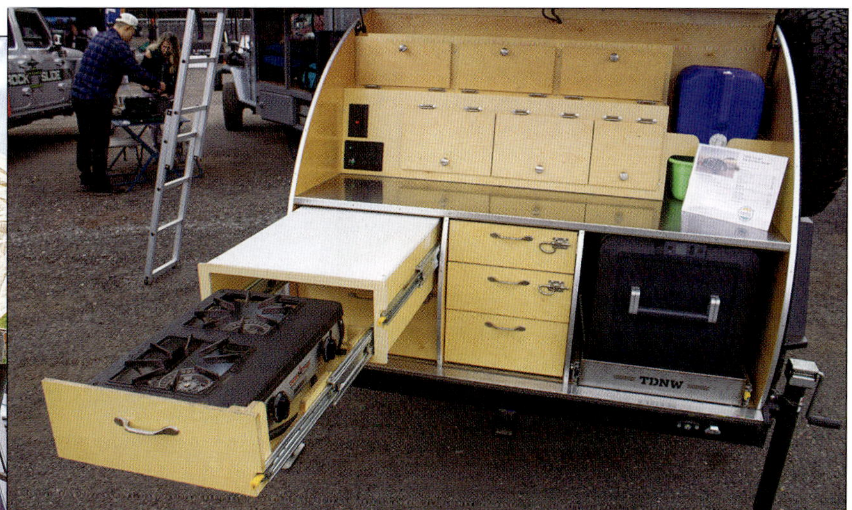

Any overlanding adventure requires gear for camping, cooking, and comfort. Long trips require more storage for gear and food. Personal preferences play a major role in determining how much gear and subsequent storage is needed.

The Ironman 4x4 IceCube fridge features an optional insulated cover to protect the refrigerator and keep the fridge cooler to reduce the electrical requirement to keep food cold.

50 watts up to 65 watts. Amperage draw varies upon load but ranges up to about 6 amps when the refrigerator is cooling. Most refrigerators have dual-power sources that use a 12-volt power port in the vehicle or a 110-volt shore power adapter when available.

Some 12-volt portable refrigerators offer separate cooling and freezer compartments with freezer temperatures as low as 0°F. Keep in mind that lower temperatures will draw higher amperage, discharge batteries more quickly, and put more strain on electrical charging systems. Most fridges use computer chips to monitor voltage. The fridge will shut down if the voltage drops too low to start the vehicle. Here are some factors to consider when selecting a 12-volt portable refrigerator for your overlanding rig:

The ARB Zero refrigerator/freezer is high quality with a price tag to match.

- Pay attention to exterior dimensions. Do you have adequate space in your rig?
- What capacity do you need for your adventures?
- How many days will pass between food replenishing opportunities?

ARB, Dometic, Type S Auto, and Alpicool are some of the many brands on the market.

Ice Chests

Ice chests provide adequate cooling for short overlanding adventures from one to two nights. Longer trips require replenishing ice or freezing ice packs. Ice packs are reusable and less messy than using actual ice. Ice chests come in both hard-shell and soft-sided designs. Hard-shell designs offer better protection from the environment and are more resistant to damage from critters. Soft-shell coolers take up less space for a given storage capacity.

Type S Auto offers the Blizzard Box portable electric cooler in a 41-quart capacity. The Blizzard Box can be used as a freezer with temperatures as low as 0°F. It operates on a 12-volt or 110-volt power source and is equipped with other features. We've been using a Blizzard Box for about three years and love it.

Dometic refrigerators have been used in the RV market for decades. They offer many choices for overlanding with capacities ranging from a 25 to 100 liters.

Dometic produces coolers as well as a huge line of camping products, including portable kitchens that are ideal for the overlander.

Many companies offer coolers. AO Coolers makes a range of soft-shell coolers. Coleman makes many sizes and styles of hard-shell coolers. Many options are available from dozens of manufacturers.

The AO Coolers soft cooler offers good capacity and cooling for short trips. We have used the AO Coolers for over three years along with Arctic Ice Chillin' Brew Series long-lasting reusable ice packs. Depending on the outside temperature, this combination can keep food cool for a few days.

Water Tanks and Pumps

Water is the most important supply to carry for overlanding adventures. The average person can survive for several days without food but only three days without water. The rule of thumb for water suggests carrying 1 gallon of water per person per day as a minimum, and don't forget about pets. Knowing where water supplies can be replenished is critical for a safe overlanding trip.

Most overlanding rigs can travel about 200 miles before needing to refuel. Most places to refuel also have water available. If you average 50 miles per day driving, you will refuel every four days. Add an extra day as a safety precaution. Two people for five days requires 10 gallons of water for drinking and cooking. Additional water will be needed for washing, showers, etc., but water for those uses does not need to be potable.

Water storage solutions range from cases of bottled water, which is inconvenient and takes up considerable space, to portable water tanks. If the water storage source is higher

A shower is a luxury when overlanding, and having warm water makes it even better. Ironman 4x4 makes a 3-gallon portable camping solar shower. Heated by the sun and powered by a foot-operated pump, the shower can also be used for cleanup after meals.

Water is a precious commodity when overlanding. Each person needs about 1 gallon (128 ounces) of water per day. Long stays in the backcountry require a source of fresh water and, in most cases, a means to purify the water before consumption. Guzzle H_2O offers water purification systems, including this Stealth 2x10 3-stage system.

Tanks for water storage are a great solution for extra water capacity. Make sure that the tank can be used for potable water that is safe for drinking.

Tailgate 'N' Go (TNG) makes a wide range of accessories for overlanders, including mounting brackets for items such as a collapsible sink and portable cutting board.

than the water outlet, gravity will work to generate flow. Otherwise, a 12-volt inline water pump will create good flow for any situation.

Slide-Out Drawers

Slide-out drawers come in a variety of sizes and have a multitude of uses. Drawers allow gear to stay organized and protected. Slide-out drawers provide ease of access. Drawer kits can be custom or premade to fit specific vehicle applications. Weight and cost are the major negative elements.

Drawer systems are the ideal storage solution for organizing gear and keeping it clean. DFG Offroad manufactures a wide range of slide-out drawer systems for a variety of vehicles. It also offers an extensive line of off-roading accessories and gear.

Electric refrigerators take up space and can be awkward to use in cramped areas. Slide-out trays are available for refrigerators, sinks, and other large storage containers.

If you own a Dodge Ram 1500/2500, or a Toyota Tundra, Alu-Cab makes the Alu-Cabin with extensive storage capacity. The Alu-Cabin includes a rooftop tent. Alu-Cab makes a complete range of overlanding products. The Alu-Cabin is available for a variety of other full-size pickups.

Savute twin drawers provide considerable storage space with a flat surface on top to easily access larger gear.

Storage Bags

Storage bags provide the ideal place to store soft goods, such as clothes, towels, blankets, sleeping bags, and recovery gear. Roll-up tool bags take up less space and allow quick access to tools when needed. Storage bags are best used inside the vehicle and away from the elements.

Small off-road trailers provide a surprising amount of gear storage capacity. Many ingenious designs are available for the overlander.

The vehicle storage and power-management system by DirtBox Gear features storage drawers, a fridge slide-out, and a slide-out for an electronic cook top. It also has a power station with a 170 amp-hour battery and a 2,000-watt pure-sine-wave inverter that can be charged from the vehicle's alternator or solar panels. The system provides both 12-volt and 120-volt output with USB ports for electronics.

Talus Expedition Gear makes a compact slide-out kitchen that features a Dometic sink with a faucet and 7-gallon water tank, a 2-burner Dometic stove with storage for a 1-pound propane bottle, and a 31-quart Dometic drawer refrigerator. The power source is a 100-amp-hour lithium-ion battery with a 450-watt Redarc inverter. The system can be recharged with a standard 120-volt plug or a 130-watt solar panel.

Mesh roll-up storage bags provide great storage for a wide range of gear, including food, cooking gear, and first aid.

Hard-shell storage cases, such as these from Front Runner Vehicle Outfitters, provide secure storage for fragile items and food. These cases clamp together for more secure storage and space saving.

Pelican makes a broad range of storage cases for just about anything. The RotopaX fluid containers are compact and durable. The white container holds potable water, and the red is for gasoline. The low roof rack is contoured to the roof line for improved aerodynamics and better fuel economy, and a lower center of gravity helps reduce the potential for rollovers.

Hard Storage Cases

Hard storage cases provide protection for electronics, camera gear, fragile items, and non-perishable food supplies. The overlanding aftermarket offers a wide selection of hard-case storage solutions at a wide range of price points. Hard storage cases fair far better for storage outside the vehicle and offer improved protection from bad weather, wind, and wild critters. Some cases fit best on roof racks, while some utilize other mounting methods.

A treated canvas storage bag, including this one from Overland Vehicle Systems, allows stowed items to be easily accessed when it is open and hanging to make compact storage easy.

The OffRoad in Mind round storage box attaches to the spare wheel/tire with straps. Holding over 800 ci, a considerable amount of gear can be tucked away for quick, easy access. The OffRoad in Mind storage box is ideal for recovery gear and a fire extinguisher. There is even a slot at the bottom to allow a tow strap to be stowed while still attached to the hitch receiver.

The Disco Series modular outdoor cooking system from iKamper provides multiple cooking options from a disc skillet (skottle) to a cast-iron pot. Heat sources range from propane to a wood fire. A Kovea propane camping stove is included. Options include a worktable and hooks for hanging utensils and propane tanks. iKamper offers a wide range of gear for overlanders.

RSi SmartCap offers several overlanding products, including the SmartCap XL bed replacement system. It provides considerable storage capacity and a variety of features, such as a fold-down kitchen. The SmartCap is available for a wide range of pickups, including those from Chevy/GMC, Ford, Ram, and Toyota, and for the Jeep Gladiator.

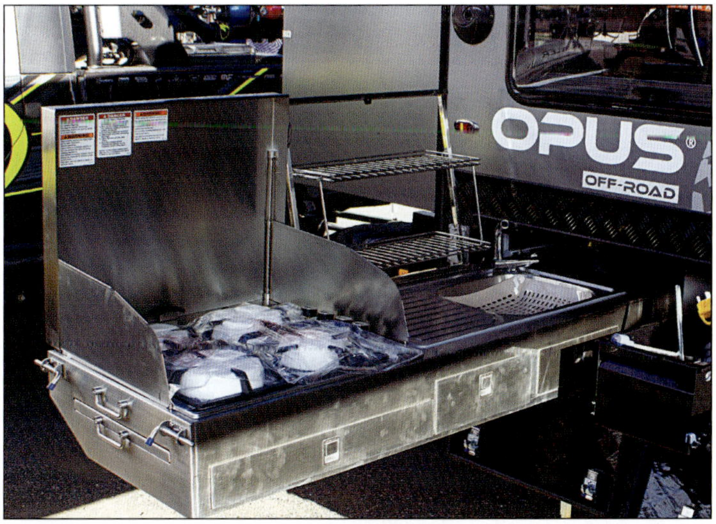

Opus Off-Road trailers offer some of the most innovative overlanding storage and kitchen solutions on the market. The slide-out stove features four burners. The sink offers drainage and a drying rack. Storage drawers are below.

Stoves, Griddles, Barbecues, and Skottles

Having a hot meal, especially for dinner and breakfast, is a wonderful treat when overlanding. The most common fuel for camping stoves is propane, although some backpacking stoves use butane. Single- and twin-burner stoves are the most common.

Some camping stoves have optional griddles for grilling or cooking breakfast staples, such as eggs, pancakes, and bacon. Table-top propane griddles are available from many sources. Small table-top propane-fueled barbecues are a nice addition for grilling and take

A TNG collapsible sink and cutting board is flanked by a propane stove (on the top right) and Blackstone griddle, which is one of the best in the world.

The Camp Chef cast-iron pot provides a great way to cook meals over hot coals, open flames, or a propane burner for large groups.

The Egoé Nestbox Roamer converts a van into a camper with a slide-in module that contains a stove, sink, and slide for a refrigerator. A bed with a fold-up mattress rests on top. Nestboxes are available for a wide variety of vans.

For limited-storage-capacity rigs, collapsible gear solves storage problems and provides great usefulness at camp. The collapsible bucket and dish pan from Ironman 4x4 fill this need perfectly. (Photo Courtesy Ironman 4x4)

Many items require propane for fuel. Power Tank makes a great mounting bracket for 10-pound propane tanks that can be mounted nearly anywhere.

up minimal space. The most popular cooking tool for overlanding is the skottle, which uses propane for fuel. Skottles are shaped like a wok and allow a complete meal to be cooked at once.

Propane Tanks and Mounts

Propane provides an efficient source of fuel for stoves, heating, and generators. Propane tanks range in size from the 1-pound propane canisters for camping and backpacking to 100-pound, long-range tanks. The most common size of tank holds 5 gallons of propane. Power Tank offers nice mounting brackets for a variety of propane tanks.

Kitchen Gear

Even short overlanding trips require kitchen gear. You probably already have many necessary items that can be repurposed for

The Wolftraders 4Wolves lightweight collapsing camping table holds up to 50 pounds on a steel frame with a strong polyester mat top and storage pockets. Wolftraders also makes a nice camping chair.

The Tailgater tire table is lightweight, quick and easy to set up, and can be used for picnics or while at camp.

Rock Slide Engineering makes a compact tailgate table for Jeep Wrangler JK and JL models as well as the Ford Bronco.

overlanding. Space is always a consideration. Many products, such as food storage, knife sets, silverware, and plates, are available in compact, lightweight sets that make storage easier. Disposable plates and silverware are not a good option. Space for trash is limited, and disposable paper and plastic items are not environmentally friendly. Here is a list of desirable (if not necessary) kitchen items:

- Reusable plastic food containers
- Picnic sets
- Cutlery
- Reusable plastic or aluminum serving dishes
- Reusable plastic plates
- Aluminum pots and pans
- Cast-iron skillets
- Coffee makers
- Collapsible sinks, buckets, kettles, and a trash receptacle

Having a complete cutlery and dinnerware set in one package, such as this picnic set from Ironman 4x4, makes great use of storage space.

CHAPTER 14

Fluid Storage, Tools, and Medical Items

Overlanding adventures require preparation to avoid disasters big and small. Tools, trail gear, fluids, tape, and other repair items save the day when Murphy's Law strikes. It may be a simple coolant leak, flat tire, or torn fabric in a tent or sleeping bag that stops your adventure in its tracks. Having the necessary tools and supplies saves the day if not the trip.

It is not possible to carry every tool, spare part, or supply to fix every possible problem, but assembling a comprehensive-but-compact kit can allow easy fixes to problems that would've previously ruined a trip and caused a major hassle. Below is a list of a few items with the potential to cause major delays and problems:

- Leaks (oil, coolant, power-steering fluid, gear lube)
- Flat tire
- Electrical issues
- Broken or bent tie-rods
- Loose tie-rod ends or ball joints
- Axles (especially independent-suspension drive axles)
- Downed trees
- Rock slides

Hopefully, trail repairs occur infrequently. They are required at times, so being prepared is important. The Hi-Lift jack is one of the most common tools on overlanding rigs. The addition of the Hi-Lift base and the Hi-Lift wheel mate make lifting a wheel and tire off the ground a snap.

Fluid Storage

Fluids are the life blood of your rig. If you travel long distances, water and fuel storage is important. If your backcountry adventures are short, the need for onboard fuel supply and bottled drinking water are adequate. There are several options for carrying water and non-flammable fluids. There are limited options for carrying gasoline due to the strict US Environmental Protection Agency (EPA) and California Air Resources Board (CARB) regulations on leakage and vapors.

The Daystar Cam Can system offers several options for non-flammable fluid storage outside

Carrying fluids is a necessary element of overlanding. Rock Slide Engineering offers a great storage solution on a rear-mounted spare tire. The EZ Rack uses two curved steel mounts (we added an extra, which is optional) that conform to the tire and are secured by a heavy-duty ratchet strap. Two Daystar Cam Cans hold water while a 2-gallon RotopaX holds gasoline and a RotopaX DLX mount attaches the fuel container to the EZ Rack. Many items can be easily mounted to the EZ Rack.

The rear window on a Jeep Wrangler JLU provides a place to mount a fuel can. The window was replaced with sheet metal that was riveted in place to mount the RotopaX.

Bed racks provide many mounting solutions for fluid storage. This Gladiator uses RotopaX mounts on the rack to hold fuel (red RotopaX) and potable water (white).

Always store fuel outside the vehicle for safety. Diesel fuel is normally contained in yellow jerry cans. Several companies, including Wavian, make NATO steel diesel cans.

Five-gallon jerry cans are the tried-and-true old-school method for fuel storage. Many styles of mounts are available.

the passenger compartment. RotopaX manufactures several sizes of gasoline containers that comply to EPA and CARB regulations. Metal and plastic containers, sometimes called "jerry cans," are another option. There are several mounting kits for all fluid storage options.

Damaging a tire's valve stem can occur in rocky terrain or when debris is left behind from heavy rainfall. The Colby valve allows a valve stem to be replaced from the outside of the rim to save you from a massive hassle.

Tire Repair Kit

While flat tires do occur off-road, they are unusual on off-road tires with a D- or E-ply rating when the tires have been aired down. If a tire goes down, two options are possible: 1) change the tire or 2) plug the puncture with a tire-repair kit. Extreme Outback, Safety Seal, and others make comprehensive tire repair kits. Simple kits are available from auto parts stores. A flat tire in a convenient location is contrary to Murphy's Law and extremely unusual.

Overlanding rigs equipped with larger tires face a difficult situation when changing a flat. Even a 35-inch-diameter M/T or A/T tire mounted on the spare tire carrier can weigh more than 100 pounds. Even on flat, stable ground, that weight creates a difficult task. Imagine changing a tire on a loose dirt hill with an off-camber slope. Just jacking up the vehicle to remove the flat becomes dangerous. A tire-repair kit can be used to plug a tire without jacking or removing the tire, and it can be done in any location as long as the puncture is exposed. Plugging the tire is easier, usually quicker, and much safer than trying to change the tire.

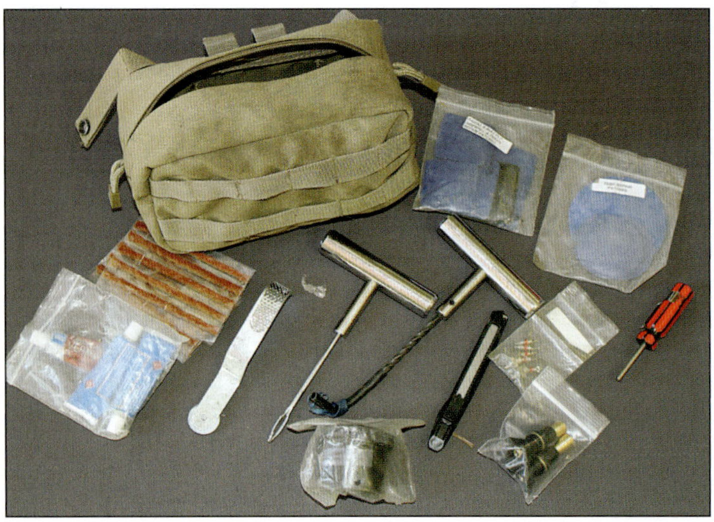

A comprehensive tire-repair kit is a must for overlanding. Most flat tires can be repaired, and the job is much easier and safer than changing the spare tire.

Occasionally, a flat tire is caused when the valve stem is damaged by a rock or a shrub branch. The Colby valve uses a unique design that secures the valve stem to the rim from the outside without removing the tire from the rim.

Tools and More

Simple tools and spare parts can save the day if you encounter problems on the trail. Here is a list of some of the items to carry in your overlanding rig:

Tools	Expendables
• Metric tool kit with combination wrenches, 1/2- and 3/8-inch-drive ratchets and breaker bars, allen and Torx wrenches, screwdrivers, pliers, adjustable pliers, locking pliers, pry bars, a large adjustable crescent-style wrench, hammers, and a chisel • Any vehicle-specific tools • Lug wrench or breaker bar and socket (and the key if your wheels have anti-theft lug nuts) • Multi-tool and knife • Electrical test light	• Spare headlight bulbs • Spare fuses • Electrical wire and connectors • Padded ground cover for working under vehicles and on the ground • Gloves • Paper shop towels • Oil-spill/fluid-absorbent pads for oil and fluid cleanup • Spray detailer and window cleaner • Microfiber towels • Trash bags • Radiator-repair sealant • Duct tape • Repair tape • Tire valve cores • Lug nuts • Silicone sealant • WD-40 • Water/coolant • Filter cleaners (for cleanable air and cabin filters) • Oil • Transmission fluid • Gear lube • Power-steering fluid

Tool rolls for a variety of hand tools are a compact and safe storage alternative.

Finding the right tool on the trail can be frustrating without an organized storage system. Tool rolls make organizing a breeze and finding the right socket quick and easy.

Fixing leaks and lubrication for rusted fasteners can make trail repairs much easier. Carry these items along with repair tape.

Folding Shovel

Folding shovels are a compact utility tool for digging out of sand, snow, and mud. The small shovel is perfect for covering smoldering campfires to make sure that the fire is

A folding long-handle or telescoping shovel makes digging out of sand, snow, and mud a little easier. If you use a recovery tool such as the Deadman anchor, a shovel is a must.

Fluid absorbent pads make trail cleanup much easier while protecting the environment.

completely extinguished. Downsides of the folding shovel include small shovel heads and short handles.

First-Aid Kit

First-aid emergencies are usually minor. Always carry a comprehensive first-aid kit to effectively deal with a variety of medical issues. Take a first-aid class and carry an emergency first-aid book or booklet. Make sure that your kit has blood-clotting pads. Include an epi pen if you have a prescription and are susceptible to allergic reactions. Carry a supply of medications large enough to last the duration of your trip or at least long enough to get to an area with a pharmacy.

Bringing a comprehensive first-aid kit is a must. Learning some basic first-aid techniques is also mandatory. Carry any special supplies and medications that you may need for your overlanding adventure.

Fire Extinguisher

Overlanding involves the use of several heat sources. Fire is always a risk. Carry a fire extinguisher or two, with one being a larger, higher-capacity version.

A fire extinguisher is a must-carry item. We carry two just in case.

Spare Parts

Carrying spare parts can make an adventure more enjoyable and less stressful. Somehow, it always seems that when you carry spares, you never need them. If you do need them, the spares can be worth their weight in gold. If you don't, you could be stranded and have to wait for parts and help.

While it is not practical to carry every conceivable spare part, a little research will allow you to make an educated guess about which parts are more prone to failure. Below is a list of common weak links that are prone to failure on many vehicles, especially older rigs:

- Axles
- U-joints
- Tie-rods
- Tie-rod ends
- Suspension joints
- Power-steering pumps
- Water pumps
- Radiator hoses
- Serpentine belt
- Hose clamps
- Zip ties

CHAPTER 15

Driving Tips and Tricks

The rapid growth of overlanding brings mostly newcomers into the off-road world. While vehicles, gear, and performance products play a major role in the overlanding experience, driving is also a critical factor. Most newcomers have little or no off-road driving experience. The key to successful and exciting backcountry adventures requires the development of driving skills to the highest level. Developing off-road driving skills minimizes the possibility of damage to your vehicle and trail or getting stuck. As with most endeavors, backcountry driving requires basic knowledge and considerable practice, which is a good thing, considering the environment where you practice.

The situations encountered when overlanding include dealing with ruts and bumps; driving on rocky terrain; climbing and descending hills; driving in sand, mud, and snow; water crossings; off-camber situations; and narrow trails. All of these situations require focus and attention as well as good driving skills. One important issue about driving off-road is that it takes some adjustments because many situations require using the controls in a way that is counterintuitive. Several examples are mentioned later in this section.

Off-road driving presents many challenges, including bumps, ruts, climbs, descents, and rock crawling, which is shown here.

Poor driving practices off-road lead to trail damage. Damage to trails is one factor that causes trail and route closures. Minimize trail damage by avoiding unnecessary wheelspin. Do this by being very gentle on the throttle pedal. Like you learned in driver's education class, pretend that there is an egg between your foot and the pedal. Squeeze the pedal gently; don't mash on it. If you do get wheelspin, back off the throttle. More wheelspin will only create more dust, splash more mud, and kick up more rocks. None of this is good for your rig or the trail.

Keep the speed down to reduce dust and trail damage that can also hurt the environment. Some dust is inevitable on many trails, but you can minimize it by keeping speeds down and controlling wheelspin. Wheelspin is covered in more detail later in this chapter.

If in doubt about a trail section, get out and look over the situation. A quick survey of the obstacle will provide a different picture than the one seen from the driver's seat. After doing this, the trail almost always looks easier, and the best path becomes more obvious. If the section is tricky and visibility is reduced because of the steepness of the trail, use a spotter (someone outside the vehicle giving the driver directions).

Discretion is the better part of valor. It is always acceptable to go back if conditions are too severe. If you're in a group, this can be a tough choice. If anyone gives you grief about that choice, ask them if they are willing to pay for any damage to your rig. That will stop the razzing.

While a spotter or other observers have valuable input, the final decision concerning the path or route is always up to the driver. It is best to rely on only one spotter.

Be responsible for your actions and those of your passengers. The backcountry provides a wonderful environment and many challenges. Damaging the trail only creates ammunition for those who would like to close all backcountry trails to motorized vehicle traffic.

Stay on designated trails. There are plenty of authorized trails. We don't need to create illegal ones or damage those that are still open. The most important factor is to pay attention to the trail and your surroundings while behind the wheel. Most accidents are caused by lack of attention by the driver.

Light application of the throttle reduces wheelspin, whereas stomping on the pedal causes more wheelspin.

Use your left foot on the brake and use your right foot on the throttle to control engine torque and speed when crawling up rocks.

Using the Controls

Use all of the controls as smoothly as possible.

Steering

Never jerk the wheel. Use smooth motions when turning. This reduces the chance of traction loss and makes the ride more comfortable. In difficult sections, use both hands on the steering wheel. Place your hands at about 2 o'clock and 10 o'clock. Do not wrap your thumbs around the wheel rim. The wheel can jerk violently over bumps and ruts and injure your thumbs.

Brakes

Apply the pedal smoothly and avoid quick, sudden braking. Avoid wheel lock-up by modulating the pedal. Minimize braking on steep descents to avoid lock-up. Descend in low range and first gear for steep slopes.

Left-foot braking when climbing hills or rocks can help reduce wheelspin and will preload the driveline. By preloading the driveline, wheelspin that is followed by a sudden increase in traction, potentially twisting a driveshaft or breaking an axle, is reduced.

Throttle

Apply the throttle smoothly to avoid wheelspin. Abrupt throttle application causes wheelspin and unnecessary damage to the trail, increases ruts and moguls, and possibly causes stone damage to your vehicle or one behind you.

Visual Fields

Pay attention to where you look. Driving in the backcountry is a slower pace than highway or city driving, but your visual field is just as important.

Part of the time you should look far ahead and take in the whole trail and environment surrounding you. Sometimes you need to look just in front of your vehicle to see the details of the trail, especially when approaching obstacles, rocks, climbs, descents, and side slopes.

Other times, you need to look to the sides to help judge the clearance when passing trees, rocks, and shrubs. Your judgment here will determine how much forest pinstriping will decorate your rig at the day's end.

You even need to look down and back at times to judge clearances. Adjust your side mirrors down so that you can see the rear tires and rear quarter panels as you pass by objects that can possibly cause damage. If you are uncertain about the best path through a tough section, get out and take a look. Use a spotter to help you see and navigate the area.

Pay attention to your surroundings and watch the trail. Keep your visual field moving to assess the entire surrounding area.

Adjust the side mirrors to see the rear tires and obstacles when moving backward.

If you are not sure about the best line through an obstacle, exit the vehicle to get a better look. The obstacle will look easier from outside.

Look as far ahead as possible, but watch your nearby surroundings as well.

Climbing Hills

While overlanding provides many driving challenges, climbing hills is arguably the greatest. The steeper the climb, the more engine torque is required for your rig to ascend, and that means more traction is necessary. Gravity combined with varying degrees of traction (and there's rarely enough) conspire to impede your progress to the top of the incline.

Naturally, the steeper the grade and the longer the slope, the greater the difficulty becomes in reaching the top. The biggest factor is traction. Most climbs feature loose dirt, loose rocks, sand, gravel, mud, and snow. None of these surfaces provide much traction when compared to asphalt or concrete. Here are the factors that need to be addressed when climbing slopes:

- Maximizing traction
- Vehicle path
- Steering inputs by the driver
- Speed and momentum
- Surface

Before we get into specifics, here are two rules to follow when climbing steep hills:

First, always go as straight as possible up the hill. Do not try to traverse steep sections unless the trail is cut into the hill on a traverse, such as on a switchback or shelf road.

Second, never attempt a U-turn on a steep hill. If you lose traction and forward progress ceases, you need to slowly back down the same way that you came up.

Granite slabs provide great traction in dry conditions. Dust, silt, and water reduce traction considerably.

Hitting a rock on a climb can cause a loss of speed on the front side and cause the tire to unweight as it crests the top of the rock. This can induce momentary wheelspin.

Finding the best balance between having enough power to climb a steep hill and too much power that causes wheelspin takes experience and feel.

Winching up the balance of the slope is an option, but make sure that the wheels are well chocked and the transmission is in park or in gear with the engine off on a manual-transmission rig while preparing to winch.

Traverses and U-turns are dangerous. Many rollovers occur because of attempting these maneuvers. Staying parallel to the fall line is the safest approach on steep sections, unless the trail is carved into the hillside.

If conditions were dry here, the slight climb would be barely noticeable. In the snow, the trail becomes very difficult, especially if conditions are icy. Using the lowest possible tire pressure (see Chapter 7) and picking a line that uses rocks, brush, and debris that protrude from the snow or ice as extra traction will help. A little momentum also helps.

Maximizing Traction

The key to completing a climb is having the most possible traction relative to the surface and grade or steepness. Without adequate traction, the completion of a climb is not possible without outside assistance by towing or using a winch. A 10-degree slope in dry summer conditions may pose no problem, but that same slope covered in mud or snow may be impassible without outside help. The steeper the grade, the more difficult the climb becomes. The narrower the trail, the more difficult the climb becomes. The slipperiness of the surface determines the traction potential, and more slippery means more difficult. You have no control over these factors.

Excessive wheelspin causes a loss of traction and momentum. Slight wheelspin is alright as long as the vehicle is moving. The driver of this Jeep is placing the left-side tires in a small rut to gain extra traction from the tire sidewalls on this steep climb. Slight left-to-right movements of the steering wheel shift the load on the tires and can help increase traction slightly.

Traction factors that you can control are the type and size of tire you use and the tire pressure in the tires. For climbing on loose, slippery surfaces, which means anything but asphalt, you need the largest possible tire contact patch and the best tires for the conditions. In most cases, the minimum best tire choice is a good all-terrain tire closely followed by mud-terrain tires, which have a distinct advantage in muddy, sandy, and loose dirt conditions. For sand dunes, you need aggressive tires at very low tire pressures. For extreme snow and ice, tire chains on all four wheels can really make a big difference. Concerning the tire contact patches, you want the largest possible unless conditions are muddy.

Getting the optimal tire contact patch area means fitting the tallest and widest tire that fits in the fender wheel wells. Low-profile tires

Driving in deep sand is one area where wheelspin can help keep the vehicle moving. Sand driving requires low tire pressure, wheelspin, and momentum to avoid getting stuck. If the vehicle stops while the tires are spinning, the tires will dig deeper holes in the sand to make extraction more difficult.

Climbing rutted hills presents a considerable challenge. The goal is to keep the vehicle as level as possible by straddling longitudinal ruts and picking a line through lateral ruts to allow the axles to articulate. A front sway-bar disconnect helps here. Keep the speed low so that the suspension can work and the tires don't crash into the front side of the ruts.

are not desirable for overlanding. Modern 4x4s come most often with 17-inch-or-taller wheels. The tallest sidewall is most desirable. You need to have tall sidewalls to air down adequately for improved traction. The second factor that you have control over is airing down your tires. Several factors determine how low of tire pressure should be. Read the section on airing down in Chapter 7.

Concerning traction on a steep climb, weight transfers off the front tires to the rear tires to give the rear tires more bite and the front tires less. The steeper the grade, the more weight transfers back. This is one of the limiting factors when climbing steep hills.

If traction is an issue and wheelspin is excessive, lockers can be used to increase overall traction. If the tires are spinning but forward motion is still possible, ease off the throttle slightly to reduce wheelspin or drag the brakes with your left foot to reduce wheelspin. Engage lockers if you have them before momentum is lost. If momentum is lost completely, stop applying power, as more power will only dig the tires into the surface more. Forward progress is no longer possible without backing down a few feet and attempting an alternate line.

Vehicle Path

The path you select to navigate the climb is important. The steeper the grade and the more slippery the surface, the more you need to select the path that provides the most traction. For example, on most dirt and small-rock trails, look for a line that

Many hillclimbs crest the top in a straight path, but some do not. Know the terrain before cresting the hill. Either use a spotter, get out and look, or follow someone with local experience.

avoids ruts and surface undulations that require significant axle articulation. This causes tire contact loading to change, which changes traction. When you hit the face of the mogul, that tire has a much steeper section to negotiate. On rocky trails, try to place the tire contact patch on top of rocks to ensure maximum ground clearance and the most level ride possible. On slippery surfaces, such as mud, snow, and ice, the edges of the trail often provide better traction. Look for small rocks, branches, and other debris along the edge of the trail for more traction.

When climbing steep hills, short and smooth left-to-right steering motions can improve traction. Knowing what is at the top of a climb is important because the driver cannot see the trail.

Steering Inputs

What you do with the steering can affect traction on a steep climb. Many 4x4 driver trainers are proponents of sawing at the steering wheel, which is making quick left-right steering inputs to find more traction, especially if you begin to sense more wheelspin and a loss of momentum. Two things happen when the driver does this. One increases traction, while the other reduces it. When you turn the steering wheel, the outside front tire becomes more heavily loaded to give it more traction. Turning the tire also allows the tire contact patch to dig into the surface slightly and possibly find a little more grip.

The flip side of this is that anytime you turn the steering wheel, drag is created at the front tires. Like putting on the brakes, it slows the vehicle. On a steep climb, this slowing effect may lose valuable momentum.

So, does sawing the wheel work? Well, yes and no. It's worth a try on a slope that you know you can climb with relative ease. In other words, practice the sawing maneuver on a slope that you've driven before. The trick is to make smooth, short turns of the steering back and forth. Too fast or too far will cause the front tires to slow the rig. You don't want the rig to change direction. This technique is best used on narrow trails where you have limited or no line choices. In most cases, the sawing is a break-even proposition, and often it is a hindrance. It is a good driving tool to carry in your bag of tricks. Only experience and practice will really tell you when and if sawing the wheel works for you.

Speed and Momentum

You need enough speed so the engine is operating in the peak torque range for maximum power while you climb. For most engines, this is between 1,500 and 3,000 rpm. If the slope is not too steep (up to about 20 degrees) and is fairly smooth, you can usually climb in low range if your vehicle is equipped with a 2-speed transfer case, or second gear in the transmission at the above engine RPM range. If the climb is steep or the surface is bumpy, keep the speed lower but stay in the peak-power RPM range by driving in low range like first gear.

Surface

The surface can make a big difference. Rocks are the easiest, and sand and loose rocks or gravel are the toughest in dry conditions. Snow, ice, and mud can make a climb impossible without chains on the tires. Analyze the surface. If you start to lose traction early on, abort the run and go back down the hill. Rethink your approach or whether you should try again at all.

Backing

If you cannot complete a climb, you have two choices: winching or backing down the hill. Backing down is not a pleasant thought, but if you lack traction to make the climb, it's either too steep or too slippery. Trying to turn around is dangerous and likely impossible on a narrow trail.

If your only option is to back down, lower your side mirrors so that

Solid rock surfaces make hillclimbs easier. Loose rock, dirt, sand, mud, snow, and ice make climbs much more difficult. Pick a line with the best traction and carry a little bit of speed. Some momentum is your friend.

you can see the trail's edge relative to the rear tires. Drive in reverse, keep the clutch engaged if driving a manual transmission-equipped 4x4, and ease down backward at the lowest possible speed without braking too much. You do not want to lock up the wheels. If you do, you can easily turn sideways and be in big trouble. Modulate the brake pedal by gently applying and easing pressure on the pedal to keep all four tires rolling. If you feel a tire slipping, ease off the amount of pedal pressure. Carrying more speed than you are comfortable with is a better option than locking the wheels.

Analyzing the Climb

The factors when approaching a steep climb are crucial: grade steepness, surface traction, and what the trail does at the top. Do you need to turn, stop, or continue once you reach the top? If you do not know what the trail does at the top of a climb, walk to the top to check it out. Many trails have drop-offs at the top or require a sharp turn. Visibility will be non-existent at the top, so you need to know what to do when you get there.

The more difficult the trail looks to you, especially if you are not familiar with it from past experience, it is always prudent to walk the climb to analyze the important factors. If the slope is slippery from rain, snow, ice, sand, or loose dirt and gravel, walk the slope to get an idea of the traction available before climbing. If you think it is impassible or dangerous, don't attempt to climb it.

Summary

- Travel straight up or down hills.
- Don't traverse the face of a hill; you may slip sideways or roll the vehicle.
- Don't turn around on narrow roads, steep terrain, or unstable ground. Back up until you find a safe place to turn around.
- Use 4WD low range for steep hills. The steeper the hill, the lower the transmission gear.
- Look for the most solid ground or rocks to find the best traction.
- Use differential lockers if your vehicle is equipped.
- Small, rapid steering-wheel movements may improve traction.
- Steeper climbs need more momentum at the bottom, but do not use excessive speed.

Descending Hills

Steep, rocky descents are tricky. Most vehicles have well over 50 percent of the weight over the front axle on level ground. The weight balance shifts more weight to the front end on a descent. The steeper the incline, the more weight transfers to the front. The situation becomes worse with a heavy load of gear, such as having a rooftop tent onboard. It is easy to lock the rear tires and cause a slide on steep descents.

For your safety, travel straight down hills. Don't traverse the face of a hill. You may slip sideways or roll your vehicle. Use 4WD and the lowest transmission gear to keep speed down on steep slopes, and minimize braking. Modulate the brake pedal to keep the tires from locking. The rear end gets lighter going downhill, which makes the rear tires more prone to locking and sliding, which can cause a rollover. Release the brakes to regain traction. Then, apply the brakes again. Keep in mind that axle lockers do not help on descents or in any braking situation. All four wheels have brakes.

If the front brakes lock up, you will have no steering control. Modulate the brakes to keep the tires rolling on both the front and rear. Make steering-wheel inputs as small as possible. It is better to carry more speed than to drive down steep slopes with any tires locked up. Some 4x4 vehicles are equipped with hill assist, which uses the antilock braking system and onboard computer to keep tires rolling and prevent wheel lockup. On a steep descent of 25 or more degrees, the hill assist will keep speed down to 2 to 3 mph when driving in low range

Descending a hill safely requires good line selection and hard braking. Rock ledge drop-offs require hard braking and steering so that both front tires descend at the same time with the steering wheel as straight as possible. Often, the drop-off must be taken one wheel at a time, and sometimes steering is necessary. Always try to turn the steering downhill so that the lower tire will act as a stabilizer and not as a fulcrum that will help roll the vehicle. Be aware of deep holes and ruts that can trip the vehicle and result in a rollover.

and first gear. Braking inputs are unnecessary, and not touching the brake pedal requires a leap of faith.

Speed should be kept very low on steep descents. The steeper the slope, the slower speeds should be kept. On slopes exceeding 20 degrees, ideal descent speeds are in the 1- to 3-mph range.

If the slope is slippery from rain, snow, ice, and/or loose dirt and gravel, walk the slope to get an idea of the traction available before descending. If you think it is impassible or dangerous, turn back if possible.

If any steering input is taking place while hard braking is underway, the back of the vehicle can slide sideways. If the vehicle gets too far sideways, the tires can grab on rocks, bumps, and ruts that lead to a rollover. Additionally, if the front tires, either independently or together, drop off a ledge or into a hole with too much speed, the front suspension will compress and cause even more weight to transfer from the rear tires to the front tires. In extreme cases, the vehicle can flip over. (Photo Courtesy Stellantis)

Rocky downhill sections provide good traction. The right front tire has dropped into a hole, but the front tires are steered to the left, which causes more weight to transfer onto the right front tire. While this scenario is not extreme, it illustrates a potential dicey situation, especially if a heavy load of gear is on the roof rack. If the driver here had steered straight or slightly to the right, the right front tire would be on top of the rock to the right of the tires and the vehicle would be more stable. As the left front tire climbs up the rock, the right front tire will drop a little more. Steering to the right here will help stabilize the vehicle.

When possible, straddle ruts parallel to the direction of travel rather than putting a tire in the rut. Placing a tire in the rut can damage the tire.

Poor articulation and less-than-optimal line selection will cause a wheel to lift off the ground in ruts and bumps. While it's not particularly dangerous, the airborne tire can slam back to earth and damage the suspension.

Approaching a bump or rut one tire at a time improves ground clearance and reduces the risk of becoming high-centered.

Ruts and Bumps

Driving in ruts and bumps requires good line selection. Good axle articulation is also helpful. The goal, while often not possible, is to keep the vehicle as level as possible. Try to straddle ruts that run parallel to the direction of travel. If ruts are located on both sides of a hump in the middle of the road, avoid straddling the hump, as the bottom of vehicle may drag or become high-centered. Place one side of the tires on the high point of the hump to ensure good ground clearance. If ruts and bumps cross the trail perpendicular to the direction of travel, slowly approach the bump or rut at an angle. This will allow optimal ground clearance as one tire at a time crosses the bump or rut. This becomes more important as the rut or bump becomes larger.

Straddle ruts, gullies, and washouts even if they are wider than your vehicle. When ruts and bumps are parallel to the direction of the road and your travel, pick a line that allows the vehicle to stay as level as possible. Good axle articulation helps keep tires planted to the road surface and improves stability. The front sway bar should be disconnected for this reason. All-terrain and mud-terrain tires have a tread on the sidewall that allows you to drive partially on the sidewalls over ruts.

Side Slopes

Side slopes are the most intimidating element of overland driving. On some trails, it is impossible to avoid driving on side slopes. Check out a side slope before driving. If there are steep drop-offs on the low side of the slope, exercise extreme caution. Turn back if you're uncertain. Wet conditions or snow make side slopes much more difficult.

Drive the path that keeps your rig as level as possible. If there is a flat shelf on the high side of the slope, place the uphill tires on the shelf. This gives the upper tires better grip to the side and reduces the chance of sliding sideways down the slope.

Most vehicles can handle a

Driving on a side slope is often necessary to avoid obstacles on a trail. Often, the rear tires can begin to slide. Trying to drive up a slope usually makes the loss of traction more severe. Climb up high and then steer downhill when the obstacle is cleared.

Side slopes can be unnerving, especially with gear stowed on a roof rack. The lower tires are in a rut and allow the Jeep to hold the line without slipping.

This section of trail is only passable by driving up the side slope. While it's uncomfortable, most vehicles are stable at up to 55 to 60 degrees of tilt. Lifted suspension and gear stored on the roof reduce the safe tilt angle.

45-degree side slope (very steep) before getting close to a rollover. Lifted rigs or those that carry considerable gear on a roof rack cannot handle as steep of a side slope. A loss of traction can cause the vehicle to slide sideways down the slope. The wider the vehicle and the lower the center of gravity, the steeper the side slope can be. If you feel the vehicle may roll over, steer down slope and accelerate gently. If you are not 100-percent certain that you can negotiate the side slope, turn around and head back. Don't turn around on narrow roads, steep terrain, or unstable ground. Back up until you find a safe place to turn around. An inclinometer can help you navigate side slopes more easily.

Water Crossings

Cross streams only at designated fording points or where the road crosses the stream. Determine the approximate depth before entering and carry a little bit of speed to create a bow wave to minimize water depth along the sides of the rig. If you carry too much speed, you will create a large surge of water that can flow over the hood and create problems as well as damage the stream and surrounding environment. A good speed for most situations is 3 to 5 mph.

If there is a strong current flowing and the water is higher than your rig's door sills at the deepest point, your vehicle can be swept away.

Most 4x4 vehicles can ford water where the depth is at or below the door sills. Keep the speed slow and steady to create a small bow wave. The wave will cause the water level to rise slightly in front of the vehicle but will lower the level along the sides of the vehicle.

Attach a winch cable or safety line to the back of the first rig and the front of the following rig in case the flow of the water moves the vehicle sideways. This process can be used in reverse for the second vehicle. Do not attempt such a crossing if you are alone.

Never enter a water crossing if the water is above the engine's air intake. If water enters the air intake, the engine will stall, and the engine will have serious damage. If you have to cross water more than 2 feet deep, an air-intake snorkel is needed to protect the engine.

Basic Rock Crawling

Cross single large rocks and other obstacles one wheel at a time slowly and at an angle if possible. Place tires over the high spots of rocks to ensure maximum ground clearance. The goal is to protect the underside, even if you have skid plates. When climbing up a rock, maintain momentum but keep the speed low.

If your rig has an automatic transmission, use your left foot on the brake and right foot on the accelerator. Apply some power for climbing and control the speed with the brake so that you crawl up the rock slowly. When dropping down from rocks or shelf sections, apply the brakes firmly so that the vehicle rolls gently down the drop-off rather than bouncing down abruptly. Try to place the tires on the tops of rocks rather than on the sloped sides if possible. This is especially important in

Placing the tires up on rocks maximizes ground clearance and provides the best traction. Rough surfaces on rocks provide good traction as long as the tire pressures are reduced so that the tire tread can wrap around the contours of the rock.

Dropping down big rocks requires heavy braking to ensure that the tires roll down the rock rather than dropping hard and causing the front springs to compress. When descending off rocks one tire at a time, try to keep the steering straight ahead or turned slightly downhill to improve stability. Turning uphill, in this case to the right, makes the downhill tire act as a fulcrum that will create instability and make a rollover more likely in extreme cases.

Select a path that keeps the tires on the high points to maximize ground clearance. Brake hard to allow the tires to roll down the drop-off and not bang down hard.

slippery conditions, such as rain, mud, snow, sand, or silt, reducing traction.

The rear tires will track inside the front tires when turning. Picking a line to accommodate the path of the rear and front tires requires good judgment and planning. Body damage and getting high-centered are the result of ignoring the line needed to clear the rear tires.

When climbing rocks and ledges, the best line often requires angling the vehicle slightly so that one front tire at a time crawls up the ledge or rock. This optimizes traction and ground clearance. In tough sections, get out to study the ideal path and use a spotter to help guide you.

Rocks can be slippery, especially large boulders with a layer of sandstone. Rigs often get stuck or damaged when one or more tires slide sideways down a rock. This can cause the rig to become high-centered or damage the underside components. Precise tire placement is crucial to avoid sliding down the side of a rock. Study the situation. One trick is to look for scrape marks on the peaks of rocks. Scrape marks are a sign that someone scraped bottom over that rock or section due to a lack of ground clearance. Place tires on the scrape marks if possible to ensure that you won't get hung up on that rock.

Using Axle Lockers

The differential housing contains the ring-and-pinion gears that transfer power from the driveshafts to the axles and then to the wheels and tires. An additional set of gears, called spider gears, allows the inside tires to rotate slower than the outside tires in a turn. Without these gears, extreme tire scrub occurs, and steering is difficult at best. The downside to the use of spider gears relates to how power is transferred. With the differential gears, power is transmitted to the tire with the least traction at each axle with 4WD engaged. In low-traction situations or when climbing hills, wheelspin is more likely since the tire with greater traction is not rotating. Lockers alleviate this issue by mechanically locking the left and right axle together so that they rotate at the same speed.

Most 4WD and AWD vehicles are not equipped with lockers, but many use the computer and anti-lock brake system to control wheelspin and improve traction. Some vehicles equipped with selectable lockers only come with a rear locker. Most often, only a rear axle locker is needed. Front axle lockers are not used as often. Some 4x4 vehicles feature both front and rear axle locks activated by air pressure or electrical current. Some traction aids, such as limited-slip differentials, work automatically. Aftermarket lockers are available for a wide range of vehicles not equipped with factory axle lockers.

One of the most common questions we are asked at the 4x4 school is when to use selectable axle lockers. It is always best to engage the rear locker before it is needed. Climbing hills with slippery surfaces, especially bumpy and rutted surfaces, is a good time to engage a rear locker. If the situation seems more extreme, engage both front and rear lockers if available.

Keep in mind that engaging the front locker will increase steering effort considerably. If steering maneuvers are required, it may be best to keep the front lock disengaged until needed. Lockers also help in sand, mud, and snow, especially when snow becomes hard packed or iced over.

Once the obstacle is cleared or conditions change to where traction is better, disengage the lockers. Lockers do not help on descents because all four tires have braking capability. Most factory-equipped vehicles with front and rear lockers don't allow only the front locker to be engaged. Aftermarket lockers do allow the front locker to be used without the rear locker engaged.

While somewhat rare, engaging only the front locker has advantages in limited situations. When climbing an obstacle, such as a rock ledge where the rear tires are on a slippery surface, having the rear locker engaged can cause the rear tires to slide sideways considerably. This can cause the line to change and lead to a situation where the vehicle can get stuck. Disengaging the rear locker reduces the possibility of the rear tires sliding sideways.

CHAPTER 16

Passage Through Tough Terrain

Spotting an off-road vehicle is an art to be taken seriously. It is always best for a driver to work with a spotter who the driver is comfortable with. It is also perfectly acceptable for the driver to stop, exit the vehicle, and take a look at the situation. Sure, this slows down the progress of the run, but not nearly as much as dealing with a rollover or even getting stuck and having to be yanked or winched off an obstacle.

The reason that spotters are necessary relates to the driver's visual field. There are many situations in off-roading where the driver cannot see obstacles. A spotter directs the driver over, through and around obstacles. For this to work, the spotter must provide clear and precise communications for the driver. The driver must trust the spotter. If trust is lacking, the driver will begin to second-guess the spotter. When this occurs, it may be better to not have a spotter at all. The trust needed at events is blind if the driver does not know the spotter. For this reason, the driver should always choose a spotter who is known to the driver whenever possible.

Good spotters are worth their weight in gold. Larry McRae is one of the best. Here, he is spotting a group on the notorious Dishpan Springs Trail near Lake Arrowhead in California.

Here's an example. Several months ago, you registered for a big 4x4 event in an area that you have not explored. The trails you preferred were available for practice. On the first day of the event, you were excited to tackle a world-famous black-diamond trail. The event organizers provided a run leader, tail gunner, and two guides to spot participants through the first difficult section. Your position in the group of 30 rigs was right in the middle. The Wrangler TJ in front of you easily made it through the second part of the obstacles. Since you were new to the area and trail, you followed the directions of the guide assigned to spot everyone through this tough section.

The spotter uses some hand signals but mostly offers verbal commands that have become commonplace: "driver" for turning to the left and "passenger" for turning to the left. About halfway through the

The spotter is well-positioned to guide the JKU through the midsection of the Gate Keeper on Big Bear Lake's John Bull Trail. The left front tire is climbing a rock. The path of the rear tire will move inside the front tire's path and should climb the center of the rock if the driver holds the steering in the same path.

The spotter should know what is happening under the vehicle in rutted and rocky terrain.

100-foot section, you lose momentum. Even with both front and rear lockers engaged, you experience significant wheelspin. Your rear differential-housing center section is against a rock just big enough to stop forward progress on the muddy soil between the bigger rocks.

One of the reasons you ended up in this spot was a miscommunication with the spotter. He yelled "driver," so you began to turn left. He then corrected himself. "I meant passenger!" By then, you were already in a tough spot but not stuck. After reversing and a couple of maneuvers, you were clear of the section.

You were surprised by the spotter's input because the rig in front of you had no issues. What you didn't know was that the driver of that rig knew the trail and ignored the spotter. He took a different line because it suited his TJ better than the line for your Wrangler JK Unlimited. You also didn't know that 12 of the 14 vehicles in front of you got the rear diff housing hung up on the same rock that you did. The other two that made it through cleanly also ignored the spotter.

This is a fairly common occurrence at large events where many volunteers are needed. Another example resulted in more dire consequences.

The trail section on the large group run is tricky, especially on the downhill sections. Two spotters were tasked with guiding 4x4s through this section. A Jeep JK Unlimited with a roof rack loaded with gear was descending this section of rock. The primary spotter was next to the driver-side door. The secondary spotter was in front off to the right and well out of the line of sight of the driver. The primary spotter guided the Jeep in a precarious position where the right rear and left front tires were up on large rocks. The rig was at full articulation with the right front tire off the rock surface. The driver was steering slightly left which was uphill. The primary spotter was not in a position to see the right front tire. As the left front and right rear continued to climb the rocks, the right front dropped but the tire was off the ground. The secondary spotter was in a perfect position to see this but was too far away and reacted too late. The outcome was a rollover. Fortunately, the injuries were minor. The spotters were out of position and most likely used verbal commands. At any point before the rollover began, the driver could have steered to the right, downhill, and avoided disaster.

Before we get into spotting techniques, it is important to understand that the ultimate responsibility rests with the driver. In the second example, while the spotters were clearly out of position, the driver contributed to the outcome. The driver should have been steering downhill, not uphill. The driver could see that the spotters were out of position, and the driver had to feel the rig getting tippy before it started to roll over. The driver could have stopped and asked the spotter for more information or to move to a safe spot in front of the vehicle. The counter argument to this is that the driver paid to participate in the event with a reasonable expectation the trail guides would provide solid guidance. That expectation was not met.

The point of these two examples relates to the difficulty of spotting.

Discussing the best line for a section is important for both the driver and spotter. Here, I converse with a student about what needs to be done to climb this rock section.

Spotting Rules

- The driver always has the option of selecting a spotter.
- The driver can fire the spotter and find someone else.
- Bystanders should be ignored unless they have pertinent info for the spotter.
- If bystanders are interfering with communications, ask them for silence.
- The driver is ultimately responsible for the outcome.
- Only one person should be spotting at a time.
- The driver must be able to see the spotter when the vehicle is moving.
- If the driver cannot see the spotter, stop.
- The spotter should be careful when moving to reposition, especially when walking backwards. Stop the vehicle if the spotter is uncertain or needs to move.
- The spotter should leave a good distance between the vehicle and the spotter's position in case a clutch is released or too much throttle is applied by accident.
- The spotter should never stand in front of the vehicle, especially when the vehicle is moving.
- The spotter should always have an escape route planned for emergencies.
- The driver and spotter need to be in agreement of what signals are used and what they mean. If the driver is unsure of the meaning of a hand signal or verbal communication, the driver should stop.
- It is the responsibility of the spotter to make sure any additional help is clear of the vehicle, such as helpers stacking rocks or moving debris.
- The spotter must have a complete picture of the situation around and under the vehicle.
- Spotting for the rear tires is just as important as for the front tires.
- In tight areas where turning is required, especially when rock crawling, lines must be planned for the rear tires and for the back portion of the vehicle to clear.
- Hand signals from the spotter must be clear, concise, and visible.
- Verbal communication should only occur when the vehicle is stationary.

Verbal Communication and Verbal Commands

Verbal communication is important but should only occur when the vehicle is stationary. Verbal discussions include choosing the best line through a difficult section, what hand signals will be used, and any possible issues that can lead to getting stuck or cause damage. This communication can be conducted between the driver and spotter in the vehicle with the spotter next to the driver's window or with the driver and spotter out of the vehicle.

Verbal commands, such as "turn left," "turn passenger," or "more driver" have become the norm in four wheeling. While using "passenger" or "driver" is less confusing than saying right or left, it still allows for miscommunication.

In the first example at the beginning of this chapter, the spotter had to correct himself several times. "Driver! No, I mean passenger!" is not helpful. Often in tight quarters or when rock crawling, an inch or two in one direction or the other can result in damage or getting stuck. In the time it takes to make a verbal correction, it is often too late.

Verbal commands can be misinterpreted, not heard, or confusing, especially if bystanders are yelling directions at the same time. Verbal commands can cause the driver to look away from the spotter which may create a problem. Military, law enforcement, and most fire agencies do not allow verbal commands. Only hand signals are used. At the Jeep 4x4 school, we encourage and use verbal communication when the vehicle is at rest. We only teach and use hand signals for spotting while the vehicle is in motion.

The spotter has stopped the driver because the driver missed the approach to the large rock. If the driver would have continued, the Jeep would have become hung up on the steering or the differential housing. The driver needs to back up a foot or two to line up one front tire to drive over the large rock for increased ground clearance.

The spotter has the front tires perfectly positioned on top of the rocks. At this steering angle, the right rear tire will track over the smaller rock in the center, and the left front tire will climb the big rock right in front of the spotter.

Hand Signals

Hand signals can take many forms. The most important element of hand signals requires that they be easily understood and agreed upon by the driver and spotter. The actual signals are less important than their clarity. The driver needs to fully understand what the spotter's hand signals mean and how they are presented. The most common form of hand signal uses pointing to the left or right. These signals should be obvious and amplified, not subtle.

An alternate form of hand signals uses mirror imaging. The spotter holds his or her hands up as if he or she was holding a steering wheel with hands in the 2 o'clock and 10 o'clock positions. When the spotter wants the driver to turn, he moves his hands as if he is turning the steering wheel. The driver mirrors the spotter's hand positions. This technique provides an additional benefit of offering precise degrees of steering as well as direction. While the degree of turn can be indicated with animated pointing, the mirroring allows more precision.

Other hand signals include "come forward," where the spotter holds his hands up with palms facing the spotter with a "come toward me" motion. Another hand signal is "stop," where the spotter holds closed fists out. Palms facing the driver held out with a pushing motion indicates to go back or back up. Palms facing the ground with an up-and-down motion indicates for the driver to slow down. Hand signals can be combined using one hand to indicate turning while the other hand is used for slowing down, coming ahead, or moving forward a small amount.

There are additional hand signals for rock crawling. We have the spotter point at the rock or obstacle being ascended or descended. If the left side is coming up, the spotter points at that tire. If it's the right side, the spotter points at the right side. If both sides, the spotter uses both hands to point at both tires. This can be the front or rear. A palm facing upward with an upward hand motion indicates that the tire (or tires) is climbing up. With the palm facing down and a downward hand motion, the tire is about to drop down the rock or obstacle.

The single most important element to hand signals is visibility. The driver needs to see the spotter's hands. If the spotter cannot see the driver, the hand signals need to be high above the head of the spotter. If the driver cannot see the spotter, the driver should stop.

Spotting Tips

Look at all of your surroundings. The spotter needs to have a complete picture of the situation including the front, sides, and back of the vehicle. The spotter also needs to know what the situation is under, and in some cases above, the vehicle.

The spotter should try to position the vehicle for maximum ground clearance while keeping the vehicle as level as possible. The spotter should look for the line with the best traction.

When spotting vehicles on side slopes, make sure the driver steers downhill as the vehicle approaches the point of a rollover. When dropping down ledges or big rocks, keep the front wheel as straight as possible or steer towards the downhill side to help stabilize the vehicle.

The spotter should try to avoid lines where the vehicle will drive

The Trails 411 Adventure Experience instructor helps guide a driver through large rocks. Hand signals provide clear and concise instructions and force the Wrangler JL driver to watch the spotter. Notice that the spotter is off to the side and out of harm's way.

The spotter's hands mimic holding a steering wheel and show a slight turn to the driver's left. This type of hand signal allows directional input and how far to turn the steering wheel. The Jeep is lined up perfectly. The driver has taken his eyes off the spotter momentarily to check the position of the left front tire. The left rear tire sidewall will slightly climb up the large rock to allow the Jeep an easy path through this difficult section on the John Bull trail.

The spotter has turned his hands fully to the left to indicate the driver needs to steer hard to stay on the optimal line.

into holes or depressions in the surface with one tire on steep sections.

When spotting for groups of vehicles on large 4x4 runs, the spotter needs to be aware of the differences between vehicles. The line for a Wrangler JKU is very different than for a CJ or Toyota pickup.

The spotter needs to keep in mind that the rear tires will not follow the tracks of the front tires in a turn. The tighter the turn, the more the rear tires will track inside the path of the front tires. This varies from vehicle to vehicle based on the wheelbase and track width.

It is best to get tires on the peak or the least-sloped section of rock so that the tires will be less likely to slide sideways down the rock.

The spotter needs be sure that no additional helpers are in harm's way before the driver moves.

It is best for the spotter to stop the vehicle if the spotter needs to reposition.

When spotting multiple vehicles, a spotter needs to be aware of changes to the trail. Rocks move, and ruts can get deeper from wheelspin.

If a spotter feels that the driver is not understanding signals and communication, the spotter should stop the driver and have a discussion.

Driving Tips

The driver can always choose a spotter. If the driver is unsure of what the spotter is doing, stop and have a conference. The driver should exit the vehicle if uncertain about the best line to take. The driver and spotter can easily evaluate the options from outside the vehicle. Lines are more clearly seen from outside the vehicle.

The driver should always see the spotter while moving. If not visible, the driver should stop. The driver needs to follow the exact instructions of the spotter and continue to follow the last instruction until the spotter gives a new instruction. Following the signals of a spotter requires a high degree of confidence from the driver. Without that confidence, the driver is likely to second-guess the spotter, which often leads to problems. If you don't trust the spotter, find a new one.

Newcomers to rock crawling often underestimate the amount of brake-pedal pressure required to control speed when descending rocks or dropping down ledges. It is much easier to ease off the brakes to move forward than to apply more brake when the drop-off speed is too much.

Most drivers, especially newcomers, expect the spotter to get them through the tough sections unscathed. That is a high expectation and one that is not likely to occur. Slipping off rocks, moving rocks, and many other situations may cause your rig to drag on the skid plates, land on rock sliders, or bounce off the bumper. That's why we have armor.

Spotting a vehicle through difficult terrain is an art form. When a driver cannot see the line, outside eyes can make a big difference. The spotter is guiding a vehicle but not operating the controls. The driver is operating the controls of the vehicle but cannot see the terrain. What could possibly go wrong!

A good spotter can make an average driver look great. A bad one can make a good driver look bad. It is a joy to work with a good spotter, but they are somewhat rare. A good spotter gives the driver confidence that the difficult sections can be traversed with minimal risk of damage or disaster. If you have a good spotter to work with, keep that person happy.

Poor spotting combined with bad driving judgment can lead to disastrous results. As with most crashes, this rollover occurred when several factors combined to create chaos. In this scenario, the left front and right rear tires are climbing up rocks. The right front and probably the left rear are off the ground. The spotter in the foreground is too far from the driver's line of sight and is doing nothing to stop the Jeep from progressing. The primary spotter is near the driver's door and unable to see the depression that the right front tire is in. This is clearly a bad line. If the driver turned sharply downhill (to the right, or passenger's side), a rollover may have been avoided. When the right front tire comes down, it will act as a fulcrum to make a rollover more likely.

The rollover has begun. As soon as the right rear tire and left front tire topped the rocks that they were ascending, the left rear and right front were off the ground. The front weight bias of the JKU forced the right front to dip heavily. While unlikely, it is possible that hard acceleration at this point could have prevented the rollover. Steering down and moderate acceleration a second earlier would have likely stabilized the Jeep enough to avert the rollover.

The rollover is nearly complete. The Jeep lands on the roof. Several factors contributed to this situation. The spotters were in poor positions and were unable to see the risk of the line where they were sending the Jeep. The driver steered in the wrong direction, which made the rollover more probable. In addition, the camping gear on the roof rack raised the center of gravity, which makes a rollover more likely.